JUSTICE IN AMERICA

JUSTICE IN AMERICA
Courts, Lawyers,
and the Judicial Process

FOURTH EDITION

HERBERT JACOB
Northwestern University

LITTLE, BROWN AND COMPANY
Boston   Toronto

Library of Congress Cataloging in Publication Data

Jacob, Herbert, 1933–
  Justice in America.

  1. Courts—United States. 2. Justice, Administration
of—United States. 3. Law and politics. I. Title.
KF8700.Z9J3   1984   347.73   83-24890
ISBN 0-316-45532-6   347.307

Library of Congress Catalog Card Number 83-24890

ISBN 0-316-45532-6

9 8 7 6 5 4 3 2

MV

Published simultaneously in Canada
by Little, Brown & Company (Canada) Limited

Printed in the United States of America

For Jenny and Max

Preface to the Fourth Edition

It is sobering to realize that this book has weathered almost two decades of use and critique and that it has served as the vehicle for introducing thousands of students to the administration of justice in the United States. This fourth edition seeks to bring the book up to date in two ways. First, it reflects the many minor changes that constantly occur in American courts and law. During the past five years, new courts have been added, many improvements have been made in the efficiency of court operations, and some important actors in the judicial arena have retired and new ones have taken their place. Second, my purpose remains to have this book reflect the best of socio-legal research on justice in America. The past five years have witnessed the publication of many studies. I could not cite all of them, but this edition does incorporate more than fifty new major research reports; and the interested reader will find the footnotes a useful guide to the best of the old as well as the new research on courts and justice.

I am grateful to my colleagues in the Law and Social Policy group in the Center for Urban Affairs and Policy Research at Northwestern University, and especially to my departmental colleagues Jerry Goldman and Wesley G. Skogan for their constant stimulation. The Center for Urban Affairs and Policy Research has provided the scholarly setting which makes my research and writing possible.

Once more I must absolve all others from errors of fact or judgment in this book. I would be pleased if readers called them to my attention for future correction.

Preface to the First Edition

This book is a political analysis of how justice is adminis-
tered in American courts. It views the courts as units of the political system. It describes the judiciary and its work on the basis
of available empirical evidence. It examines trial courts and those
who participate in trials, as well as appellate courts and proceedings.

I view the courts as political institutions, performing functions
that are similar to those of legislative bodies and executive agencies but operating under different sets of decision-making rules.
This perspective is a break with the traditional manner in which
political scientists and lawyers have examined the judiciary, but
my point of view is not new. Professor Jack Peltason suggested
much the same in his *Federal Courts in the Political Process*[1]
almost ten years ago. The present volume extends Peltason's
analysis to state courts and to all participants in the judicial process.

My approach differs from the traditional legal approach in that
it focuses on courts rather than on the law. I do not deny that if
one is interested in analyzing the meaning of legal doctrine and
the logical relation of one doctrine to another, it is useful to abstract the law from the courts that interpret it. But my primary

[1] New York: Random House, 1955.

purpose is to describe the courts, not the law. While it is useful to entertain the fiction that courts are independent agencies when one analyzes legal doctrine, this fiction obscures a clear understanding of how courts operate and what functions they perform. Consequently, I have emphasized what traditional scholars often neglect. This is an essential corrective if students, lawyers, and citizens are to understand how their courts function.

A secondary purpose of this book is to integrate the vast body of research available on the courts so that we may better realize what we know and what we still need to learn. Most research on the judiciary has been undertaken by legal scholars and sociologists; this book should also serve to introduce political scientists to studies which are in journals normally beyond their purview.

I am personally indebted to a number of colleagues who read a manuscript version of this book and made numerous helpful suggestions. They are Professors Joel Grossman (University of Wisconsin), Lawrence M. Friedman (University of Wisconsin Law School), Harry Kalven, Jr. (University of Chicago Law School), James R. Klonoski (University of Oregon), C. Peter Magrath (Brown University), Walter F. Murphy (Princeton University), and Kenneth N. Vines (Tulane University). Professor Jerome C. Carlin of the University of California at Berkeley read the section on legal ethics and permitted me to use his research, which will be published shortly. None of these colleagues entirely agree with me; all errors that remain and the responsibility for interpreting that data rest with the author alone.

Contents

I

INTRODUCTION   **1**

1

Justice and the Political Arena   **3**

The Courts as Guarantors of the Political Structure   4
Arenas for Symbolic Issues   6
Institutions of Racism and Class Domination   7
Repositories of Legal Culture   9
The Courts as Political Institutions   13
Conclusions   20

II

THE FUNCTIONS OF COURTS   **23**

2

Enforcing Norms   **25**

Characteristics of Norm Enforcement   26
Consequences of Judicial Norm Enforcement   28
Lawmaking in the Enforcement Process   32

3
Policymaking by the Courts · 35

Interest Groups and Judicial Policymaking 39
Characteristics of Judicial Policies 42
Consequences of Judicial Policymaking 45

III
PARTICIPANTS IN THE JUDICIAL PROCESS · 47

4
Lawyers and the Bar · 49

Bar Associations 50
The Training of Lawyers 52
Admission to the Bar 56
Legal Ethics and the Economic Status of Lawyers 59
Bar Associations and Politics 63
The Availability of Legal Services 67
What Lawyers Do 76
Conclusions 82

5
Attorneys for the Public · 85

Lawyers for the Federal Government 85
Government Lawyers in the States 92
Conclusions 100

6
Judges · 101

The Functions of a Judge 101
The Recruitment of Judges 113
The Removal of Judges 127
The Impact of Selection Procedures 130

7

The Public in Court 135

Juries 136
Interest Groups in the Judicial Process 149
The Media and the Judicial Process 152
Conclusions 158

IV

THE STRUCTURE AND RULES OF THE JUDICIAL PROCESS 159

8

The Organization of Courts in the United States 161

The Structure of American Courts 164
Consequences of the Dual Court System 169
The Administrative Organization of Courts 170
The Courts' Resistance to Change 174
The Traditional Independence of the Courts 179

9

Criminal Trials and Plea Bargains 182

The Scope of the Problem 183
Criminal Prosecutions as an
    Organizational Process 186
What Happens to Defendants? 196
The Effects of Reform 203
Conclusions 208

10

Civil Justice and Economic Discrimination 210

The Flow of Cases in Civil Proceedings 213
Who Sues? 218
Who Benefits from Civil Proceedings? 223

The Impact of Reform on Civil Justice 227
Conclusions 229

11
Appellate Proceedings   **230**

Federal Courts of Appeals 231
State Appellate Courts 236
United States Supreme Court 239
Outcomes 248
Conclusions 250

V
CONCLUSION   **253**

12
A Personal Assessment   **255**

Index of Authors and Cases   **263**
Subject Index   **269**

I

Introduction

1
Justice and the Political Arena

Justice in America has many faces. For some Americans, she is the blindfolded woman holding scales, evenly dispensing sanctions without regard to social position, power, interests, race, or sex. But other Americans perceive justice differently. They notice that criminal courts are peopled by the poor and by blacks, while civil courtrooms are filled with the well-dressed middle class. They ask themselves whether justice instead reflects the institutional racism or the class biases of the society at large. Still other Americans react strongly to court rulings that strike at the heart of their life styles or belief structures. They are either incensed or elated at court decisions on such matters as the busing of their children to achieve racial integration, the right to have an abortion, or the imposition of the death penalty. These are emotion-laden issues on which people readily take positions and which have fueled political discussions across the country for decades. Finally, a few notice that the courts also engage themselves in fundamental conflicts over governmental structure and process. Representation in legislatures, the government's right to suppress information, the right of corrupt officials to hold office, and the relative power of Congress and the President have

3

been the subjects of other court rulings. Indeed, President Nixon resigned from office as a direct result of the Supreme Court decision forcing him to release a tape of conversation widely considered to contain the "smoking gun" that would have sealed his impeachment.

Each of these faces of justice reflects a segment of reality. Together they compose a complex and sometimes contradictory picture. Without an understanding of these contradictions, one cannot fully understand either American justice or American politics.

The Courts as Guarantors of the Political Structure

Since courts are part of the general governmental structure, they are inevitably drawn into a nation's political life. In addition, they possess many unique features that enable them to play a special role in the political process.

Ever since *Marbury v. Madison* in 1803, United States courts have asserted the right to be authoritative interpreters of the Constitution, and most other political participants have conceded them that power. The Constitution is now what the courts say it is; presidents, congressmen, state officials, bureaucrats, and all other Americans are obligated to act in accordance with court interpretations of the federal and state constitutions. If the courts interpret the Constitution to say that judges may not exclude the press from open hearings, no judge may do so.[1] If the courts decide that the New Jersey legislature must pass a new tax to finance public schools, the legislature must stay in session until it has accomplished that end.[2] During the final days of the Nixon administration, the courts had to decide on the relative power of the courts and the presidency. President Nixon claimed that because of his "executive privilege" he did not have to provide courts with information that might harm his relationships with his subordinates, although the special prosecutor claimed that this information was necessary to establish the innocence or guilt of the Watergate defendants. The courts ruled that Nixon's conception of executive privilege could not be read into the Con-

[1] *Nebraska Press Association v. Stuart*, 427 U.S. 539 (1976).
[2] *Wall Street Journal*, June 22, 1976, p. 18.

stitution and that he could not therefore resist subpoenas for the relevant documents and tape recordings.[3] The President complied and subsequently resigned his office.

Since American courts are the authoritative interpreters of constitutional provisions, many fundamental issues of governmental structure and political procedures come before them. Even such partisan matters as the financing of election campaigns can become issues of constitutional law and interpretation. When the Supreme Court in 1976 struck down certain parts of the Campaign Finance Reform Act, this decision had the effect of permitting wealthy candidates to spend as much of their own money as they liked while limiting outside contributors to $1,000 apiece.[4] Consequently, candidates who had personal wealth could spend an almost unlimited amount, whereas less affluent competitors could spend only what they could raise from the public under the limitations still permitted by the Court's decision. Elections themselves may be decided by court decisions, as was the 1982 gubernatorial election in Illinois. The vote count produced a microscopic margin of less than two-tenths of one percent for incumbent Governor James Thompson, and it was challenged by his opponent, Adlai Stevenson III. The outcome remained in doubt for two months after the election until the weekend before the inauguration, when the Illinois Supreme Court declared the recount statute unconstitutional. (Uncharacteristically, the court split almost exactly along partisan lines.) Only then did Stevenson concede defeat.[5]

Such involvement in partisan matters is not unusual for American courts, but courts concern themselves even more frequently with issues of civil liberties and civil rights. The details of how Americans may enjoy freedom of press, assembly, and religion are constantly the object of litigation and court rulings. Likewise, the courts continuously interpret the rights of Americans in criminal trials in the light of the provisions in the Fifth and Sixth Amendments to the federal Constitution and their counterparts in state constitutions. The courts also play a substantial role in upholding the right of all to be treated equally, without regard

[3] *Nixon v. U.S.*, 41 L. Ed., 2d, 1039.
[4] *Buckley v. Valeo*, 96 S. Ct. 612 (1976).
[5] *Chicago Tribune*, Jan. 8, 1983, p. 1.

to their race. Many Americans perceive the courts as the guarantors of their fundamental rights against incursions, either by a Congress that might yield to temporary majorities or by a power-hungry President, whose personal interpretation of the public interest clashes with the fundamental rights protected by the Constitution.

The courts' role in interpreting constitutional provisions regarding governmental structure, civil liberties, and civil rights inevitably propels the judiciary into the center of political controversy. The courts cannot issue rulings on these matters without favoring some elements in American society and harming others. Although legal scholars may argue for neutral principles of constitutional interpretation, no decision has a neutral effect. Indeed, such issues do not reach the court by accident; rather, the individual or group hoping to benefit from a favorable court ruling usually seizes the initiative and brings the issue to the courts. For many people, litigation is another way of waging a partisan political battle. Especially for those who feel themselves disadvantaged in electoral campaigns, underrepresented in Congress, or neglected by the presidency, litigation for a favorable constitutional interpretation may be their optimal political strategy.

Arenas for Symbolic Issues

Constitutional interpretation often involves fundamental issues on which people feel deeply. Praying in school, busing for racial integration, abortion, and the death penalty are only a few of the issues over which many people become excited. Public concern reflects the symbolic potency of such issues: these matters touch core values that are intensely held. White middle- and working-class parents feel severely threatened when they see their children bused to schools that they consider inferior in neighborhoods from which they have recently fled. Many individuals base their opposition to abortion on religious beliefs about the sanctity of all life, even that which is only nascent; they think of abortion as murder. Still others have strong views about capital punishment. Whether or not they are convinced that it deters crime, many respond to heinous crimes with the urge to wreak revenge upon those who commit them.

Each of these issues and many others that come before American courts spill over into other political arenas. Typically, those who lose in court attempt to recoup their losses, either by forcing the adoption of a constitutional amendment that would undo the court's interpretation or by gaining remedial legislation. For instance, those opposing abortion found it easier to convince Congress to adopt the Hyde amendment, which severely curtailed the use of federal funds to pay for abortions, than to convince the Supreme Court to overturn its *Roe v. Wade*[6] decision. Such issues migrate from one arena to another. Some initially go to court and then move to the legislative, executive, or electoral arena; others begin in one of the other institutions of government before emerging in the courts. Only after passions are spent by many years of conflict and compromise do such issues fade from the political scene.

Institutions of Racism and Class Domination

Other manifestations of the judicial process lead some observers to think of the courts as instruments of social control that are manipulated by ruling elites. Such scholars as E. P. Thompson[7] in England and David Balbus[8] in the United States have asserted that the underlying motives of many court actions are to promote the objectives of dominant economic and political elites. They see much criminal and civil law as having the effect of controlling the availability of the labor force and maintaining the degree of social order necessary for entrepreneurial activity. Such observers point out that criminal courts are populated mostly by the poor, whereas civil courts are used principally by middle-class citizens and business enterprises to (from the observers' viewpoint) exploit the less fortunate. In the United States, this means that the victims of such justice are not only predominantly poor but also predominantly black or Hispanic.

[6] *Congressional Quarterly Weekly Report*, April 19, 1980, pp. 1038–39.

[7] E. P. Thompson, *Whigs and Hunters* (London: Penguin Books, 1975), pp. 258–69.

[8] Isaac D. Balbus, *The Dialectics of Legal Repression* (New York: Russell Sage Foundation, 1973); Isaac D. Balbus, "Commodity Form and Legal Form: An Essay on the Relative Autonomy of the Law," *Law and Society Review*, 11 (1977), 571.

The common crimes that criminal courts process are disproportionately committed by the poor and by blacks, who themselves comprise a disproportionate fraction of the poor. By contrast, white-collar crimes are less frequently prosecuted, and those convicted of them frequently receive less severe penalties. Judges often think that short jail terms and the stigma of conviction are sufficient punishment for a corporate vice-president or a city councilman convicted of embezzlement, whereas they give a burglar or thief two years in the state penitentiary.

At the same time, civil courts appear to be the domain of the middle class. The upper classes seem to use these courts to settle property disputes among themselves and to borrow the power of the state to extract payment from those working-class and poor customers who have become delinquent in their credit obligations.

Like other government institutions, courts reflect some of the biases and values of those who dominate the political process. Western criminal law has always protected property rights; that is, it has favored those who possess property. Common criminals have always been disproportionately drawn from the ranks of the poor, so that criminal courts appear directed against them. Whether the courts actually treat blacks and whites differently is an empirical question that will be addressed in later chapters. It is easy to jump to conclusions based on superficial observations; the reality is quite complicated. However, it is an undeniable fact that many persons believe that justice in the United States is both color sensitive and class prejudiced.

In addition, some perceive the criminal law as an instrument of political suppression. These perceptions were particularly nurtured during the Nixon administration's drive against radical opponents of the Vietnam war. Although the Justice Department won few convictions against those whom it accused of conspiring against the government, the prosecutions themselves cast a pall over the exercise of dissent. Such use of the criminal courts is not unusual in American history. Threats to the governing elite have frequently been perceived as subversive, conspiratorial, and, therefore, criminal. The Alien and Sedition Acts were passed to counter the revolutionary fever emanating from France after 1789 and domestic political opposition by the Jeffersonians;

industrial unrest in the 1880s and 1890s was met by the arrest of union and socialist leaders; the "red menace" of the 1920s was countered with a series of criminal charges against those whom the Attorney General considered the most dangerous leaders. In each instance, the criminal process was turned against political opposition. At the same time, would-be radicals have engaged in criminal acts and sought to turn their trials into political events.

Repositories of Legal Culture

The courts, however, are not simply instruments of political conflict. Courts and law occupy a special position in Western nations as objects of peculiar reverence and distinctive expectations. Courts respond to social and political crises differently from executive institutions, and proceed by rules and rituals that have few parallels in other governmental processes. These peculiarities of the legal culture must also be accounted for in an examination of the judiciary.

An appreciation of the special position of law in Western societies is fundamental to an understanding of the administration of American justice.[9] Law still is perceived as partly sacred, although all laws that American courts enforce have a secular origin. The quasi-sacred nature of law comes from its origins in Western tradition. The Mosaic legal and moral code was not entirely renounced by Christianity. Much law until the Reformation was sacred Roman Catholic canon law interpreted by church lawyers and enforced by church courts. Laws enforced by secular authorities were endowed with quasi-sacred character because the monarchs who enforced them derived their right to rule by divine will. Much law, of course, came from Roman sources, but it was covered by the patina of sacred authority through the church or monarchy. The doctrine of natural law as a derivative of divine law and as commanding obedience because it was morally correct carried the quasi-sacred character of law into the secular industrial age. In the nineteenth and twentieth centuries, neither religion nor natural law provided the moral underpinning of American law. That function was taken over by the doctrine

[9] Adda B. Bozeman, *The Future of Law in a Multi-cultural World* (Princeton, N.J.: Princeton University Press, 1971), pp. 35–49.

of popular sovereignty, which asserted that the authority of the state emanated from the consent of the governed as expressed in democratic elections.

Twentieth century American law possesses none of the outward characteristics of the divine; it is entirely a secular creation. Yet it continues to benefit from popular respect for the sacred. People are taught to respect law alone among the institutions of government, simply because it is law. One may speak disparagingly about presidents, congressmen, and generals; indeed, the quadrennial presidential election campaign encourages harsh rhetoric against such authorities. One may insult the President at the White House and only be condemned as a boor, but disrespect for the lowliest judge in the courtroom will bring a jail sentence. Respect for the law is urged by many people — even if one disagrees with it and seeks to change it — as a necessary barrier to anarchy.

The special respect that law engenders makes the struggle to enact laws so important. Laws are important not only because they authorize a particular distribution of values but also because of their symbolic effect. Once enacted, they command obedience even from those who opposed them. Once a proposal becomes law, it magically leaves the partisan arena and enters the legal pantheon.

The distinctive respect for law has many consequences for the judicial process. It imbues many court proceedings with a dignity and a ritualism that is unmatched in American government. Courtrooms are built to resemble temples; they tend to be dark, richly paneled, and high ceilinged — violating most precepts of the functional design that pervades so many other public structures. The courtroom is built so that attention is focused on the judge, who sits on a pedestal above the other participants. No visitors' gallery rises above the judge; those who work in the courtroom are not allowed to sit or stand at the same level; everyone else operates below. The judge is the only official in the courtroom who wears a special costume — a robe. Everyone must rise when judges enter or leave the courtroom. They are addressed as "Your Honor," even though individual attorneys may despise them as persons. Attorneys are considered officers of the court and are subject to its discipline. Ordinary citizens who come to court for redress of grievances are labeled "petitioners," or, if they stand accused of a crime or a civil offense, "defendants." Thus, architecture, dress, behavior, and language reinforce respect for the law and for the courts.[10]

The rules of courtroom procedure and the concepts underlying them are also much less contemporary than many other governmental processes. They resulted not only from conflicts that contemporaries can remember and may have participated in but also from ancient conflicts that have been mythologized. For instance, almost every public official subscribes to the adversary process as the proper one for resolving disputes in a courtroom. By *adversary proceeding*, most people mean that two sides confront each other according to elaborate rules. Almost all public officials agree that hearsay evidence should not be admitted in court; that the right to confront one's accuser is an important one; that the presumption of innocence in criminal trials is desirable. We shall see later in this book that many of these presumptions are not observed in the actual disposition of court cases. Nevertheless, they are honored as traditions, and departures from them are considered undesirable deviations.

Moreover, these rules and presumptions distribute advantages in the judicial arena quite differently from the rules and presumptions in administrative or legislative procedures. When an issue comes to trial, the two parties are on a more nearly equal plane than elsewhere in the political process. The same rules for presenting evidence apply to both the government and the defense in criminal trials, so the government has no formal advantage. Indeed, the opposite is true: the defense has the advantage of the presumption of innocence. The government must therefore prove beyond a reasonable doubt that the offense occurred and was committed by the defendant. The defendant does not need to prove his innocence; judges and juries must decide on the facts and on the law presented to them. If they respond to external pressures — such as from their immediate constituency or from the press — or if they indicate a willingness to link decisions, trading one person's guilt for another's innocence (parallel to

---

[10] Thurman W. Arnold, *The Symbols of Government* (New York: Harcourt, Brace and World, 1935, 1962).

legislative logrolling), their decision is considered illegitimate and corrupted, although each of these influences is considered proper in the administrative or legislative arenas.

The adversary form of judicial proceedings also forces disputes into the mold of a two-party conflict. Judicial proceedings do not lend themselves well to the consideration of multifaceted disputes. In challenge to a zoning law brought by neighbors who are resisting a public housing project the court cannot easily consider alternative land uses or produce a compromise whereby another piece of land is used for the public housing project and the disputed land is used for a shopping center. The adversary proceeding oversimplifies many conflicts, and consequently many disputes are brought to court only as one stage in their ultimate resolution. After the court has decided the outcome of one two-sided dispute, other disputants are likely to seek alternative solutions through the legislative or administrative processes.

Tradition — modified by current legislative compromises — also regulates access to the courts along different principles than access to other government agencies. Self-interest must generally be demonstrated to obtain a hearing in court, which means that a plaintiff must show his personal stake in the decision. The disinterested do-gooder often cannot win a hearing in court, as he might in other government agencies. Further, the courts are by tradition limited to ruling on those cases that others bring to them. Judges, of course, may hint that they would rule favorably in certain kinds of cases if brought to them, but they cannot rectify an injustice unless the cases heard raise the particular issues they favor. Consequently, courts appear to be more passive institutions than many other governmental agencies: they can only respond to, rather than initiate, those cases that interest them.

One other element of the legal culture is particularly important in understanding the judicial process. All persons with substantial authority in the courts come from the legal profession, and almost all decisions are made in the presence of lawyers and by them. No other governmental institution is so dominated by a single profession.

To be sure, all lawyers are not alike in social background, school ties, social outlook, or professional activity. Yet they are subject to a single code of conduct and are the products of training programs that, if not identical, are fundamentally similar. Most lawyers are graduates of American law schools where they have learned legal doctrine and legal method from a common set of case materials; most have been admitted to the bar after passing similar examinations. The consequences of lawyers' dominance in the judicial process are manifold. A legal jargon allows lawyers to communicate easily with one another without the general public understanding it fully. Although lawyers oppose each other in particular cases, they are part of a common guild and help protect each other against competition or attack from the outside. The same bond links lawyers to judges, for all judges have risen from the ranks of the bar and many maintain social ties with their former associates. Their common training has developed an almost universal agreement that the presumptions of the legal culture are legitimate and appropriate. Moreover, because their special training has developed a close familiarity with these presumptions and because attorneys feel comfortable using the legal jargon, lawyers are often intensely defensive of their culture.[11]

These elements of the legal culture place a distinctive stamp on the judicial process. They help distinguish politics in the judicial arena from politics in the legislative and executive arenas. They lend credence to the view that courts and law stand above politics as ordinarily defined.

The Courts as Political Institutions

Throughout United States history, courts have been regarded as the third branch of government. Courts depend on the same political processes that sustain legislative and executive institutions.

Each component of the judicial process is the product of political conflict. In many cases the conflict occurred many decades ago, and the structure that we use today is a relic of that conflict. For instance, many people take for granted the present structure of federal courts: trial courts in large districts, appellate courts serving entire regions, and a single Supreme Court rendering

[11] For a fuller discussion, see Chap. 4.

decisions for the entire nation. This structure, however, was not readily accepted in the nineteenth century as the one that was clearly best for the nation. It emerged through long and bitter struggles — first at the Constitutional Convention, later in the First Congress when the Judiciary Act of 1789 was debated, and then over the next century until the circuit courts of appeals were finally established in 1891.[12] Since then, the general structure of the federal courts has remained stable and has won wide acceptance, but details of court organization still stir heated controversy. During the early 1960s, Southern conservatives sought to shield themselves from the more liberal judges in the Fourth Circuit by taking South Carolina and Virginia from it and adding them to the Fifth Circuit. Their attempt evoked heated opposition from civil rights advocates who did not want the appeals courts to become more conservative.[13] In 1981, when those controversies had faded somewhat, the Fifth Circuit was split into two with little notice.[14] The location of district courts and the number of judges serving each court also are matters of considerable interest and of controversy to those who are affected by court actions.

State and local court structures were produced by similar conflicts. Some states possess many specialized courts that represent tokens of victory for special interests, which believe such courts give them advantages in pursuing their interests. Juvenile courts were sought and obtained by social reformers concerned that the ordinary courts would not show adequate concern for juvenile delinquents.[15] Housing courts were obtained by those who hoped that special forums would lead to more effective enforcement of housing codes.[16] Probate courts — an ancient legacy — have been retained through the efforts of attorneys, who earn

[12] James Willard Hurst, *The Growth of American Law* (Boston: Little, Brown, 1950), pp. 88–121; Richard J. Richardson and Kenneth N. Vines, *The Politics of Federal Courts* (Boston: Little, Brown, 1970), pp. 16–35.

[13] Richardson and Vines, *op. cit.*, pp. 17–18, 36–54.

[14] *The New York Times*, Oct. 2, 1981, p. 14.

[15] Margaret K. Rosenheim (ed.), *Justice for the Child* (New York: Free Press of Glencoe, 1962), pp. 1–43; Anthony Platt, *The Child Savers* (Chicago: University of Chicago Press, 1969); Ellen Ryerson, *The Best Laid Plans: America's Juvenile Court Experiment* (New York: Hill and Wang, 1978).

[16] See Lawrence Friedman, *Government and Slum Housing* (Chicago: Rand McNally, 1968), pp. 25–72, for a general discussion of housing code enforcement.

considerable fees through the probating of wills, and by political parties, which collect high patronage tolls from the probate process.[17]

Seemingly technical elements of the judicial process — such as the rules by which one may bring a problem to court and the rules of evidence at a trial — are similarly the product of past political conflict. The fundamentals of those rules grew out of the struggle between the English crown and the barons and later the commercial classes before United States independence. Most rules were accepted as reflecting the interests of the dominant political elite during the American Revolution. But these rules have not remained constant. They are always being changed in response to new demands on the political process. Proposals for preventive detention of suspects who are likely to commit additional crimes while awaiting trial or who are deemed particularly dangerous are one example of this process of change.[18] Another is the suggestion to limit the scope of the exclusionary rule, which prohibits the introduction of evidence obtained illegally by police.[19] Such proposals reflect the concern of many people that the courts are not effective in controlling criminality and do not effectively safeguard against crime in the streets.

Changes in procedure are not limited to the criminal process. After a long period, during which employers used the courts to combat unions and prohibit strikes, organized labor finally amassed sufficient political strength in 1932 to prohibit courts from issuing injunctions against unions in ordinary strikes.[20] An important element of the civil rights conflicts of the 1960s was a determination of who might go to court and what courts might be used to challenge alleged racial discrimination or denial of

[17] Wallace S. Sayre and Herbert Kaufman, *Governing New York City* (New York: Norton, 1960), pp. 540–41.

[18] Richard Harris, *Justice* (New York: Avon Books, 1969, 1970), pp. 213–34. The proposal was adopted for the District of Columbia in 1970 and suggested for the remainder of the nation in 1971.

[19] *The New York Times*, March 2, 1983, p. 9.

[20] Herbert Jacob, "The Courts as Political Agencies — An Historical Analysis," in Kenneth N. Vines and Herbert Jacob, *Studies in Judicial Politics*, Tulane Studies in Political Science, Vol. 8 (New Orleans: Tulane University, 1963), pp. 33–35. See also Lawrence M. Friedman, *A History of American Law* (New York: Simon and Schuster, 1973), pp. 486–89.

civil rights.[21] Debates during the 1970s over antipollution laws in the states and nation included the issue of whether ordinary citizens or only government officials could obtain court injunctions against polluters.[22]

The constitutional and structural positions of the courts in the political arena make them vulnerable to political conflict, but these positions do not sufficiently explain the concern of political interest groups with the judiciary. The courts are attractive political targets because they exercise considerable influence on the distribution of valued services and goods. Courts in the United States have more power than most governmental institutions to stigmatize or legitimize behavior. An accusation by an executive official that someone has engaged in criminal behavior is only a charge; a similar accusation by a legislator is discounted by most people as "politics" or "headline hunting." A determination of criminal behavior by a judge, however, carries with it stinging penalties, not the least of which is the stigma attached to such a court conviction. A record of conviction may deprive one of many privileges of citizenship, such as the right to vote or inherit property, and it limits one's possibilities for finding a job. Obversely, when a court determines that an activity is legal, the ruling usually shields it from further official harassment. City officials, for instance, may claim that adult bookstores are illegal operations and raid them. But when a court holds them to be legal, further raids or other interferences are less likely to occur; when they do occur, the operators often have recourse to the courts. Conduct of doubtful legitimacy — such as performing an abortion — may be legitimized by a court when it rules that an antiabortion statute is unconstitutional. City officials may seek to prohibit protest demonstrations; but when a court holds the protests to be constitutional exercises of guaranteed freedoms, the demonstrations gain the legitimacy that they previously lacked in the eyes of many people.

---

[21] *Congressional Quarterly Almanac, 1965* (Washington, D.C.: Congressional Quarterly, 1966), p. 563; Voting Rights Act of 1965, PL89–110.

[22] *Congressional Quarterly Weekly Report*, April 24, 1970, p. 1116, and September 25, 1970, p. 2319. On the general matter of class action suits in federal courts, see *Eisen v. Carlisle and Jacquelin*, 40 L. Ed. 2d, 732 (1974).

In addition to legitimacy and stigma, the courts distribute many thousands of dollars through their decisions. The conflict over who could sue industrial polluters was not an ivory-tower exercise in legal technicalities: it meant that even if an industry won an accommodation from a government official (and therefore obtained exemption from antipollution regulations), it might face court suits from angry citizens and subsequently have to invest millions of dollars in installing antipollution devices. Product liability and a manufacturer's responsibility for the health of its employees involve huge sums that may threaten the viability of large-scale enterprises, such as the Johns Manville Corporation, which filed for protection under the bankruptcy law when it faced millions of dollars of potential damages because it had exposed workers and customers to asbestos and the attendant health hazards.[23] On the other hand, when the courts protect corporations from such damage actions, innocent users and workers suffer the consequences of ill health without compensation. The conflict over whether disputes resulting from automobile accident injuries should go to court or whether compensation should be paid automatically by insurance companies involves the annual distribution of hundreds of millions of dollars and the livelihood of a substantial segment of the American bar. With no-fault insurance, many fewer attorneys would be required to process claims. Legislation concerning leases and consumer contracts often involves the right of various parties to resort to court action. The eviction suit is a significant weapon of landlords; the courts' approval of the seizure of wages or bank accounts to pay overdue bills is important in the arsenal of credit merchants. All these matters, though individually small, aggregate to billions of dollars.

The manner in which courts distribute values differs from the ways in which legislators or executive officials distribute them. But the fact that the courts distribute values sought by many groups makes the judiciary the object of intense conflict. Those who seek the preferments distributed by courts try to insure success by obtaining legislation that gives them an advantage in the court structure and in the operating rules. The constitutional fact

---

[23] *The New York Times*, Aug. 27, 1982, p. 1.

that courts are part of the governmental structure is used by those who seek favors from them; it allows such people to influence court structure and procedures through political processes.

Conflict not only surges around judicial structure and procedures but also surrounds questions of staffing and resources. Unlike the practice in many other countries, judges in the United States are not career officials. American judges are recruited for the bench while in their forties and fifties; they come from private careers as attorneys and possess no special training to be judges. Their selection from the ranks of ordinary lawyers is far from random: most judges have engaged in political activity by running for elective office, by holding legislative and law-enforcement offices or by managing or contributing to campaigns. Lawyers become judges because they have the proper partisan credentials in addition to possessing the formal qualifications. For many judgeships, successful candidates must also have political opinions that coincide with those of their appointing or slating authority. For Supreme Court appointments a person generally is not only associated with the President's party but also tends to share his outlook on government. It was no accident that President Lyndon Johnson appointed Abe Fortas to the Supreme Court, that President Nixon named William Rehnquist, or that President Reagan brought Sandra Day O'Connor to the Court. Consequently, courts are often linked to partisan political conflicts through the judges. Judges do not come from an ivory tower; they are not political neophytes. On the contrary, they are familiar with current issues and acquainted with many political leaders. Often those who hold important executive and legislative positions were once close political allies of judges. Thus, the courts have considerably greater understanding of contemporary partisan conflicts than is often credited to them.

Such close political relationships are reinforced by the courts' dependence on legislatures and executive officials for their other resources. The buildings they occupy, the equipment they use, their authorization to hire staff, the bailiffs who protect the courtrooms, and even the judges' own salaries — all are subject to the ordinary appropriation process.[24] Although constitutions typi-

---

[24] See Carl Baar, *Separate but Subservient* (Lexington, Mass.: Lexington Books, 1975).

cally prevent the reduction of judges' salaries, other items are subject to legislative whim and are a means of attempting to influence the flow of judicial decisions. The law that increased the salaries of high-level federal officials in 1964 pointedly neglected to increase the salaries of Supreme Court justices as much as those of other officials, in order to express Congress's displeasure with many of the Warren Court's rulings. At the local level, judges often have difficulty obtaining the resources they desire to operate in the style they would like.

Other resources also require political connections. A juvenile judge cannot require psychiatric treatment if none of the public or private facilities will take the child — or, being forced to take him, will not treat him effectively.[25] A judge cannot place a man on strict probation if the probation department does not have the staff to supervise the probationer carefully; what was strict probation in the judge's sentence may become lax supervision. Moreover, when a judge's ruling is unpopular and requires the positive assistance of executive officials to become effective, that cooperation may be absent. For more than two years, for instance, President Eisenhower did little to support the Supreme Court's decision that Southern public schools be desegregated; as another example, many school officials have ignored the Court's ban on public prayer in school classes. Thus the courts depend on other government organs not only for the resources to sustain them but also for the power to carry out court decisions.

Decisions to increase the court staff, to give courts more resources, and to enforce judicial decisions vigorously (or with laxity) come from political processes outside the judiciary. The interests that stand to gain from judicial action are likely to support the courts' quest for resources; those that stand to lose from judicial action are likely to oppose the expenditure of additional resources. For instance, proposals to increase the number of federal judges are unlikely to be considered by Democratic Congresses if a Republican president proposes them and if a Democrat may soon succeed him. Democrats prefer to wait until their candidate is in the White House, when their partisans can be

[25] Robert M. Emerson, *Judging Delinquents* (Chicago: Aldine, 1969), pp. 57–80.

rewarded with judgeships. Republicans act in the same manner. Similarly, Southern congressmen were reluctant to support improvements for the federal judiciary — especially those that might bring more Northern judges to the South — as long as the federal courts were spearheading the drive against racial segregation in the South.

These many links to other political processes make complete judicial independence impossible. The courts are influenced by political forces and social crises that engulf executive and legislative officials. In addition, they are vulnerable to exploitation by other government officials. Given appropriate laws (which are the product of legislative politics) and accommodating judges (who are appointed or elected with the help of executive and legislative officials), a president or governor may use the courts to promote his policies. The goals may be those of an Attorney General John Mitchell, who wished to crush opposition he considered subversive; or they may be those of an Attorney General Ramsey Clark, who insisted he wished to assist the disadvantaged by promoting voting rights for blacks in the South. In each case the goals are legitimated by law. They are political objectives pursued outside the judicial process as well as through it. In each case the courts are used as an instrument of political conflict.

Conclusions

The ambivalent feelings that many Americans have about their courts stem from the conflicting roles that American courts seem to play. Are they truly guarantors of the political structure or are they arenas for symbolic issues? Are they racist institutions, repositories of the legal culture, or simply political institutions? To some Americans one of these roles predominates; others see different faces of justice when they pass a courthouse.

Unless one is willing to oversimplify unmercifully, one must conclude that the distribution of justice does not simply result from partisan politics, social cleavages, interest-group activity, or election outcomes. Moreover, the pure categories of legalists also do not describe the distribution of justice well: justice is not simply the outcome of the adversary process, of neutral legal principles, or of the lawyers' expertise in legal problems. Many considerations interact to produce decisions that distribute the values associated with justice.

In the following chapters, we shall examine the individual facets of American judicial institutions and practices and observe the manner in which legal traditions interact with political processes. First, we shall examine the functions that courts perform: both in enforcing norms and in making policy, the legal and political characteristics of judicial institutions combine to produce distinctive results. In subsequent chapters, we shall describe the participants of the judicial process and the resources they bring to the judicial arena. Finally, we shall examine the structures, rules, and processes that govern judicial decisions in America.

II

The Functions of Courts

2
Enforcing Norms

The administration of justice is essential to an ordered society. Administering justice generally means that norms are enforced in an evenhanded way so that the same standards are applied to all persons. However, that does not mean that the courts are neutral referees of social conflict. The laws they administer are themselves the product of political conflict and reflect the values predominating at the moment. That such norms need a formal enforcement mechanism such as the courts suggests that they are supported with less than unanimity. Although some who violate the norms agree to their validity, others do not. Few murderers disagree with the law prohibiting murder, but many drug users do challenge the validity of the prohibition against drug use.[1] Laws that require registration for the draft cloak ideological conflict over the legitimate claims of government to require military service. In much litigation, the parties agree on the legitimacy of the norms while disagreeing about factual matters that would permit or prohibit invocation of the law. Other lawsuits question the validity of the norms themselves. Thus, courts are

[1] *The New York Times* (Midwest ed.), March 21, 1983, pp. 1 and 9.

25

not politically neutral when they enforce norms; they are engaged in an activity that helps support the values of the dominant groups in the United States. They are part of the mechanism that sustains the political system.

Characteristics of Norm Enforcement

The norms that courts enforce are embodied in administrative regulations, in statutes, in prior decisions of other courts (that is, in common law), and in the tradition of the community. One distinctive feature of the twentieth century is the growing importance of administrative and statutory law in relation to common law and simple community tradition. The growing complexity of social relations has led legislatures to define more norms in the form of enacted laws and to delegate to administrative agencies the task of formulating detailed provisions that have the force of law. Thus, courts are presented with a much larger body of norms that have been politically approved than was true in earlier times.

Irrespective of the source or the embodiment of the norms, lawyers have generally categorized them in terms of criminal law and civil law. Violations of criminal codes vary widely in their significance and in their treatment by the courts. Many offenses are considered misdemeanors and are punishable by only a small fine, a short sentence in the local jail, or both. Serious offenses are classified as felonies. Conviction on a felony charge may result in a fine of several hundred or thousand dollars, a long prison sentence in the state penitentiary, or a combination of the two. The courts also enforce community norms in civil litigation. When a person is injured through someone else's negligence, he may not only demand reimbursement for his injuries, but he may also request punitive damages, a common practice in libel suits. The person who feels he has been libeled seeks not only compensation for his damaged reputation but often a much larger amount for punitive damage. When a court awards such damages, it does so to recognize that an important norm of the community has been violated by the libel. The same may occur in antitrust cases. A firm whose business has been harmed by the illegal practices of a competitor may sue not only for compensation of the damages but also for triple the amount as punishment, because practices declared by the law to be unfair violate norms thought to be essential to preserving the American private enterprise system.

According to many observers of the judicial process, enforcing community norms is the principal function of the judiciary. Indeed, the volume of criminal cases is staggering. In the federal courts alone, 28,000 criminal charges were commenced in 1980.[2] Many more criminal cases come before state courts, for few federal laws invoke criminal sanctions. For instance, in California alone, 65,000 criminal charges were filed in the major trial courts in the year between July 1, 1979 and June 30, 1980; additional thousands were disposed of in the minor courts of the state.[3] Statistics in most states are too incomplete to count criminal cases accurately. However, the FBI estimated for 1980 that more than 8.9 million arrests took place — with 2.1 million representing the most serious felony charges.[4] In addition, millions of traffic charges must be added to the courts' work of enforcing community norms. Overtime parking, running a red light, or exceeding the speed limit are not usually classified as criminal offenses, although they violate norms that are essential to orderly living in an urban, motorized society. They are almost always enforced by a court. Adding all the categories together, the work of the criminal and traffic courts clearly affects millions of citizens and plays a major role in bringing legal norms to bear on the lives of Americans.

The number of civil cases that involve norm enforcement is also large. In 1979 there were 2.3 million divorces,[5] and 5.7 million people were injured in automobile accidents.[6] Most such cases are as routine as petty criminal cases; although suits are filed in court, they are usually settled out of court, either by an agreement not to contest in the divorce cases or by a monetary settlement in the auto accident cases. In a growing number of states, the courts no longer handle all such disputes. Some are

[2] U.S. Bureau of the Census, *Statistical Abstract of the United States, 1981* (Washington, D.C.: Government Printing Office, 1981), table 322, p. 186.

[3] Judicial Council of California, *Annual Report* (1981), p. 70.

[4] *Statistical Abstract, 1981*, table 310, p. 180.

[5] *Statistical Abstract, 1981*, table 124, p. 80.

[6] *Statistical Abstract, 1981*, table 1081, p. 622.

diverted to mediation; others are routinely negotiated between parties on the basis of "no-fault" statutes. Nevertheless, the amount of litigation has grown considerably. In the federal courts, which handle only a small portion of all cases but for which we have reliable data, the number of civil cases filed leaped from 59,000 in 1960 to 168,000 in 1980. Relatively few of these went to trial. Nevertheless, the number of trials rose from 7,100 in 1960 to 10,100 in 1980.[7] The workload of state courts has risen similarly, indicating that the courts play an increasingly important role in enforcing norms in American society.

Consequences of Judicial Norm Enforcement

Court enforcement of existing norms sometimes involves the judiciary in heated controversy. An excellent example is the role of the courts in labor relations during the early part of the twentieth century.[8] As a consequence of the growing industrialization of the country after the Civil War, workers began to join trade unions for the purposes of bargaining collectively, raising their wages, and improving their working conditions. Unions met bitter opposition from most American captains of industry. When workers struck, management replied with lockouts, use of scab labor, and removal of the factory from the locale. Strikes were frequently peaceful, but occasionally they evoked violence.

The courts became involved toward the end of the century when employers discovered a new weapon in their arsenal — the injunction. The first prominent use of the injunction was during the famous Pullman strike led by Eugene Debs in 1894. Although workers only refused to connect Pullman cars, the federal government and the railroads won federal court injunctions on the claim that the mail was being obstructed. The injunctions broke the strike. Thereafter federal courts issued injunctions on either similar grounds or the ground that interstate commerce was impeded. State courts issued innumerable injunctions on the allegation that irreparable damage was threatened by the strike and that therefore an injunction should be issued. As a remedy

[7] *Statistical Abstract, 1981*, table 322, p. 186.

[8] Edwin E. Witte, "Social Consequences of the Use of Injunctions in Labor Disputes," *Illinois Law Review*, 24 (1930), 772–85; Felix Frankfurter and Nathan Greene, *The Labor Injunction* (New York: Macmillan, 1930).

of equity law, the injunction could be issued on the basis of *ex parte* affidavits alone; that is, on the basis of sworn statements by employers without evidence from labor's side and without a hearing.[9] Such injunctive orders were ordinarily in the form of a temporary restraining order or temporary injunction; after a hearing the order could be made permanent. In labor disputes, if employers could halt a strike temporarily, unions were often unable to resume it even when the injunction expired. In addition, many workers misunderstood the temporary injunction; they thought it made their strike permanently illegal. Not eager to get into trouble with the law, they were unwilling to strike at a later date.[10]

Judicial statistics are too incomplete to estimate with great accuracy the number of injunctions issued in the half century following the Civil War. Between 1901 and 1929, records show 118 applications for federal injunctions, of which 100 were granted. The ratio of reported to unreported injunctions appeared to be about 1:10 in federal courts, making it likely that over a thousand injunctions were granted by them. State courts issued even more injunctions.[11]

In granting injunctions in labor disputes, the courts entered a highly controversial field where almost no substantive statutory law existed. The courts acted on the basis of ancient principles of equity, even though these principles had been developed under quite different circumstances. The fact that a laborer and his employer were not equals in the marketplace was not usually entertained by the courts. The realization that, when a change is sought, an injunction preserving the *status quo ante* prejudices the case of one party did not appear to trouble the courts. Consequently, injunctions doomed many strikes to impotence. The judicial policy of granting injunctions resulted in placing courts squarely in the political arena in the eyes of many Americans. Some unions tried to use the ballot box to unseat those they called

[9] Frankfurter and Greene, *op. cit.*, pp. 53–81.

[10] Edwin E. Witte, *The Government in Labor Disputes* (New York: Macmillan, 1932), pp. 117–22.

[11] Frankfurter and Greene, *op. cit.*, pp. 49–53; Edwin E. Witte, "Report to the U.S. Commission on Industrial Relations on Injunctions in Labor Disputes" (typewritten manuscript, Wisconsin State Historical Society Library), p. 22.

"injunction judges" and to replace them with more friendly jurists. Others supported the recall of unfriendly judges. In Congress and state legislatures, unions sought legislation that would overrule unfavorable judicial decisions and take away from the courts their power to grant injunctions in labor disputes. However, until such legislation was passed by Congress in 1932, the courts remained a principal arena for the settlement of labor disputes. Court decisions not only set the agenda for other political agencies but also vitally affected the balance of political power.

Enforcement decisions have also propelled ambitious individuals to higher public office. District attorneys may win acclaim through their handling of particular cases and thus obtain the publicity necessary to capture higher offices. Earl Warren began his political career as a district attorney in California. James Thompson won prominence in Illinois as U.S. Attorney and used that as a springboard to the governorship.

Moreover, politically influential individuals may be caught in the web of the judicial process, and their careers marred. In recent years the clearest example was the fate of Senator Edward M. Kennedy of Massachusetts, who pleaded guilty to leaving the scene of an accident. He was given a suspended sentence in a case involving the death of a secretary, who was drowned when he drove his car off a low bridge on Chappaquiddick Island. That incident dimmed his political future and, although he continued to win reelection as Senator, he lost his position as a front-runner for the Democratic presidential nomination. Involvement in the Abscam scandals cost several congressmen their seats in the late 1970s. Yet court convictions do not always end political careers, as demonstrated by the career of Harold Washington. Not only did he win a congressional seat after a conviction on income tax evasion charges, but that court record also did not prevent his winning the race for mayor of Chicago in 1983.

Judicial enforcement of societal norms has other tangible consequences. Thousands of convicted criminals are incarcerated behind prison walls. Their removal from the rest of society enhances to some degree the safety of law-abiding citizens. Yet the high crime rate in the United States indicates that the public's safety is by no means assured by imprisoning proven lawbreakers. Ingrained criminality and social circumstances combine to produce new criminals as rapidly as the courts imprison old ones. Despite the efforts of thousands of law enforcement officers and the imprisonment of several hundred thousand violators of the law, the losses resulting from criminality have risen sharply in the last decade. In 1971, 429,000 crimes of violence killed or injured people, according to police reports; ten years later those same police reports recorded 760,000 such crimes.[12] During 1981, crimes against property cost more than 9.1 billion dollars.[13] In addition, organized rackets earn hundreds of millions of dollars from traffic in narcotics, liquor, and gambling. These activities involve not only several thousand criminals but additional thousands of law-abiding citizens, who either have to pay for protection from gang attacks or are milked through the gambling activities of racketeers. The criminal courts have clearly had little success in eradicating such activities. Like higher-status defendants, racketeers often have sufficient resources to escape judicially prescribed punishment.

Court enforcement of community norms has imposed an enormous expense on society. As a consequence of court action, 369,000 law violators spent some time in prison in 1981.[14] The cost of operating prisons in the United States during that year amounted to more than $3.9 billion.[15] In addition, one should count the cost of parole and probation services for those prisoners who were released under minimal custody.

Norm enforcement through civil cases also has a great economic impact. In 1980 alone, insurance companies paid $23.6

[12] *Statistical Abstract, 1981*, table 293, p. 173. The data refer to murders, forcible rapes, and aggravated assaults.

[13] Federal Bureau of Investigation, *Uniform Crime Reports 1981* (Washington, D.C.: Government Printing Office, 1982), p. 150.

[14] Bureau of Justice Statistics, *Prisoners in 1981*, Bulletin NCJ-82262 (Washington, D.C.: U.S. Department of Justice, May 1982). This is an underestimate because it does not include prisoners in local jails or persons who were held for a portion of the year and released before December 31. The local jail population numbered 158,000 in 1976; Timothy J. Flanagan, David J. van Alstyne, and Michael R. Gottfredson (eds.), *Sourcebook of Criminal Justice Statistics, 1981* (Washington, D.C.: U.S. Department of Justice, Bureau of Justice Statistics; Government Printing Office, 1982), table 6.14, p. 461.

[15] Joan Mullen and Bradford Smith, *American Prisons and Jails, Vol. III: Conditions and Costs of Confinement* (Washington, D.C.: National Institute of Justice, 1980), p. 132.

billion for damage and injury claims resulting from automobile accidents.[16] What happens in court also has a perceptible impact on drivers who do not have accidents, for almost all of them are insured. Insurance rates reflect the number of accidents and the amount of damages that insurance companies must pay. When many claims are made and paid, insurance rates for the rest of the driving population increase.

Lawmaking in the Enforcement Process

The manner in which judges apply legal norms gives them an influential voice in molding the norms. It is true, of course, that many laws are applied quite mechanically in court. Traffic courts are often little more than cashier windows at which persons accused of a violation pay their fines. Yet even such norms are not always applied mechanically. A great deal of discretion is exercised by policemen, as every driver knows who has sought to convince a patrolman not to issue him a ticket. A winning smile on the part of a young woman or the proper insignia on the car (often a decal indicating that the driver has contributed to a policemen's benefit association) may be sufficient to escape the traffic ticket. In addition, violations that are not seen are not punished. The judge also exercises some discretion in traffic cases, though only a small proportion of such cases reach his attention. He may reduce the charge or, if he feels it is unreasonable, he may even dismiss it. For instance, in one college town that required a $.50 license tag on bicycles to prevent their theft, the police issued $12.00 tickets to students who did not possess the tag. The traffic judge, however, dismissed the charge, commenting that the punishment was excessive for the "crime."

More serious violations grant the judge or prosecutor a higher degree of influence in the sanctioning process. The prosecutor may dismiss or reduce the charge against a defendant; the judge may accept or reject the prosecutor's action. A judge may influence the course of a trial by his behavior. Most important of all, he may impose light or stiff sentences on those convicted. By imposing heavy penalties, he may put real teeth into the law

---

[16] *Statistical Abstract, 1981*, table 1084, p. 623.

enforcement process. By suspending sentence or placing the convict on probation, he may make the law (or norm) almost meaningless.

Moreover, those responsible for enforcing the law must often decide which laws to enforce at a given time. The norms embodied in law usually conflict with the beliefs of part of the community to which they are supposed to apply. Although gambling is prohibited in many communities, churches sponsor bingo games, prominent citizens enjoy poker in their homes, and horse-racing fans place bets on the races. A decision to arrest and prosecute bookies but not priests, poker players, or horse-racing fans means that the law on its face is unequally applied. Yet such decisions are often made by law enforcement officials, for they recognize the need to adapt legal norms to community values. Courts are placed in similar predicaments when there are laws punishing homosexuality or alcoholism. Some courts (together with the police) ignore such laws; others treat the offenses as medical rather than penal problems; a few administer the law with brutal exactitude.

It would exaggerate the process to say that trial judges make policy when they exercise their discretion in administering justice. They do not make policy, for they do not declare a general standard for treating all like cases that come before them. They have no need to make such a statement. They proceed case by case. Examining a long series of cases, one may discover consistencies that resemble the application of clear-cut policy statements. For instance, few judges appear to issue evictions during the weeks immediately preceding Christmas; some policemen make prostitution arrests mainly to ensure that the women working the trade receive regular medical examinations; some judges use bail as an instrument of pretrial punishment by setting it especially high for alleged crimes that are particularly repulsive to them. In other instances, one would discover inconsistent actions, indicating that the judges and police neither intended to establish implicit policy nor in fact did so.

Whether a judge behaves consistently or inconsistently in exercising his discretion, he influences the adoption of community norms and gradually helps to mold them by his enforcement activities. In this way judges and courts play a far more influential role in society than a mechanical view of the law enforcement process would attribute to them. They enforce laws, and by the manner in which they do so they sometimes mold community norms.

3
Policymaking by the Courts

The courts do more than enforce norms; they do more than evolve new norms through the accretion of decisions. They also create new norms through conscious policymaking. That is not a recent development; American courts have been significant participants in the policymaking process since the founding of the nation. In the nineteenth century, both federal and state courts played a key role in establishing the legal framework that made possible the growth of the American economy. Such concepts as compensation for the taking of property and the freedom to use property for new purposes were not part of the law until nineteenth century courts adopted them.[1]

In more recent years, federal courts have seized more of the policymaking role than the state courts. They have focused their activity less in the economic sphere and more in the areas of civil rights, criminal justice, and the integrity of the institutions of American government. The judiciary led the way in establishing new policies in interracial relations with its decisions forbidding

---

[1] Morton J. Horwitz, *The Transformation of American Law* (Cambridge, Mass.: Harvard University Press, 1977), pp. 31–62.

official segregation in public schools.[2] It also established a new set of norms for processing criminal cases by requiring that indigents be given attorneys at public expense in all cases where the defendant faces possible imprisonment,[3] that defendants be warned that whatever they say to the police may be used against them, and that defendants be permitted attorneys during police interrogation if they request them.[4] The judiciary also established that juveniles be given some of the same rights as adult offenders in hearings that may lead to their imprisonment.[5] Reapportionment of national, state, and local legislative bodies has followed the Supreme Court's *Baker v. Carr* decision, which required that all legislative districts have approximately the same population.[6] The Court declared public prayer in the schools unconstitutional and struck down state laws that prohibited all abortions.[7] In business affairs, the judiciary constantly defines the bounds of fair competition and sets policy regulating labor–management relations.[8] It rigorously constrains official harassment of the press by limiting the use of libel laws by public officials against newspapers.[9]

The distinction between law enforcement and policymaking rests on qualitative differences. In enforcing laws, the courts intend each decision to apply only to a particular case. Such decisions (usually by trial courts) are not designed to create precedent or set policy. Often they are unaccompanied by an opinion; or, if opinions are written, they remain unpublished. Because they are inaccessible, these decisions usually cannot be cited as

[2] *Brown v. Board of Education*, 347 U.S. 483 (1954).
[3] *Gideon v. Wainwright*, 372 U.S. 335 (1963); *Argersinger v. Hamlin*, 92 S. Ct. 2006.
[4] *Miranda v. Arizona*, 348 U.S. 436 (1966).
[5] *In re Gault*, 387 U.S. 1 (1967).
[6] *Baker v. Carr*, 369 U.S. 186 (1962). For the dozens of decisions implementing and broadening the application of this rule, see National Municipal League, *Apportionment in the Nineteen Sixties* (New York: n.d., looseleaf).
[7] *Engel v. Vitale*, 370 U.S. 421 (1962); *Abington School District v. Schempp*, 374 U.S. 203 (1963); *Roe v. Wade*, 410 U.S. 113 (1973).
[8] Martin Shapiro, *The Supreme Court and Administrative Agencies* (New York: Free Press of Glencoe, 1968); Arthur Selwyn Miller, *The Supreme Court and American Capitalism* (New York: Free Press of Glencoe, 1968); Alfred W. Blumrosen, "Legal Process and Labor Law," in William M. Evan (ed.), *Law and Sociology* (New York: Free Press of Glencoe, 1962), pp. 185–220.
[9] *New York Times v. Sullivan*, 376 U.S. 254 (1964).

precedent.[10] Although a series of norm-enforcement decisions may constitute a trend and change the law slowly through judicial usage, judges who make such decisions are often unaware of the direction or pace of the trend. This is true not only in the administration of criminal justice but also in cases concerning divorce and other familial matters, personal injury litigation, and labor disputes.

When they make policy, the courts do not exercise more discretion than when they enforce community norms. The difference lies in the intended impact of the decision. Policy decisions are intended to be guideposts for future actions; norm-enforcement decisions are aimed at the particular case at hand. Policymaking decisions are usually accompanied by published opinions to which other lawyers can refer in other courts. Appellate courts most frequently make policy decisions. Trial courts set policy only occasionally.

Opportunities for judicial policymaking arise less frequently than occasions for enforcing norms. Every case affords the chance to enforce a norm. Only when a norm itself is challenged can the courts engage in policymaking. Such occasions may require the courts to interpret statutes or to interpret constitutional provisions.

In interpreting statutes, American courts determine the effects of legislative decisions. To many judges a legislative enactment is not law until enforced and interpreted by the courts. In most instances the courts interpret statutes routinely, for most cases fall squarely inside or outside the law's provisions. Yet the legislature's intent is ambiguous in some cases; these provide the courts an opportunity to engage in policymaking. For instance, in 1970 the Wisconsin Supreme Court decided that the state's usury law prohibited retail stores from charging more than 12 percent annual interest on revolving charge accounts; the stores had routinely been charging 18 percent.[11] Sometimes a legislature intentionally enacts an ambiguous statute, leaving its detailed interpretation to the courts. New York's 1980 divorce law requires "equitable distribution" of assets between husband and

[10] Indeed, some courts prohibit the citation of such cases. See Rule 28 of the 7th Circuit of the U.S. Court of Appeals; *The Third Branch*, 8 (1976), 9–10.

[11] *State v. J. C. Penney Co.*, 179 NW 2d, 641.

wife. Determining what is equitable involves hundreds of judgments, which become standardized only after many years of litigation. Such things as licenses, pension rights, and tax shelters must be fitted into the scheme. Antitrust statutes are another example of judicial policymaking, because Congress has enacted only the most general guides to policy. Exactly what constitutes a restraint of trade or monopolization is a question that the courts determine. In doing so, courts not only make law but usually set explicit policy to guide other businesses and government agencies.

The courts are often called on to interpret the Constitution. Every controversial statute and many controversial executive actions are challenged in court on grounds of unconstitutionality. When deciding on the constitutionality of a government action, the courts must choose what meaning they wish to give the Constitution and what social objectives to pursue. The Supreme Court, for instance, has given quite different interpretations to the "due process of law" clauses of the Fifth and Fourteenth Amendments, ranging from a guarantee of property against governmental intervention to a guarantee of civil rights against official abuse.

Federal courts have become more involved in policymaking than the state courts for several reasons. One is that the national Constitution is more ambiguous in many of its key provisions. State constitutions, by contrast, are much more detailed documents and leave less room for judicial interpretation. In addition, the United States has become more homogenous than ever before, with nationwide enterprises playing the dominant role in the economy. These enterprises litigate policy issues in the federal courts in order to establish national policy. Federal courts also enjoy a better reputation for legal expertise.

Even though Americans do not usually perceive their courts as policymakers, they often bring important controversies to them. The power of courts to review the constitutionality of legislative and executive action, commonly called the power of "judicial review," constantly involves American courts in conscious policymaking.

Interest Groups and Judicial Policymaking

Judicial policymaking is not distinguished from other court actions only by the intent of judges, the form of their decisions, and the impact of their actions. It is also characterized by a different array of participants. Whereas norm-enforcement decisions usually concern only the immediate litigants, policy decisions draw a wider group of participants to the courtroom. They especially attract the concern of organized interest groups. In part this is because it is difficult and expensive to engage in litigation; it requires the commitment of considerable financial resources as well as the willingness to wait patiently until the case has been won. Consequently, litigants who are more interested in changing policy than in correcting a single wrong seldom stand by themselves.

Moreover, not everyone may sue in court. To litigate, one must have "standing" — that is, one must be personally involved in the sense that one's own person or property has been threatened. Therefore, those who wish to test a law in court often violate the law's provisions intentionally to provide an opportunity to sue in court. Such "test" cases are instigated to test the constitutionality of a law or to give judges an opportunity to interpret statutes in such a manner that the group no longer feels threatened by them.[12]

Interest groups sometimes search for a person who is willing to serve as the formal plaintiff or defendant in a test case. They must find someone who can maintain standing as a litigant and who can be counted on to stick with the court fight over the several years that are required to bring a case to an appellate court. If litigants are fighting segregation in schools, for instance, they must have a child so young that it still is in school when the case reaches the high court; otherwise, the case will be declared moot, for they no longer have a personal interest in the

---

[12] The use of test cases is carefully discussed by Clement E. Vose in "Litigation as a Form of Pressure Group Activity," *Annals of the American Academy of Political and Social Science*, 319 (1958), 20–31, and in *Caucasians Only* (Berkeley: University of California Press, 1959). See also David R. Manwaring, *Render unto Caesar* (Chicago: University of Chicago Press, 1962).

matter. Such litigants must also be firmly settled in their locale, for moving to another city or state might render the case moot.

A test case not only requires careful selection of the individual litigant whose name is lent to the suit but also necessitates careful planning of courtroom strategy. The action protested must be challengeable only on constitutional grounds. If a judge rules that the objectionable action is wrong because some procedure has not been followed or because the law does not apply to the particular case in question, the group will have won its case without gaining its broader policy objective. Such a victory is Pyrrhic, for other officials may still proceed against the group as before. The group's lawyers, therefore, must plan its case so that a decision can only be reached on constitutional grounds. All other avenues of deciding the case must be foreclosed; no gaps may remain open that might allow a court to avoid the issue the group wishes to press on it.

The technique of instituting test cases was perfected by the National Association for the Advancement of Colored People (NAACP) and by Jehovah's Witnesses. It is responsible for their marked success in winning important policy changes for themselves. For Jehovah's Witnesses, it won a new measure of religious freedom; for the NAACP, the technique abolished discrimination by state and local governments. Test cases, however, do not guarantee that an appellate court will hear the case or that a court will respond to the challenge presented by the case. Despite whatever skill has been invested in preparation, an appellate court may simply refuse to review the case or may find legal technicalities that allow it to avoid the policy issue that the group wishes to resolve. For instance, for many years most courts stated that reapportionment issues were not justiciable; consequently, cases involving malapportionment were rarely successful. In such instances judges felt that they could provide no legal remedy for what was admitted to be a moral wrong. Not until 1962 in the *Baker v. Carr* case were litigants successful in convincing the Supreme Court that the issue was justiciable. The earlier failure of groups to convince the Court was not the result of less skillful presentations; it seems more plausible that the Court was prepared in 1962 to decide a matter that it had not been ready to act on earlier. Yet, the Court would have been unable to render such a decision without the willingness of litigants to press their test case through the courts. Likewise, prior to 1954 the NAACP and other groups were unable to press the courts into overruling their 1896 decision that separate but equal public facilities were constitutionally valid. In many cases after 1938, black litigants won admission to particular facilities but did not win a general statement from the Court declaring separate but equal facilities unconstitutional. Only in 1954 did the Supreme Court render the policy decision that the NAACP had sought for so many years.

One should not, however, assume that pro–civil rights groups always seek judicial remedies for their grievances. That depends on the stance of the Court. The Burger Court, dominated by the conservative justices appointed by President Nixon, was much less hospitable to civil rights claims in the late 1970s than the Warren Court had been in the 1960s. Consequently, civil rights groups began to select their cases more carefully and tried to avoid bringing cases which might elicit damaging policy pronouncements from the Court. On the other hand, conservative groups were emboldened and pursued their own litigation strategy to bring cases to the Court that might evoke policies that they favored.

Test cases are not the sole means by which groups participate in the policymaking activities of the courts. Some cases involving policy reach the courts without initial group participation. Appeals by defendants in criminal cases, for instance, are often instigated by the defendant himself, not by a group — even though his appeal may raise policy questions. Moreover, groups other than the one that initiates a test case sometimes want to be heard in court. Under such circumstances groups may participate by submitting an *amicus curiae* (friend of the court) brief to the court.[13] Such briefs are most often filed with an appellate court. In the decade between 1970 and 1980, more than half of all noncommercial cases decided by the Supreme Court with a full opinion had one or more amicus briefs.[14] To file such a brief, a group

---

[13] Karen O'Connor and Lee Epstein, "Amicus Curiae Participation in U.S. Supreme Court Litigation: An Appraisal of Hakman's 'Folklore,'" *Law and Society Review*, 16 (1981–82), 311–20;

[14] O'Connor and Epstein, *op. cit.*, p. 316.

must first obtain permission from the litigants in the case or, failing that, from the court.

An *amicus* brief places the group's opinions and attitudes on the record. It gives a court additional information on which it may decide a case. Sometimes — especially when the original litigant has inadequate counsel — *amicus* briefs present more substantial legal arguments than the litigant himself. In other cases *amicus* briefs inform the court of the probable consequences of an adverse decision.

Amicus curiae briefs involve groups more casually than do test cases. They parallel to a striking degree the principal technique of lobbyists before executive agencies and legislatures, for they rely on the utility of information. It is hoped that giving the courts information will incline them to rule in favor of the group's interest. Furthermore, an *amicus curiae* brief is an effective means of showing a group's support for a particular cause that has reached the court through someone else's initiative. It satisfies a group's own members by dramatically demonstrating the organization's activity in behalf of causes about which they are concerned. On the other hand, presenting such a brief to an appellate court involves fewer risks and less cost than making a test case. No member of the group is personally threatened with imprisonment or the other consequences of a lost lawsuit; the group's own interests are usually not so directly involved that a reversal in court would lastingly damage them. However, although the tactic is less dangerous, it is also less effective. *Amicus curiae* briefs on one side of a case often evoke similar briefs on the other side. There is little evidence that judges are particularly influenced by these briefs. Occasionally an opinion will quote material from an *amicus* brief or follow the logic suggested in it, but the judge might have come to the same conclusions without the brief.

Characteristics of Judicial Policies

The participation of interest groups in judicial policymaking illustrates one similarity between judicial and other governmental policymaking. There are important differences as well. Judicial policies have a narrower scope; they often are directed at government agencies rather than the public at large; and their impact is often more ambiguous than that of legislative policies.

Some issues are almost never raised in courtrooms, so that the courts rarely formulate policies with regard to them. Foreign affairs, although increasingly important to the American political system, are ordinarily beyond the scope of court action. Although many Congressmen and political commentators sharply challenged American participation in the Vietnam war, the Supreme Court by a 6–3 vote refused to rule on its constitutionality.[15] With very few exceptions (involving cases questioning the validity of treaties), courts have not become involved in foreign affairs. Judicial policymaking is restricted to domestic affairs.

Even in the domestic arena, judicial policies do not touch on all matters. The appropriation of funds and the levying of taxes are almost never successfully challenged in court. Moreover, courts rarely demand that funds be appropriated for a particular purpose. Such issues remain the almost exclusive domain of legislative and executive decision making. However, during the waning days of the Nixon administration, the courts actively intervened in conflicts over the spending of money appropriated by Congress but impounded by the President. In several instances, appellate courts ordered the spending of such funds, and Congress subsequently enacted legislation making the impoundment of funds by the executive more difficult.[16]

Most judicial policies are concerned with the regulatory activities of government. Judicial concern with government regulation arises from the constitutional guarantees of individual freedom and the right to hold property subject only to government action through the due process of law. All regulatory policies restrict freedom and property. Therefore, courts have often been asked to determine whether such regulations were imposed through due process or not. Such conflicts have required the courts to develop judicial policies restricting government regulation to reasonable acts adopted through lawful procedures.[17]

---

[15] *Massachusetts v. Laird*, 400 U.S. 886 (1970); see *The New York Times*, November 10, 1970, p. 1.

[16] *Congressional Quarterly Almanac, 1973* (Washington, D.C.: Congressional Quarterly, 1974), p. 253.

[17] Shapiro, *op. cit.*

Judicial policymaking, moreover, is usually directed at other
government agencies rather than at private individuals — another consequence of the interpretive role that courts play. They
interpret statutes and constitutional provisions; in so doing, they
permit or prohibit the action of other government agencies. For
instance, they have prohibited racial discrimination by government agencies in schools, parks, elections, and similar affairs;
but they have not prohibited on constitutional grounds racial discrimination by private individuals. The latter prohibitions, in-
sofar as they have been enacted, are the consequences of legislative and executive policymaking.

A third important characteristic of judicial policies is that their
intended scope is often quite ambiguous — a consequence of
the process by which policies are adopted. Courts make policy
in response to the particular factual situations raised by the cases
they are considering. Although judges may informally consider
a much wider range of facts than those present in a case, the
decision itself is based on the facts of the case under consideration. The judges who write the opinion may intend their decision to apply to many similar situations, but that intention is
usually not clear until other cases have been litigated and until
the new doctrine has been extended to them. In the meantime,
the policy's extent can be quite uncertain because its phraseology
has been necessarily ambiguous. Although legislative policy is
always ambiguous, its ambiguities arise from other causes. Legislative policy is not usually adopted because of a single incident,
and precedents that are themselves ambiguous do not play as
large a role in justifying the policy.[18]

The ambiguity of judicial policy statements leads to a rhythm
of actions typical in judicial policymaking. A high court will declare a new policy in a case involving one constellation of facts.
A series of cases then follows in which the high court or lower
ones extend the policy to other fact situations. After a few years
the scope of the policy becomes more certain.

[18] Donald L. Horowitz, *The Courts and Social Policy* (Washington, D.C.:
Brookings Institution, 1977).

Consequences of Judicial Policymaking

The fact that courts make policy conditions the political process in the United States. It opens another avenue for seeking favorable decisions for those who are unsuccessful with the legislature or executive. If a group fails to capture or hold a legislative majority, and if it fails to elect its candidate as chief executive of the state or nation, it may nevertheless seek to alter public policy through litigation. Access to the courts and success before them depend not on electoral victories but on legal skill and on sufficient financial resources.

Because the courts constitute an additional policymaking arena, there is further uncertainty about public policy in the United States. A controversial matter is not necessarily settled when Congress enacts a law and the President decides to enforce it. The courts may also be called to approve the policy. At the very least in such instances, judicial participation in the process delays decisions by several months. At the most, it stymies Congress and the President and leads to enacting policies favored by judges.

The fragmentation of the policymaking process in the United States has another consequence besides delaying action. It allows certain people who would otherwise be excluded from politics to have a voice in making public decisions. Convicts not only have no right to vote but also are not a very respectable constituency for any legislator or executive. Yet they have played an important role in creating safeguards in criminal law that protect all members of society. Through their appeals, the Supreme Court has decided that searches and seizures must be carried out with a proper warrant if the evidence so obtained is to be used in court, that all defendants must have the opportunity to have legal counsel, and that the prohibition against self-incrimination applies in state as well as federal courts. Other groups almost as unpopular in their locale have, in a like manner, won a voice in policymaking. Although almost disfranchised in Southern states, blacks won the right to use public facilities and public schools on a desegregated basis through court action before Congress or the President gave their cause additional support. Jehovah's Witnesses, a militant Protestant sect whose members make themselves unpopular through their evangelistic fervor, won the right to refuse to salute the flag in school. Atheists and other minority religious groups convinced the courts to outlaw public prayer in the schools. Had such groups been limited to legislative or executive action, there is little doubt that they could not have won adoption of the policies that they obtained through court action.

Finally, the policymaking activities of the courts place them squarely in the center of the political arena. Although court decisions are usually not identified with partisan causes, they are often highly controversial. Although the judiciary's norm-enforcement activities are almost universally accepted, its policymaking function — despite its long history — is not. To many citizens, legislators, executive officials, and even some judges, judicial policymaking is an illegitimate activity, a usurpation of legislative functions. Consequently, the courts attract even more opposition to their policy decisions than the substance of those decisions might have generated by itself. Those who are opposed to a judicial policy win allies from those who are opposed to judicial policymaking in any matter.

III
Participants in the Judicial Process

4
Lawyers and the Bar

Lawyers are the key group in molding the administration of justice and all other legal work. No others may practice before the courts; no others may perform out-of-court legal tasks.

At last count there were more than 622,000 lawyers in the United States.[1] Although some lawyers earn very handsome incomes, most earn less than many professionals. Starting salaries in Wall Street firms were as high as $50,000 in 1982.[2] In 1976 17 percent of the members of the Chicago bar earned more than $60,000, but more than 25 percent earned less than half that amount. Lawyers' incomes lag considerably behind those of physicians; on the average they are closer to those of accountants. In 1976 the median income of attorneys was approximately $30,000, whereas that of physicians was $50,000.[3]

---

[1] Barbara Curran, "The Legal Profession in the 1980's" (address to the American Bar Association), July 30, 1983.

[2] *The New York Times*, May 4, 1982, section IV, p. 2.

[3] John P. Heinz, Edward O. Laumann, Charles L. Cappell, Terence C. Halliday, and Michael H. Schaalman, "Diversity, Representation, and Leadership in an Urban Bar: A First Report of a Survey of the Chicago Bar," *American Bar Foundation Research Journal* (1976), 727; *The New York Times*, May 16, 1977, p. 35.

In recent years there has been a growing feeling that the bar is overcrowded and that too many lawyers are competing for a limited amount of business.[4] Although lawyers have made many efforts to improve their standing they still occupy an ambiguous status position in American society and suffer from the shyster image.

To improve the legal profession and its image, lawyers have organized themselves into bar associations so that they could foster better law schools, eliminate the actual shysters in the profession, and improve legal services to the public. Bar associations have been equally energetic in seeking to raise the economic status of lawyers by restricting entry into the profession, eliminating competition from nonlawyers, and imposing fee schedules on lawyers and clients. Such activities have made bar associations influential in molding the role of lawyers in the American judicial process.

Bar Associations

Bar associations were originally organized to combat judicial corruption in large cities.[5] The Association of the Bar of the City of New York was organized to free New York courts from the clutches of the Tweed Ring. The Chicago Bar Association was organized about the same time to improve the administration of justice in Chicago. The American Bar Association was organized only a few years later, in 1878, to work for the improvement of legal education and of the legal profession in general. Originally it consisted only of individual members scattered throughout the country. Since 1936 its membership has included state and local bar associations, and it has become the national organ of these associations.

[4] *The New York Times*, May 16, 1977, p. 1 and May 17, 1977, p. 1. On fluctuations in the supply of lawyers, also see the *1967 Lawyer Statistical Report* (Chicago: American Bar Foundation, 1968).
[5] For the history of bar associations see Charles Warren, *A History of the American Bar* (Boston: Little, Brown, 1911); M. Louise Rutherford, *The Influence of the American Bar on Public Opinion and Legislation* (Philadelphia: published by author, 1937), pp. 1–21; James W. Hurst, *The Growth of American Law* (Boston: Little, Brown, 1950), pp. 285–94; Edson R. Sunderland, *History of the American Bar Association* (Ann Arbor, Mich.: n.p., 1953).

For many years membership in bar associations was entirely voluntary. The lawyers interested in their activities joined; the remainder abstained. Membership grew very slowly under such conditions. In most states barely a quarter of the lawyers belonged to local associations in the 1920s; even fewer belonged to the American Bar Association.[6] Unlike medical societies, bar associations had no control over facilities vital to lawyers. Hospitals normally restricted use of their facilities to those who belonged to the county medical society, but all lawyers admitted to the bar could practice in court whether they were members of a bar association or not.

Legal reformers recognized that if the bar were to become more influential in political decisions regarding the courts, such as the selection of judges, the profession would have to organize itself better, improve its educational standards, and impose stricter discipline on its members. To obtain these objectives a small group of prominent attorneys, led by Herbert Harley, established the American Judicature Society in 1913; its purpose was to work for the improvement of the bar and the courts. Harley himself was much impressed with the Law Society of Upper Canada, in which membership was compulsory for all lawyers practicing in the area. He quickly turned the Judicature Society into an instrument for promoting compulsory membership in bar associations in the United States. Rather than call such a system a "closed shop" or "compulsory membership" — both terms having bad connotations in the antiunion atmosphere of the early twentieth century — Harley campaigned for what he termed an "integrated" bar.[7]

In 1921, North Dakota became the first state to integrate its bar. Its legislature took the initiative by passing a statute requiring all practicing lawyers to become members. A number of other states followed this procedure, until the Oklahoma legislature adopted and then repealed its statute integrating the bar in 1939. The Oklahoma Supreme Court reacted to this setback by issuing a court order requiring bar membership for practice before the Oklahoma courts. Thereafter, other supreme courts

[6] Dayton McKean, in *The Integrated Bar* (Boston: Houghton, Mifflin, 1963), p. 40, quotes a former president of the ABA on state membership.
[7] *Ibid.*, pp. 35–41.

followed suit, either using specific statutory authority or relying on their inherent power as the highest tribunal of the state.[8] As McKean points out, integration of the bar through a court order makes bar associations completely independent of state legislatures. The bar can lobby before legislatures without fear of reprisal, for their membership funds and their operating rules are beyond the reach of legislative action. Only the Supreme Court can regulate bar association activities in the states that have integrated the bar through a court order.

The bar associations of 33 states, including such populous ones as California and Michigan, are now integrated.[9] When the bar is integrated, every lawyer who wishes to practice his profession must join the state bar association, pay its dues, and subject himself to its rules.

Both integrated and voluntary bar associations have directed much of their effort toward improving the quality of legal services available to the public. Part of their activity has been directed toward improving legal education; part of it has been focused on tightening admission requirements to the profession.

The Training of Lawyers

Like doctors, contemporary lawyers must submit to a long period of training before becoming eligible to practice. This, however, is a twentieth century development in the United States. Throughout the nineteenth century legal training was haphazard. Most lawyers received their training in the office of a practicing attorney; they worked for him as a clerk and, by doing so, learned the trade themselves. When they felt ready to strike out on their own, they sought admission to the bar from a court and proceeded to establish their own practice. Only a few law schools existed. Some were connected with a university, but legal training was not generally considered a legitimate part of the classical education that most universities dispensed. Some law schools were independent, like the Litchfield Law School,

[8] *Ibid.*, pp. 40–51. This gives a brief account of the growth of the movement to integrate the bar.

[9] *Ibid.*, p. 21. McKean notes twenty-seven states. After his book was published, six additional states acted to integrate their bars. Private communication with Sharon Palmer, Bar Services Department, ABA, August 24, 1983.

but they survived for only a short time. In both types of law school, students listened to lectures on the law, read treatises, and prepared themselves in a general way for legal work. Such legal training was almost always capped by a period of apprenticeship with a practicing attorney before the fledgling sought to practice on his own.[10]

After the Civil War university law school training became more acceptable as the result of efforts to systematize legal studies by using the "case method." Espoused chiefly by Dean C. C. Langdell of Harvard, the study of cases was said to make legal research and education scientific. Adoption of the Langdell case approach transformed legal education into the study of appellate cases. Collections of such cases in "casebooks" gave the student his raw materials. His task as a fledgling lawyer was to learn how to separate fact from rule, the governing facts from the incidental ones, and the *ratio decidendi* (the rule of the case) from *obiter dicta* (incidental comments) in order to understand the principles that underlie the common law and govern the development of case law. The method was applied to all substantive fields of law; thus, the student learned torts, contracts, property, estates and wills, and procedure by examining cases instead of through an office apprenticeship or lectures or treatises.

Although the case method gave law schools a respectable place in universities' academic departments, university-connected law schools did not immediately attract most would-be lawyers. Until after World War I apprenticeships in law offices remained the dominant method of induction into the legal profession. After the war, a larger proportion of those who desired to become attorneys went to a law school, but most went to unaccredited, proprietary law schools. These were profit-making institutions that held their classes at night to accommodate students who had to earn their living at another job during the day. Such schools required little beyond literacy for admission. Their law course took as little as two years of part-time work. Because they

[10] Legal education in the nineteenth century is well described in Hurst, *op. cit.*, pp. 256–76; Albert J. Harno, *Legal Education in the U.S.* (San Francisco: Bancroft-Whitney, 1953), pp. 35–50.

depended on the tuition of the student for their economic success, they failed few students.[11]

The quality of lawyers produced by this patchwork educational system varied tremendously. Those prepared by Harvard, Yale, Michigan, or other nationally oriented university law schools possessed a thorough, if not very practical, preparation. Some of those who graduated from night schools were brilliant, ambitious men who compensated for their poor preparation by prodigious effort. Many, however, were unqualified when they began to practice. To remedy this situation, the American Bar Association (ABA) sought to upgrade law schools by accrediting those institutions that met its standards. In 1917 it required its schools to exclude students who lacked two years of college preparation; it also gradually lengthened the law school course. In 1900 the ABA helped to organize the American Association of Law Schools (AALS), an accrediting association controlled by the law schools themselves.[12] By the mid-twentieth century the ABA and the AALS had succeeded in convincing law schools to restrict entry to college juniors and to require three years for full-time legal education.[13] Part-time attendance lengthened the required period. Moreover, the activity of the AALS and ABA eventually drove most of the unaccredited, profit-making schools out of business. In the academic year 1936–1937, eighty-eight unapproved schools educated 38 percent of the nation's law school students. Twenty years later only thirty-seven such schools remained, and they had less than 10 percent of the nation's law school students.[14] By 1980, very few states permitted graduates of non-ABA-accredited law schools to take their bar examinations. Only a handful of states allowed students to substitute an apprenticeship program for law school, and this option was rarely used.[15]

[11] Alfred Z. Reed, *Present-Day Law Schools in the U.S. and Canada*, Bulletin No. 21 (New York: Carnegie Foundation for the Advancement of Teaching, 1928), pp. 110–28.

[12] Rutherford, *op. cit.*, pp. 35–55.

[13] Albert P. Blaustein and Charles O. Porter, *The American Lawyer* (Chicago: University of Chicago Press, 1954), pp. 185–86.

[14] Joseph T. Tinnelly, *Part-Time Legal Education in the U.S.* (Brooklyn: Foundation Press, 1957), pp. 24–25; Blaustein and Porter, *op. cit.*, pp. 176–79.

[15] Frances K. Zemans and Victor G. Rosenblum, *The Making of a Public Profession* (Chicago: American Bar Foundation, 1981), p. 7.

As attendance at approved law schools became the predominant mode of legal education, the curriculum came under increasing attack.[16] New subjects — administrative law, tax law, patent law, and other specializations — were piled atop the traditional fields. The case method came to be viewed as a new orthodoxy and was criticized for its abstraction from real life and its failure to teach law students many matters necessary for a successful legal practice.

Consequently, legal education continues to be in flux. The case method still predominates: law students can be distinguished on any campus by the massive tomes they carry to and from class. However, other legal materials, such as statutes and administrative rules, are also included in many texts. A few schools use materials from the social sciences, although teaching students to understand the social context of legal work is not yet part of the mainstream of legal education.[17] Finally, students are given increasing opportunities to get a taste of the practice of law through summer internships, moot trials, and preparation of cases for indigents.

Another change in legal education is the growing tendency to require the continuing education of attorneys and judges after they have been admitted to the bar. By court order in a number of states, lawyers and judges must attend a prescribed number of class hours every year or two to win renewal of their license to practice.[18] Although such continuing education courses are

---

[16] An excellent description of legal education and a summary of criticisms of it can be found in "Modern Trends in Legal Education," *Columbia Law Review*, 64 (1964), 710–34. See also Blaustein and Porter, *op. cit.*, pp. 170–73; Harno, *op. cit.*, pp. 122–60. Some early trends are noted by Esther L. Brown, *Lawyers and the Promotion of Justice* (New York: Russell Sage Foundation, 1938), pp. 66–103.

[17] An indication of how slowly legal education has accepted social science techniques is a statement by Fred L. Strodtbeck concerning the impact of the University of Chicago Jury Project on the curriculum of the law school. He writes, "As a point of interest, the existence of the project in the Law School has not affected law teaching in any way, save that during some of our early difficulties the regular faculty had less time to devot to it." "Social Process, the Law, and Jury Functioning," in William M. Evan (ed.), *Law and Sociology* (New York: Free Press of Glencoe, 1962), p. 148, note 6.

[18] In 1983 Minnesota, Iowa, Wisconsin, and nine other states required continuing legal education for renewal of one's bar license. Personal communication with William Wheeler, ABA, October 26, 1983.

not likely to be integrated with the preprofessional training of law students, they promote regular contact between the law school and practicing attorneys — and may exert a subtle influence on legal education in the United States.

Admission to the Bar

Possessing a law degree by itself does not usually entitle the holder to practice law. Because an attorney is technically a court official, he must, in addition to possessing legal training, be admitted to practice by a court. In the same way that legal education was haphazard for most of the nineteenth century, admission to the bar depended more on the charity or leniency of a local judge than on the application of a set of strict standards. The lack of standards is reflected in the memoirs of Salmon P. Chase, a lawyer who eventually served as Chief Justice of the Supreme Court. He wrote:

> Very seldom, I imagine, has any candidate for admission to the bar presented himself for examination with a slenderer stock of learning. I was examined in open court. The venerable and excellent Justice Cranch put the questions. I answered as well as I was able — how well or how ill I cannot say — but certainly, I think, not very well. Finally, the Judge asked me how long I had studied. I replied that, including the time employed in reading in college and the scraps devoted to legal reading before I regularly commenced the study, and the time since, I thought three years might be made up. The Judge smiled and said, "We think, Mr. Chase, that you must study another year and present yourself again for examination." "Please, your honors," said I deprecatingly, "I have made all my arrangements to go to the western country and practice law." The kind Judge yielded to this appeal and turning to the Clerk said, "Swear in Mr. Chase." Perhaps he would have been less facile if he had not known me personally and very well.[19]

Normally, to be admitted by one court was sufficient to practice before any court in the state, for each judge respected his colleagues' actions in admission proceedings. Thus, the standards of the most lenient judge in a state became the minimum standards for admission.[20]

[19] Quoted by Hurst, *op. cit.*, p. 281.
[20] *Ibid.*, pp. 276–85.

This practice, like the weaknesses in legal education, attracted the attention of the ABA and the state bars.[21] Their interest was twofold. Easy admission allowed the entry of unqualified and unscrupulous attorneys, whose work blemished the reputation of all lawyers. Moreover, easy entrance into the legal profession allowed more lawyers to compete for the available legal work and depressed the income of lawyers. Unlike most other professions, which remained beyond the reach of second-generation Americans because of costly training or restrictive admission practices, the legal profession became a favorite avenue of advancement for immigrants' sons. This is reflected in the admission statistics for the 1920s, the first decade in which sons of immigrants who had entered the United States during the preceding thirty years were likely to become eligible to practice law. Admissions jumped from 52 for every one million in the population in 1920 to 82 in 1928 and 79 in 1929.[22]

In 1975 many lawyers in Chicago still came from relatively modest backgrounds. Whereas the fathers of most lawyers had themselves been members of the middle class, more than a third of the most recent law school graduates came from lower-middle-class white-collar and blue-collar backgrounds.[23] Moreover, a much larger number of blacks and women entered the bar in the 1970s than ever before.

Entry of new groups into the legal profession came despite obstacles that were erected by the organized bar to restrict entry. Early in the twentieth century, the bar had obtained legislation to lengthen the required legal training before application for admission could be accepted. By 1917, thirty-six states prescribed definite training requirements; by 1921, twenty-eight states already required three years of law school training.[24]

Most efforts to restrict entry into the bar, however, were focused on requiring applicants to pass a standardized bar examination. Every state now uses such a bar examination either for all applicants or for those who have not attended state-approved

---

[21] Rutherford, *op cit.*, pp. 55–86.
[22] *1961 Lawyer Statistical Report*, p. 89.
[23] Zemans and Rosenblum, *op. cit.*, p. 39.
[24] Rutherford, *op. cit.*, pp. 39–41.

law schools.[25] In a few states, notably California and North Carolina, the integrated bar association itself conducts the examination.[26] In other states, a board of bar examiners is appointed by the governor for this purpose. Bar examinations have reduced admissions to the legal profession. For instance, in California, since the bar association was given control over admissions in 1927, the number of lawyers has not kept pace with the population. While the California population more than tripled, the number of lawyers increased more slowly.[27] For the country as a whole, however, the number of lawyers has gradually increased. In 1960 there was one practicing lawyer for every 949 Americans; by 1980 the number of lawyers had increased so that there was one for every 410 people.[28]

Bar examinations have also had an unanticipated consequence. Because law schools are accredited according to, among other things, the number of students who pass the exam and are often rated by students according to this standard, legal education has become very much examination oriented in many states. Subjects included in the examination are required of the students, and courses in these subjects are often molded according to the questions asked on the examinations. Other subjects — likely to be new ones — that are not on the examinations are electives, which few students feel they can afford to take. Consequently, bar examinations have stifled changes in legal education in many states in which they are given. Students from schools that do not specifically prepare them for the bar (such national law schools as Yale emphasize national rather than local law) attend cram schools before taking the examinations.[29]

Bar associations have not restricted their interest in admission procedures to the educational qualifications of would-be law-

---

[25] On current practice, see Blaustein and Porter, *op. cit.*, pp. 210–39.

[26] McKean, *op. cit.*, p. 24.

[27] *1971 Lawyer Statistical Report*, p. 63.

[28] Barbara Curran, "Lawyer Demographics" (address to the American Bar Association), Aug. 8, 1981. By comparison there were 476 Americans per physician providng patient care in 1979: U.S. Bureau of the Census, *Statistical Abstract of the United States*, 1981 (Washington, D.C.: Government Printing Office, 1981), table 163, p. 105.

[29] McKean discusses the impact of bar examinations on legal education, *op. cit.*, pp. 64–66.

yers. They have also sought to restrict entry to those who are morally fit to become lawyers. Each applicant for admission to the bar must have "good moral character." However, this standard has been vague.[30] At the very least it means that no one who has a serious criminal record can be admitted to the practice of law. In some cases it has led to the refusal of a board of examiners to admit someone who has held (or still holds) unpopular political views. Although the standards are vague, the Supreme Court has usually upheld the authority of state courts to refuse admission to persons the state deems unworthy to practice law.[31] Admission is a privilege that a court may withhold. Through such actions the bar has successfully prevented the entry of some individuals who might have embarrassed the legal profession.

Legal Ethics and the Economic Status of Lawyers

Another long-term concern of the ABA and state and local bar associations has been the ethical norms under which attorneys operate. Recognizing its obligation to assist the courts in rendering justice and smarting under the public image of shyster, the organized bar turned its attention in the early twentieth century to adopting a code of ethics. In 1907 it adopted one for attorneys; later it also adopted a code for judges.

The Code of Professional Responsibility concerns itself with various matters.[32] One group of rules involves the conduct of lawyers toward their clients and the general public. These rules reflect the conflict that lawyers often experience between doing their utmost for their clients and supporting the law. Thus, when an updating of these rules was considered (in the aftermath of Watergate) the ABA debated them vigorously. The rules that were finally adopted in 1983 did not substantially increase the obligation of lawyers to represent the public interest rather than their clients'. The revision did not include the proposed requirement that attorneys reveal to law enforcement officials their

[30] Blaustein and Porter, *op. cit.*, pp. 212–18.

[31] Harry Kalven, Jr., and Roscoe T. Steffen, "The Bar Admission Cases: An Unfinished Debate Between Justice Harlan and Justice Black," *Law in Transition*, 21 (1961), 155–91.

[32] The following categories are similar to those proposed by Jerome Carlin, *Lawyers' Ethics* (New York: Russell Sage Foundation, 1966).

clients' intentions to defraud the public. That decision by the bar was made partly out of fear. A prominent Chicago attorney, Albert Jenner, gave one example. He had just represented an alleged crime syndicate financier who had been murdered. Mr. Jenner explained that his client had told him "everything." Under the proposed rule, he said, "I could have been required to disclose. I don't want to be assassinated."[33] In addition, such a revision of the rule threatened the confidential relationship between attorneys and corporate clients. Lawyers feared that corporations would hesitate to employ them in negotiating intricate arrangements that might have dubious legality. Thus, these rules were not changed, and attorneys remain obligated to represent their clients zealously but within the bounds of the law.

Other rules seek to regulate attorneys' relationships with their colleagues and to protect their monopoly on legal services. For example, some rules prohibit the division of fees with other attorneys and forbid lawyers to assist nonprofessionals in the "unauthorized practice" of law. Such rules reflect the deep concern of the bar with protecting its economic position and professional status. A major change in this set of rules during the late 1970s was a vast relaxation of the rule against advertisement. Whereas 20 years earlier all advertisements were banned, by 1980 only the most extravagant commercials elicited professional concern.

A third set of rules seeks to prevent the perpetration of fraud upon the court and interference with the administration of justice. Several rules govern the attorney's release of information to the press — to avoid trial by press instead of in the courtroom.[34] Another rule exhorts the attorney not to engage in undignified or discourteous conduct degrading to a tribunal.

Every state has a procedure to enforce these rules.[35] The states' supreme courts impose the formal sanctions, but in most

---

[33] *Wall Street Journal* (Midwest ed.), Feb. 8, 1983, p. 6.

[34] Disciplinary Rule 7-107.

[35] The following relies heavily on Eric H. Steele and Raymond T. Nimmer, "Lawyer, Clients, and Professional Regulation," *American Bar Foundation Research Journal* (1976), 917–1019. See also F. Raymond Marks and Darlene Cathcart, "Discipline within the Legal Profession: Is It Self-Regulation," *Illinois Law Forum* (1974), 193–236; and Michael C. Dorf, "Disbarment in the United States: Who Shall Do the Noisome Work," *Columbia Journal of Law and Social Problems*, 12 (1975), 1–75.

states the bar associations themselves conduct all preliminary investigations and hearings.[36] They principally rely on complaints from clients, although some cases come from other lawyers or nonprofessionals involved in the case. Disciplinary agencies also take up cases coming to their attention from the news media, for example, when an attorney is convicted of a crime or when a prominent person, such as former President Nixon, is accused of unethical conduct.

The heavy reliance on clients to bring complaints has two important consequences. First, much potentially unethical conduct goes unreported because clients do not know whom to contact with their complaints.[37] Second, many complaints do not in fact involve unethical conduct but rather concern contractual disputes with the attorney involved. Despite increased public and professional concern about legal ethics, the sanctioning of attorneys has not become uniformly more frequent or severe. Whereas 11 attorneys out of every 10,000 were disbarred or resigned in 1940, the number was approximately half that in 1974.[38] Moreover, an increasing number of the sanctions fall short of disbarment and consist instead of temporary suspension and public or private reprimand. More than 90 percent of all complaints are dismissed without investigation — a reflection of the small, often voluntary, staffs of the disciplinary agencies and of the contractual nature of many complaints.[39] Less than 1 percent of the original complaints lead to disbarment.[40]

Fewer lawyers abide by the code than these statistics suggest. Carlin's study in New York City showed that only those norms that prohibit interference with the administration of justice through fraud or bribery or that condemn taking advantage of clients were widely accepted by lawyers.[41] Fewer lawyers accepted the rules prohibiting various forms of solicitation. The

---

[36] Steele and Nimmer, *op. cit.*, pp. 921–33.

[37] For instance, a survey of clients who had serious problems with their lawyers showed only 2 percent going to the bar association as a remedy for their complaint. *Ibid.*, p. 958.

[38] *Ibid.*, p. 939.

[39] *Ibid.*, p. 982.

[40] *Ibid.*

[41] Jerome Carlin, *Lawyers on Their Own* (New Brunswick, N.J.: Rutgers University Press, 1962), pp. 47–48 and 49–132 *passim*.

degree to which they were accepted depended in New York on the status of the lawyer and the nature of his practice. High-status lawyers, who worked in large firms and practiced before the federal courts — when they entered a court at all — were most likely to conform to the rules. Lower-status lawyers, who were usually engaged in solo practice before state courts, were less likely to accept the norms. Indeed, the more contact such lawyers had with lower-level courts, the less likely they were to conform to legal ethics. The culture of the lower courts — waiting around, exchanging gossip, litigating petty criminal and civil cases — promoted unethical actions.

The most frequent complaint made to the Association of the Bar of the City of New York's grievance committee concerned neglect of cases by lawyers. Charges of converting or misappropriating funds and of client neglect constituted the most frequent complaints adjudicated against lawyers.[42] To meet such complaints, New York in 1982 established a special Clients' Security Fund, financed by registration fees of attorneys, to reimburse clients who were defrauded by their lawyers.[43]

Another rule that has disturbed lawyers a great deal prohibits the "unauthorized practice" of law. Unauthorized practice is the activity by individuals who are not lawyers in some phase of work that lawyers do. Unauthorized representation of a client before a court almost never occurs. Rather, the bar is concerned about real estate agents who fill out legal forms closing a sale, trust company officers who advise their customers about the drawing of a will, and accountants who give tax advice to their clients. Each of these activities could be performed just as well by a lawyer.

Bar associations have attacked such unauthorized practices by disciplining lawyers associated with them. Thus, a lawyer who is employed by a tax-accounting firm and gives legal advice to the firm's clients may be disciplined by disbarment proceedings against him.[44] Another line of attack has been to seek legislation prohibiting others from doing lawyers' work. Bar association

[42] Carlin, *Lawyers' Ethics*, p. 154.
[43] *The New York Times* (Midwest ed.), July 27, 1982, p. 3.
[44] "Opinion No. 297, Professional Ethics Committee," *American Bar Association Journal*, 47 (1961), 527–28; Disciplinary Rule 3-101.

strategy apparently has been to seek legislation that is as vague as possible, leaving to the courts the precise definition of what is unauthorized practice of law, for the bar associations are confident that judges will be sympathetic to their professional interests.[45] Other state laws prohibit nonlawyers from specific kinds of activities. In 1963, for instance, the United States Supreme Court upheld a Kansas statute prohibiting anyone except lawyers from engaging in the activity called debt-adjusting — reorganizing an individual's or company's debt in such a way that it might be paid over a period of time.[46]

State courts have also acted to prevent unauthorized practice, but with less success, as demonstrated in Arizona in 1962. The Arizona Supreme Court had decided that when realtors or title companies prepared instruments of conveyance in connection with property sales, they were engaging in unauthorized practice, which was punishable in court. The court listed as unlawful forty-four other activities commonly performed by realtors. Stung by this rebuke, Arizona realtors spearheaded a drive to initiate a constitutional amendment specifically authorizing realtors and title companies to continue drawing up sales contracts. They collected 107,420 signatures, placed the amendment on the ballot, and won the subsequent election.[47] Such incidents emphasize the weakness of a bar association when it is forced into the general political arena.

Bar Associations and Politics

Bar associations are more than guild groups that restrict entry into the profession and seek to control the activity of their members. They are also political interest groups, actively engaged in lobbying for proposals that the bar considers vital to its interests.

Much of the bar's political activity concerns the organization and personnel of the courts. The bar claims a more immediate interest than any other organized group in the organization of the courts, for lawyers may deal with courts every day whereas

---

[45] Rutherford, op. cit., p. 97; Blaustein and Porter, op. cit., pp. 126–29.

[46] Ferguson v. Skrupa, 372 U.S. 726 (1963).

[47] Merton E. Marks, "The Lawyers and the Realtors: Arizona's Experience," American Bar Association Journal, 49 (1963), 139–41.

ordinary citizens use the courts at most once or twice during their lifetime. Moreover, lawyers assert that their constant contact with courts gives them a better understanding of how the judiciary ought to be organized. Consequently, bar associations have invested much of their energy in devising and promoting court reorganization schemes. Bar association efforts to reorganize the courts, however, also illustrate the weakness of the bar as a political lobby, for lawyers seldom unite behind the reform proposals. Some lawyers oppose reorganization plans because changes in court structure upset their routine, force them to learn new procedures, and occasionally deprive them of advantages they possess under the status quo. Only where changes eliminate nonprofessional elements in the judicial process has the legal profession been united in its support. Thus, moves to abolish the office of justice of the peace — a minor judicial officer who often is not a lawyer — usually win the enthusiastic backing of the organized bar. In contrast, changes in court procedure or reorganization of major trial courts win the backing of only some attorneys.[48]

The organized bar has also been very active in seeking to influence the selection of judges. On the state level, where judges are often elected on a partisan or nonpartisan ballot, the bar association has frequently lobbied for a change in selection procedures that would give the bar a greater voice. Generally bar associations have supported "merit selection" (also called the Missouri Plan), under which the bar together with laypeople nominate a panel of candidates from which the governor appoints the judge. In areas where the bar is unable to win approval of such a plan, it seeks to establish its influence with the voting public by holding "bar primaries." In these polls, lawyers belonging to the bar association vote on the fitness of candidates to judicial office. The results of the polls are then publicly announced in the hope of influencing the electorate. In cases where judges are appointed or where the bar can obtain access to party

[48] The role of the ABA is described in somewhat uncritical terms by Rutherford, op. cit., pp. 131–244; the opposition of lawyers is described by Sidney Schulman in *Toward Judicial Reform in Pennsylvania* (Philadelphia: University of Pennsylvania Law School, 1962), pp. 218–21.

nominating conventions, the bar seeks to establish its influence with the officials who appoint or nominate judges.[49]

The bar has used a different strategy with respect to federal judges, who are appointed by the President after senatorial confirmation. It tries to influence the President and the Attorney General as they make their initial nomination. The ABA has met with a large measure of success in this effort. Since President Eisenhower's administration, the ABA has exerted considerable influence in the Justice Department's initial screening procedure. It has become standard procedure for the Attorney General to seek the ABA's opinion about potential nominees when choosing a name for submission by the President to the senate.[50] Although Presidents do not always accept the ABA's advice, they invite bar association comment before nominating judges. Under Eisenhower, the ABA attained the stature of a veto group; he gave his Attorney General instruction not to submit names disapproved by the ABA.[51] Nevertheless, a few judges were nominated by the Eisenhower administration over the opposition of the ABA. Since then, as Figure 4.1 shows, the ABA has had considerable success in obtaining judicial appointments for candidates it regarded as qualified. The bar association rated about half the appointees as exceptionally well qualified or well qualified. The ABA disagreed with the administration in only a small proportion of nominations.

Yet, with respect to selecting judges, the legal profession is not always united in its support of bar association proposals or candiates. Lawyers represent different clients and develop opposing points of view. The large section of the bar that often handles damage cases is especially divided, between lawyers representing insurance companies ("the defense bar") and lawyers representing injured clients ("the plaintiff bar"). These two groups of lawyers seldom agree on methods of selecting judges;

---

[49] Rutherford, op. cit., pp. 155–61; Hurst, op. cit., pp. 128–34; Edward M. Martin, *The Role of the Bar in Electing the Bench in Chicago* (Chicago: University of Chicago Press, 1936). See Chap. 6 for a fuller discussion of these matters.

[50] Elliot E. Slotnick, "The ABA Standing Committee on the Federal Judiciary," *Judicature*, 66 (1983), 348–62.

[51] The role of the ABA in selecting federal judges is best described by Joel B. Grossman, *Lawyers and Judges: The A.B.A. and the Politics of Judicial Selection* (New York: John Wiley, 1965).

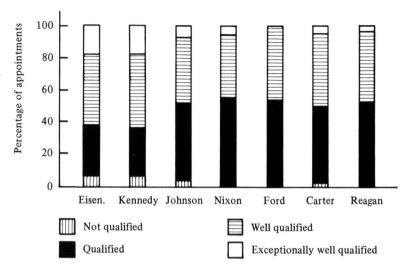

FIGURE 4.1
ABA Ratings of District Court Appointees, by Administration

Sources: For the Eisenhower and Kennedy administrations, Harold W. Chase, "Johnson Administration Judicial Appointments 1963–1966," *Minnesota Law Review*, 52 (1968), 987; reprinted by permission. For the other administrations, Sheldon Goldman, "Reagan's Judicial Appointments at Mid-term," *Judicature*, 66 (1983), 338–339. Reprinted by permission.

they often disagree about individual candidates for the bench. Consequently, even in this sphere of political action, bar associations often do not represent the united opinion of the legal profession. Their efforts to control the selection of judges are severely hampered by such internal divisions among lawyers.

The bar is also active in promoting legislation that will benefit both lawyers and the administration of justice. The bar has staunchly supported legal assistance programs for the poor that are federally financed, despite the staunch opposition of President Reagan. In a more self-interested matter, it has sought to require legal representation before administrative bodies and to require compulsory membership in state bar associations.

Finally, bar associations concern themselves with general policy matters not directly related to the courts or the administration of justice. Earlier in the century the ABA opposed bills in Congress restricting court jurisdiction in labor cases or establishing welfare programs.[52] Later, the ABA supported the Bricker Amendment, which restricted the President's treaty-making power, and took other conservative stands on public issues.[53] At each national convention the ABA passes on matters of current controversy; its journal publishes a listing each month of legislation pending before Congress on which the association has taken a stand.[54] No evidence indicates that its influence is great on such matters, but the ABA does not hesitate to speak.

In their many activities bar associations have sought to mold the conditions under which courts are available to the public. On the one hand, they have strenuously sought to improve the quality of legal services by improving legal education, by reforming the structure of the courts, by promoting the selection of able lawyers for judgeships, and by establishing a stringent ethical code of conduct for lawyers. On the other hand, the bar's activities have tended to make legal services available on a more restricted basis. The bar's campaign against unauthorized practice is an attempt to safeguard its monopoly over legal services. Bar association concern with political issues shows that these groups are not just oriented toward legal reform; they often act like other interest groups in pressing for adoption of measures desired by their members.

The Availability of Legal Services

The quality of legal services depends on more than the number of lawyers and the training they have received. It also de-

---

[52] Rutherford, *op. cit.*, pp. 131–244, describes the ABA's opposition to measures sponsored by "liberals" to restrict the jurisdiction of the federal courts. Such legislation would have made it more difficult for the courts to strike down state social welfare legislation. See also Felix Frankfurter and Nathan Greene, *The Labor Injunction* (New York: Macmillan, 1930), pp. 150–81.

[53] *The New York Times*, Feb. 20, 1957, p. 15.

[54] In January 1976, this list included no-fault auto insurance, Administration Procedure Act amendments, additional judgeships, judicial circuits, three-judge courts, judicial tenure, open government laws, gun control, federal criminal code revision, consumer protection, Real Estate Settlement Procedure Act amendments, workmen's compensation, medical malpractice insurance, criminal justice information, privacy, LEAA extension, fair trade laws, antitrust laws. *American Bar Association Journal*, 62 (1976), 15.

pends on their availability to those who need legal services. Since lawyers perform many services that do not entail courtroom appearances, people who need lawyers are not necessarily those caught in the toils of the law.

Legal advice, like medical attention, is often preventive: it is aimed at keeping the client out of court rather than bringing him before it. The preventive nature of legal services is particularly obvious with regard to civil cases. People form businesses, collect debts, clarify their titles to property, collect compensation for damages, enforce contracts, probate wills, obtain divorces, and adopt children. Each of these actions requires the services of a lawyer; only some of them necessitate an appearance in court.

The availability of lawyers is partly a matter of how lawyers are perceived by the public. Are people as used to walking into a lawyer's office as into a doctor's? Do they know how to find a lawyer? Do they have realistic perceptions of how much legal advice will cost?

All available evidence indicates that the general public is not well informed about legal services.[55] Most people believe lawyers will charge them considerably more than they actually do.[56] Most people turn to friends, relatives, and neighbors for advice on choosing an attorney, and a sizable proportion simply turn to the yellow pages of their telephone directory.[57] About one-third of the population has never visited a lawyer.[58] Most problems, except for the drafting of wills, are resolved without the help of attorneys;[59] people who have problems requiring an attorney often do not see a lawyer even though they might be able to afford minimum fees.

[55] Much of this paragraph is based on Barbara A. Curran, *The Legal Needs of the Public* (Chicago: American Bar Foundation, 1977).

[56] *Ibid.*, p. 231. See also Roger B. Hunting and Gloria S. Neuwirth, *Who Sues in New York City* (New York: Columbia University Press, 1962), pp. 49–52; George Buckner, 2d, "What Your Clients Think of You," *Journal of the Missouri Bar*, 17 (1961), 468–69.

[57] Curran, *Legal Needs*, pp. 200–203.

[58] *Ibid.*, p. 147.

[59] *Ibid.*, pp. 138–43. See also Cyril A. Fox, Jr., "Providing Legal Services for the Middle Class in Civil Matters," *University of Pittsburgh Law Review*, 26 (1965), 811–47; Barlow F. Christenson, *Lawyers for People of Moderate Means* (Chicago: American Bar Foundation, 1970); Bruce Campbell and Susette Talarico, "Access to Legal Services," *Judicature*, 66 (1983), 313–18.

The organization of the legal profession seems to aggravate this situation considerably. Unlike medicine, the legal profession has not traditionally recognized specialization. Although several states — California among them — now permit certification in a limited number of specialties, most do not.[60] Consequently, although an attorney may do most of his work in one or two areas of the law and know little about others, he is not obliged to limit his practice to his areas of expertise. A layperson has no easy way of knowing whether his attorney is competent to handle his particular problems. In addition, lawyers have been reticent to advertise their services even though most legal restrictions over advertisement were lifted in the late 1970s. The American consumer is flooded with appeals to buy, but he seldom sees claims by lawyers that their services might be useful. Moreover, the lawyer's professional reluctance to advertise apparently inhibits his offering additional services to his clients. Whereas the doctor might tell a patient who complains of a cold that he needs a complete examination, a lawyer who sees a client about a will is not likely to examine other aspects of the client's legal relationships or to offer his services. A recent survey indicates that most clients would not mind — indeed, many would welcome — such additional services.[61] However, most lawyers feel that it is unprofessional to probe into a client's affairs; they wait for the client to complain of some difficulty before offering advice. Only when a client explicitly comes in for an "annual legal checkup" is the lawyer likely to examine the entire range of legal problems that the client may have.

The difficulties facing clients who can pay for legal services are multiplied for those who are indigent. Justice is available only to those who have legal assistance, except where administrative procedures and small claims courts are available. Those who are indigent must either forgo justice or seek help in procuring legal assistance. In the early 1960s, an estimate of the individuals requiring legal assistance was placed conservatively

---

[60] In 1983, nine states provided specialty certification. Personal communication with William Wheeler, ABA, October 26, 1983.

[61] Buckner, *op. cit.*, p. 482.

at more than 900,000; less than half of these people in fact received legal aid.[62]

Several private organizations exist in the United States to provide legal assistance to indigents. The most numerous are the legal aid societies, which specialize in providing legal assistance to indigents. In addition there are the legal aid bureaus that are part of general charitable organizations (such as settlement houses), bar association legal aid offices, law school clinics that provide legal assistance, and (in a handful of localities) tax-supported legal aid bureaus.[63] In 1959, 96 legal aid groups were staffed by salaried personnel and 41 groups staffed by volunteers. They were located principally in metropolitan areas and served 72.9 million of America's 177 million population.[64] In short, legal aid was available to less than 42 percent of the population. On the other hand, in 1961 only 13 of the 130 cities with a population over 100,000 had no legal aid organization.[65]

Since the middle of the 1960s, federally funded legal assistance offices have assumed a major role in providing legal services for the poor. Originally funded by the Office of Economic Opportunity, legal service offices were located in many of the poorest neighborhoods and in centers of rural poverty. In 1967, the federal government funded 299 programs at $30.4 million.[66] Approximately 1,800 full-time attorneys each handled 500 cases per year and altogether served nearly 300,000 clients.[67] Although many of the programs of the "war on poverty" were dismantled

[62] Emory A. Brownell, *Legal Aid in the U.S.* (Rochester, N.Y.: Lawyers Cooperative Publishing Co., 1951), p. 37; and Emory A. Brownell, *Supplement to Legal Aid in the U.S.* (Rochester, N.Y.: Lawyers Co-operative Publishing Co., 1961), p. 46.

[63] The various legal aid organizations are described by Brownell, *Legal Aid*, pp. 8 ff.

[64] Brownell, *Supplement*, p. 33. Population statistics are from *Statistical Abstract*, 1962, p. 9.

[65] *Reports of the American Bar Association*, 86 (1961), 139.

[66] Harry P. Stumpf, "Law and Poverty: A Political Perspective," *Wisconsin Law Review* (1968), 698–99. By contrast, private legal aid agencies were funded at only $4.5 million in 1959; Brownell, *Supplement*, p. 46.

[67] Stumpf, *op. cit.*; Harry P. Stumpf and Robert J. Janowitz "Judges and the Poor: Bench Response to Federally Financed Legal Services," *Stanford Law Review*, 21 (1969), 1059. See also "Neighborhood Law Offices," *Harvard Law Review*, 80 (1967), 805 ff.; and "Rural Poverty and the Law in Southern Colorado," *Denver Law Journal*, 47 (1970), 82 ff.

by the Nixon and Ford administrations, legal aid for the poor survived, through a transfer to the new Legal Services Corporation, which received $88 million from Congress for its first year of operation in 1976.[68] The Reagan administration tried to abolish the Corporation and shift the financing of legal assistance to state and local governments. Though it failed to kill the federal program entirely, it succeeded in restricting the activities of the Corporation's lawyers. Under legislation passed in 1981, they could no longer accept test cases that challenged the actions of government agencies affecting their clients.

To be eligible for legal assistance, potential clients must meet two general requirements. First, they must be too poor to engage their own counsel. Poverty, of course, is relative, especially for those requiring legal assistance: legal aid may enable a client to remain off the welfare rolls by making it possible for him to collect debts and wages or to avoid payments that he would otherwise have to make. Poverty is also relative to the area in which an individual lives. One needs more money to live in a large metropolitan center than in a small village; one needs more money on the West Coast than in the South. Throughout the country, however, only those with very low incomes are usually eligible to receive legal aid.

Second, the applicant for legal aid must have the sort of case that the agency he has approached is willing to handle. Where legal aid organizations define their role as helping people with family matters or in housing disputes, they are unlikely to attract clients with claims of sex or age discrimination. Thus, the very manner in which legal aid agencies define their role also determines the kinds of clients they attract and the needs which they fill, as well as the needs they neglect.[69] Agency rules about accepting cases vary considerably. Almost all agencies refuse cases that would normally involve a contingent fee, because a private attorney generally will take such a case even for a poor client. In addition, many private agencies will not accept bankruptcy

---

[68] Statement by Thomas Ehrlich at Hearings before Subcommittee of the House Appropriations Committee, 2d Supplemental Appropriation Bill, 1976, 94th Congress, 2d Session, p. 88.

[69] Leon H. Mayhew, "Institutions of Representation: Civil Justice and the Public," *Law and Society Review*, 9 (1975), 401–30.

cases, and some do not take divorces. Government-financed legal service programs are generally more willing to accept such cases.[70]

Once a case is accepted, the legal aid office provides many of the same services offered by private attorneys to their clients, but private and government-sponsored offices vary in their practices. Private agencies are less willing than government-financed agencies to bring cases to court. Almost one-quarter of the work of government-financed agencies was representation of clients in court.[71] In addition, these agencies sponsored important test cases and carried them to the Supreme Court in the 1970s. Thus, it was a government-sponsored agency that brought the case that led the Supreme Court to declare unconstitutional the residency requirements for welfare clients;[72] another case eliminated court costs for the poor when they file for a divorce.[73] Such advocacy before appellate courts changed the law for the poor by providing them with realistic remedies and restricting discrimination based on wealth.

Providing legal assistance for indigents who wish to take or defend a civil action meets only part of the need for free legal services. Equally pressing is the need of indigents who are accused of a criminal offense. Threatened with loss of their job and often their freedom, faced by professionally trained adversaries, indigent defendants are at a grave disadvantage unless they can secure adequate legal assistance. Some legal aid societies provide aid in criminal cases; most do not. Most states utilize public defender offices in their large cities and assigned counsel in rural areas — although the trend is toward heavier reliance on full-time public defenders.[74] The public defender office (usually supported from tax funds) specializes in handling criminal cases. Assigned counsel are private lawyers assigned to particular cases by judges. Sometimes these attorneys are specialists in criminal

---

[70] Stumpf, *op. cit.*, p. 700; on private agencies, see Brownell, *Legal Aid*, pp. 72 ff.

[71] Stumpf, *op. cit.*

[72] *Shapiro v. Thompson*, 394 U.S. 618 (1969).

[73] *The New York Times*, March 3, 1971, p. 1.

[74] The latest data are for 1977, at which time 47 states used public defenders in at least some jurisdictions. *Sourcebook of Criminal Justice Statistics, 1981* (Washington, D.C.: Government Printing Office, 1982), table 1.2, p. 3.

proceedings; more often they are young attorneys who need the fees paid by the court. At other times they are drawn randomly from a list of all attorneys in the judicial district. In 1979, $597 million was spent throughout the United States, for the defense of indigents; this represents more than three times the amount spent in 1975.[75] However, only 9,000 full-time persons were employed to defend indigents; part-time assigned counsel continued to do much of the work.[76]

As in civil cases, assistance for defense against criminal accusations requires both proof of indigency and involvement in the proper sort of case. Proof of indigency is usually sought by an affidavit, sworn by the defendant, that he cannot afford to engage counsel and that he has no relatives who will do so. A more operational test, used in most cases, is whether the defendant provided his own bail. The presumption in many localities is that if the defendant can afford bail, he can afford an attorney — even though it is quite clear that some defendants have resources only for the one and not for the other.[77] Thus, a frequent requirement for getting free legal assistance in criminal cases is that the defendant must submit to pretrial imprisonment. In addition, the defendant must be accused of a sufficiently serious crime to warrant legal representation. Although indigents charged with misdemeanors are usually eligible for free legal assistance according to Supreme Court decisions, many do not receive it.[78]

Even when a defendant is eligible for legal assistance, the quality of help he receives and the benefits he derives from it vary greatly across the country. Assigned counsel operate at a grave disadvantage. Since they often work without adequate compensation or without any fee at all, they cannot always afford to take time away from their paying practice. Even if they are conscientious, they usually lack funds for investigative purposes.

[75] *Statistical Abstract, 1981*, table 313, p. 182.
[76] *Ibid.*
[77] "Legal Aid to Indigent Criminal Defendants in Philadelphia and New Jersey," *University of Pennsylvania Law Review*, 107 (1959), 843–44.
[78] *Gideon v. Wainwright*, 372 U.S. 335 (1963). Moreover, except when the defendant is charged with a heinous crime, his assigned counsel may not receive any compensation at all. See "Legal Aid to Indigent Criminal Defendants," *op. cit.*, pp. 820–21.

They must rely on the defendant's story and on inspirational guesses while examining the prosecution's witnesses. Since most cases, however, do not get to court but are compromised outside the courtroom, the defense attorney does not even have a chance to shake the prosecution's case. The defense is thus often in a decidedly disadvantageous position.[79]

Moreover, many lawyers assigned to defend indigents are not well qualified in criminal law. Those who are just out of law school know only what they have learned in class; they have had no court experience. Many of those drawn from a list of all the lawyers in a county are office lawyers who do not even have the advantage of recent classroom exposure to criminal proceedings and law.[80]

Indigents who have a public defender are often more fortunate.[81] Whether publicly or privately supported, defender offices are staffed by professionals who are as specialized and skilled as the prosecutor's staff. The office attracts men of greater ability than assigned-counsel systems, for it provides not only a regular livelihood but also, in some instances, a chance for advancement. In Los Angeles, for instance, three of the five men who held the office prior to 1961 were elevated to the bench.[82] Moreover, defender offices have some funds available for investigations, so that the defendant is likely to fare better in negotiations with the

[79] The best (although outdated) survey of actual practice in providing counsel to indigent defendants is Lee Silverstein, *Defense of the Poor in Criminal Cases in American State Courts: A Preliminary Summary* (Chicago: American Bar Foundation, 1964). See also "Legal Aid to Indigent Criminal Defendants," *op. cit.*; Special Committee of the Association of the Bar of the City of New York and the National Legal Aid and Defender Association, *Equal Justice for the Accused* (Garden City, N.Y.: Doubleday, 1959); Bertram F. Willcox and Edward J. Bloustein, "Account of a Field Study in a Rural Area of the Representation of Indigents Accused of a Crime," *Columbia Law Review*, 59 (April 1959), 551–83.

[80] Willcox and Bloustein, *op. cit.*, pp. 563–66. New Jersey systems are described in "Legal Aid to Indigent Criminal Defendants."

[81] The evidence indicates that large local variations exist in the efficacy of public defenders, appointed counsel, and privately retained attorneys. For Chicago, see Dallin H. Oaks and Warren Lehman, "Lawyers for the Poor," in Abraham S. Blumberg (ed.), *The Scales of Justice* (Chicago: Aldine, 1970), pp. 91–104. For other areas see "Representation of Indigents in California: A Field Study of the Public Defender and Assigned Counsel Systems," *Stanford Law Review*, 13 (1961), 522–65; Yale Kamisar and Jesse H. Choper, "The Right to Counsel in Minnesota," *Minnesota Law Review*, 48 (1963), 1–117.

[82] "Representation of Indigents in California," *op. cit.*, p. 541, note 127.

district attorney if the case does not go to trial. If the case goes to trial, the opportunity to conduct an independent investigation permits a more vigorous defense.[83] Despite the sums spent on investigation and the constant availability of the defender, defender offices do not cost more than paid assigned-counsel systems; economies of scale apparently make them somewhat cheaper.[84]

However, indigent defendants suffer from the fact that they usually obtain counsel only after several days, or weeks, of imprisonment. Counsel is often assigned only after indigent defendants have made a statement to the police or district attorney — a statement that might severely, and unfairly, prejudice the case against them.[85] The requirement that counsel be made available almost immediately after arrest is more frequently honored in Supreme Court cases than in lower-court practice.[86] Moreover, defendants often feel that public defenders are part of the government team and cannot be fully trusted. They envy the control that clients appear to have over the lawyers that clients themselves hire.[87]

In summary, the availability of legal services depends first on the public's knowledge of where lawyers can be found and how much they are likely to cost. Second, its availability depends on the resources that litigants command. For those who cannot afford a lawyer, legal service offices, assigned counsel, and public defenders provide some assistance; but in civil matters less than half of those who need the help get it. In civil cases the help seems to be fairly effective; in criminal cases it is much less so except when provided by a public defender.

[83] *Ibid.*, p. 559.

[84] *Ibid.*, p. 563; Kamisar and Choper, *op. cit.*, pp. 115–16.

[85] Special Committee, *op. cit.*, pp. 72 ff.

[86] Neal Milner, "Comparative Analysis of Patterns of Compliance with Supreme Court Decisions: 'Miranda' and the Police in Four Communities," *Law and Society Review*, 5 (1970), 129. See also Willcox and Bloustein, *op. cit.*, pp. 558–59; and "Legal Aid to Indigent Criminal Defendants," *op. cit.*, p. 827.

[87] Jonathan Casper, *American Criminal Justice* (Englewood Cliffs, N.J.: Prentice-Hall, 1972); Jonathan Casper, *Criminal Courts: The Defendant's Perspective* (Washington, D.C.: U.S. Department of Justice, Law Enforcement Assistance Administration, 1978), Malcolm M. Feeley, *The Process Is the Punishment: Handling of Cases in a Lower Criminal Court* (New York: Russell Sage Foundation, 1979), p. 91.

What Lawyers Do

The fact that legal aid workers take so few cases to court reflects the general nature of legal work. Although the popular image of the lawyer is that of an attorney fighting a case before judge and jury, many lawyers rarely see a courtroom. Most of their work takes place inside their offices. Attorneys write contracts for their clients so that, if trouble arises, the contracts will be enforceable in a court. They arrange the sale of a client's property or, inversely, the purchase of some property for a client. They write wills and arrange trusts. They advise on tax problems. Lawyers handle matters before governmental agencies, such as arranging to rezone a small tract of land or helping to float a multimillion-dollar stock issue.

When a client comes to a lawyer, the first action the attorney takes is to see whether the matter can be settled without litigation. The attorney may file a suit to indicate how seriously his client regards the matter, but most such suits are settled long before they reach the courtroom. Although a lawyer must be prepared to act like a gladiator, most of the time he assumes the role of adviser and negotiator. This role has become increasingly conspicuous for lawyers. One large Chicago firm, Jenner and Block, organized a special mediation group in 1983; its task was to negotiate on behalf of its clients in commercial cases.[88] In other matters, such as divorce, lawyers also increasingly mediate settlements, sometimes in conjunction with a mental health professional.

The growing complexity of American law and the need for highly specialized legal services have led to profound changes in the conditions under which legal services are offered.[89] Before World War I the typical lawyer ran his own office. He probably had a clerk or two and perhaps even a young associate. The law office was principally a one-man operation. The typical lawyer took a great variety of cases, and every case received his personal attention.

[88] *Chicago Law Journal*, January 31, 1983, p. 1.
[89] An excellent general discussion of these changes appears in Hurst, *op. cit.*, pp. 306–11. See also Carlin, *Lawyers on Their Own*.

In 1980 slightly less than half of the country's lawyers in private practice were on their own.[90] The remainder practiced law in the nation's 41,000 law firms. Most of these firms, however, were quite small; only 7 percent (or approximately 2,600) had as many as ten lawyers.[91] A few firms in large cities had more than a hundred lawyers; many of these megafirms also became national firms in the 1970s, with branch offices in Washington and in several other cities.

Approximately 9 percent of all lawyers in 1980 worked for the government. The proportion of the bar working for governmental agencies has not changed in the last twenty years, but as the number of lawyers has increased, so has the number of government lawyers. Another 10 percent of all lawyers worked for private industry or business, often as house counsel.[92]

Practicing law in a large firm is quite different from practicing on one's own.[93] Such firms do complicated work for wealthy clients, many of whom retain the firm on a continuing basis. Large law firms operate in the legal field as clinics do in medicine: they allow lawyers to specialize and to economize on the overhead expenses (office, library, clerical help) of legal practice. Each partner in a firm is likely to be a specialist in a particular aspect of the law. When a technical problem arises, it is sent to the appropriate specialist in the firm; however, contact with the client is likely to remain with the partner who initiated the case. New lawyers for the firms are recruited from the leading law schools of the country. Young lawyers are hired as associates. Only one of six or seven new associates eventually becomes a partner. The remainder leave for another firm, begin their own

[90] Curran, "Legal Profession."
[91] Ibid.
[92] Ibid.
[93] The work of large firms is described by: Spencer Klaw, "The Wall Street Lawyers," Fortune, 57 (1958), 140–44; Martin Mayer, "The Wall Street Lawyers," Harper's Magazine, 212 (1956), 31–37, 50–56; Emily P. Dodge, "Evolution of a City Law Office," Wisconsin Law Review (1955), pp. 180–207, and (1956), pp. 35–56; Erwin O. Smigel, The Wall Street Lawyer (New York: Free Press of Glencoe, 1964), pp. 141–310; Joseph C. Goulden, The Superlawyers (New York: Weybright and Talley, 1971); and James B. Stewart, The Partners (New York: Simon and Schuster, 1983). However, the differences noted in the text are not as large in smaller cities; see Joel Handler, The Lawyer and His Community (Madison: University of Wisconsin Press, 1967).

practice, or frequently take positions with business corporations as a house counsel or as an executive.

The position of house counsel is relatively new. Lawyers in such positions are employees; they handle only the work of their corporate employer. Some very large corporations possess legal departments that vie in size and excellence with those of the largest law firms. The difference is that house counsel serve only one master, their corporate employer, and must serve him regardless of their personal estimate of the matter. In some cases such counsel enable the corporation to do without outside legal work; the company can obtain whatever legal services it needs without divulging its secrets to outsiders.

Still another service that lawyers perform is advising businessmen on other than strictly legal problems. Although a business may at first engage a lawyer's service to solve legal difficulties, it often finds that as the result of his legal work the attorney has gained a good deal of insight into the company's operations and its position vis-à-vis competitors. Thus, the lawyer may become a business counselor, advising clients on economic matters, the introduction of new products, and marketing strategies.

One consequence of the specialization of legal work and the shift of most lawyers from individual practice to large partnerships is that relatively few lawyers are prepared to practice before the courts. This is most strikingly true in criminal law. As in other fields, criminal law has become a specialty of its own. Whereas becoming a tax specialist in a large firm gives a lawyer prestige, becoming a criminal lawyer is likely to cost the attorney whatever prestige he has acquired.[94] A criminal law practice requires close contact with the seamy side of life. In many cases the work does not pay very well, for the clients are not wealthy. If the lawyer defends a notorious criminal, the community may misunderstand and associate the lawyer with his client. For these reasons, rel-

[94] A. L. Wood, "Informal Relations in the Practice of Criminal Law," *American Journal of Sociology*, 62 (1956), 48–55; on the prestige structure of the bar in one large city, see John P. Heinz and Edward O. Laumann, *Chicago Lawyers: The Social Structure of the Bar* (New York and Chicago: Russell Sage Foundation and American Bar Foundation, 1982), pp. 59–126.

atively few lawyers desire criminal cases; when at all possible they avoid taking them.

Until recently litigation in civil cases had become less frequent. Lawyers from large firms that specialized in business cases rarely found themselves before a judge. In one midwestern firm that catered to business clients, litigation declined from a relative low of 19 percent of its affairs in 1908 to an even lower 11 percent in 1950. By contrast, 28 percent of the firm's business involved counseling in 1908, and such activities increased to 47 percent in 1950. However, in the 1970s litigation once more increased; litigation departments of large law firms showed the greatest growth. This was the result of both a greater tendency of clients to litigate private disputes and passage of many new and complicated federal laws which invite litigation.[95] In addition, large law firms employ attorneys who specialize in regulatory matters handled by particular federal and state agencies. Such a practice is much like concentrating on litigation in court.

Most lawyers are not well prepared to appear in the courtroom or before regulatory agencies. To overcome that problem some courts — most notably the Northern Federal District Court of Illinois — have imposed special requirements on lawyers appearing before them. The problem is felt by appellate courts as well. Appellate judges have long complained about the quality of oral arguments.[96] Appellate courts depend less and less on oral arguments because, in part, they find that many attorneys who bring appellate cases are ill prepared to engage in a give-and-take colloquy. Thus, one consequence of the specialization of the bar and its withdrawal to the office is that the character of the judicial process is slowly being changed.

Perhaps the most striking difference today between "firm" lawyers and "solo" lawyers lies in the backgrounds of the attorneys and the kinds of cases they handle. Firm lawyers come from the best law schools and handle the affairs of wealthy clients. Solo practitioners — at least in metropolitan areas — more often are lawyers who have graduated from substandard law schools,

[95] Dodge, *op. cit.*, p. 48; *The New York Times*, May 18, 1977, p. 1.
[96] "The Second Circuit: Federal Judicial Administration in Microcosm," *Columbia Law Review*, 63 (1963), 890.

that is, either proprietary or night law schools.[97] Although the firm lawyers are likely to have come from upper-middle-class families, solo practitioners more often come from immigrant ethnic groups and from working-class or small-merchant families. Typically the firm lawyer makes a much higher income than the solo practitioner.

The solo practitioner's legal business is quite different from the firm lawyer's. The individual practitioner's clients are likely to be small businesses or private individuals with legal problems. Many of his clients come to him by chance: he locates himself on a busy street and depends on "walk-up" clients. In large metropolitan areas, solo practitioners are forced by their limited opportunities to specialize in petty matters, which sometimes require unethical practices. Sometimes they handle doubtful automobile accident claims. Sometimes they rely on ambulance chasers — euphemistically called investigators — as one of the ways in which they can procure cases. They split fees with other lawyers because they feel that they must pay to get further referrals. They distribute bonuses at Christmas to court clerks and other administrative officials because they know that, unless they do so, their cases will be held back; and their clients will leave them, dissatisfied.[98] All these activities are condemned by the organized bar as unethical. Yet it appears that in some metropolitan areas — and perhaps all of them — prominent bar members who work in large firms promote these activities by sending cases that require fixes to solo practitioners, apparently sensing or knowing how the solo lawyer will handle the case. Upper-status lawyers themselves undermine what they consider to be the essential ethics of the legal profession by referring questionable cases to other lawyers. A small-firm lawyer explained

[97] This and the other differences mentioned below are discussed at length by Carlin, *Lawyers on Their Own*, pp. 41–122; Jack Ladinsky, "Careers of Lawyers, Law Practice, and Legal Institutions," *American Sociological Review*, 28 (1963), 47–54; Jack Ladinsky, "Career Development Among Lawyers: A Study of Social Factors in the Allocation of Professional Labor" (unpubl. Ph.D. dissertation, University of Michigan, 1963); Dan C. Lortie, "The Striving Young Lawyer: A Study of Early Career Differentiation in the Chicago Bar" (unpubl. Ph.D. dissertation, University of Chicago, 1958); Heinz *et al.*, "Diversity," pp. 717–85; Heinz and Laumann, *Chicago Lawyers*, pp. 167–208.
[98] Carlin, *Lawyers on Their Own*, pp. 155–67.

his experience: "It's a case of noblesse oblige — I remember being asked by a big firm to fix up a phony divorce. I refused; they didn't want to soil their hands."[99] Whereas large-firm lawyers find it disadvantageous to violate legal ethics, some small-firm lawyers and solo practitioners cannot afford to abide by the canons.

The rather sharp distinctions between firm and solo practitioners are reflected in the limited number of lawyers who become active in politics.[100] Large-firm lawyers — the cream of the bar — rarely run for public office. Law firms do not find political activity a wise investment of time for associates or partners. Lawyers in a firm have relatively little need to go into politics: their clients are obtained through social and business connections, not through politics. When firm lawyers become politically active, it is usually to seek or be appointed to high national office. Many Wall Street firm lawyers have received cabinet or subcabinet positions in Washington. It is rare, however, to find a firm lawyer in local or state politics.[101]

The lawyers engaged in local politics are for the most part solo practitioners and criminal lawyers.[102] Both find that political activity produces useful contacts, which help to build up an individual practice. The criminal lawyer must get to know the police well, as a matter of professional concern, because he must deal with them every day. He must negotiate constantly with the prosecutor. If the criminal lawyer is a political ally of the district attorney, he will at least receive more courteous treatment than if he is politically inactive. Other solo practitioners find politics a useful way to supplement their incomes. Many receive appointments to sinecure positions, which supplement their meager law income. Others obtain cases from governmental agencies

[99] Smigel, op. cit., pp. 270–71.

[100] Walter J. Wardwall and Arthur J. Wood, "The Extra-Professional Role of the Lawyer," American Journal of Sociology, 61 (1956), 340–47.

[101] It is significant that although political activity occupies a prominent role in Carlin's description of solo lawyers, Smigel scarcely mentions it.

[102] Carlin, Lawyers on Their Own, pp. 133–35; Wood, op. cit., pp. 48–55. For a more critical view of the role of the lawyer in politics, see Joseph A. Schlesinger, "Lawyers and American Politics: A Clarified View," Midwest Journal of Political Science, 1 (1957), 26–39; Heinz Eulau and John D. Sprague, Lawyers in Politics (Indianapolis, Ind.: Bobbs-Merrill, 1964), pp. 11–86.

or from judges whom they have met through their political activity. A solo practitioner has most to gain from running for public office. He may seek the district attorney's post because it allows him to obtain free publicity without facing disciplinary action by the bar association. If he wins, the office will bring him enough contacts so that he can eventually retire from it. Likewise, legislative positions enable a young attorney to publicize his name, become known to business concerns that lobby in the state capital, and supplement his income until his legal practice can stand on its own or until he is defeated.[103] Some of these lawyer-politicians are lured into politics as a career; most, however, retire from active politics as soon as it becomes financially possible.

Accordingly, the best-trained minds of the legal profession and the highest-status members of the bar do not ordinarily seek public office or engage in political activity. Lawyers engaged in public service are more likely to represent the lower echelons. Often they render distinguished service. Rarely, however, do they live up to the expectation that they are experts in the law and therefore especially qualified to serve in the legislature or other public office. As a whole, they render no better and no worse service than other occupational groups.

Conclusions

The quality of justice depends on the quality of legal service and the conditions under which it is available to those who need it. In this connection, the education of lawyers has improved vastly over the last fifty years. More stringent requirements for admission to the bar also make it less likely that untrained individuals will enter the legal profession.

Despite the much-improved delivery of legal services to needy individuals, poverty remains a barrier to their obtaining equal justice. When facing criminal charges, a poor person often must prove his need for free counsel by awaiting disposition of his case in jail. When the free counsel is an assigned attorney rather than a public defender, the defendant is less likely to re-

[103] This is indicated clearly in the author's own research on Wisconsin lawyers in politics. See Chap. 5 for details.

ceive highly qualified legal assistance. Thus, the quality of criminal justice still depends on one's wealth.

The same is true for those who cannot afford an attorney for civil cases. Legal offices provide minimal assistance to some clients, but in no city do they provide all the help that is needed. Sometimes the help they give is not as good as that which can be bought with private resources. In many cities legal aid societies refuse to take certain kinds of cases; often they cannot afford to take a case when court action is necessary.

That the legal profession is highly organized also has important consequences for the judiciary. The bar associations that dot the country make significant efforts to improve court organization, the quality of judges, and the procedures governing legal processes. They provide a convenient mechanism for disciplining attorneys who violate the Code of Professional Responsibility. Unfortunately, the private government of the bar associations sometimes impedes the administration of justice. Bar associations are sometimes as much concerned with protecting the livelihood of their members as they are with improving the quality of justice. Associations occasionally are more concerned with reducing unauthorized practice than with preventing the miscarriage of justice. In many communities the inadequacy of legal aid for indigents is directly attributable to bar association fears that more effective legal aid would lead to increased government control of the legal profession. A semiofficial publication of the ABA expressed this fear in the following terms:

> Whenever the government in any form is a party to litigation, its lawyer is paid out of the public treasury. This is where the question touches the issue of legal aid. If lawyers for all the poor are to be paid out of public funds, would the next step be to provide persons of moderate means with lawyers paid wholly or in part out of the public treasury? How far could we go in this direction and not destroy the independence of the bar? Thus at the bottom of the legal aid problem lies this question: If legal aid attorneys receive their fees from public funds, will that be the first step, the entering wedge, into "socialization" of the legal profession? There appears to be no ready answer to that question.[104]

---

[104] Blaustein and Porter, *op. cit.*, p. 89.

The specialization of legal work and its concentration in large firms where specialists can be usefully employed have had a great impact on the administration of justice. Specialization has taken the ordinary lawyer out of the courtrooms; instead, he carries on his work in his office. For most lawyers, litigation is a last recourse. Directed to seek out-of-court settlement by the canons of legal ethics, the attorney also seeks to avoid courtroom appearances because he finds trials expensive and because he is not particularly well prepared to engage in such a duel. Nevertheless, one cannot say that justice is always thwarted by avoiding trials and concentrating legal talent in large firms. Those who can afford to engage a large firm usually obtain excellent legal advice and services, better than an individual practitioner might have rendered.

Especially significant for the quality of legal services provided the average American is the fate of solo practitioners and lawyers working in small firms. Unless they can develop the same degree of specialization that characterizes large firms servicing corporations and wealthy clients, such attorneys cannot meet the legal needs of ordinary people effectively.

5
Attorneys for the Public

Not all lawyers engaged in litigation are private entrepreneurs. Many are government employees. The government — whether the federal government, state government, or federal, state, or local agency — is frequently involved in litigation and must have its own representatives before the courts. The government plays a dominant role in criminal cases, for it prosecutes them. It participates in important civil litigation, for when cases involve public policy, the government is concerned.

Each level of government in the United States possesses its own legal agents. Their role in the judicial process varies with their formal functions and their informal position in the political system.

Lawyers for the Federal Government

As the scope of federal activity has grown in the twentieth century, the range of litigation involving the federal government has also increased. In 1980 more than 23,000 lawyers worked for the federal government.[1] Some serve particular agencies, such

---

[1] Barbara Curran, "Lawyer Demographics" (address to the American Bar Association), Aug. 8, 1981.

as the regulatory commissions, the Department of Agriculture, and the Department of Defense. The largest single civilian group works in the government's principal legal office, the Department of Justice.

The Justice Department was not organized until 1870, although its head, the Attorney General, was one of the original cabinet officials authorized by Congress in 1789. Until after the Civil War, litigation involving the federal government did not justify a separate department: the Attorney General could operate in a small office. Today, however, he supervises ninety-four United States Attorneys — one attached to each district court — an equal number of United States Marshals, the FBI, and several thousand attorneys in Washington.

The Justice Department's impact on the judiciary is manifold. The Attorney General is a key participant in the selection of federal judges.[2] He supervises the prosecution of all violations of federal criminal law and the initiation of major civil litigation to carry out the President's antitrust and civil rights policies. Another official of the department, the Solicitor General, supervises the appeal of government cases to the Courts of Appeals and to the Supreme Court.

Since the Civil War the scope of criminal statutes passed by Congress has increased greatly. They prohibit interfering with federal elections, transporting stolen cars over state lines, white slavery, bank robbery, mail fraud, kidnaping, tax fraud, and similar offenses. All persons charged with a federal crime are arraigned before a federal magistrate. Their cases are turned over to the United States Attorney attached to the United States district court, who functions much like a district attorney, preparing the prosecution case, negotiating with the defendant, and conducting the trial.

United States Attorneys also handle a large number of civil cases for the federal government. The government initiates numerous suits over its contracts for materials and service, tax matters, and its regulatory programs. Private individuals also sue the government over such matters. Of the 168,769 civil cases begun

[2] See Chap. 6.

in federal district courts in 1980, 36 percent involved the federal government as either plaintiff or defendant.[3]

Many civil cases are handled by government attorneys employed by operating agencies rather than by the Justice Department.[4] Some of their legal staffs are quite sizable and process thousands of claims. The legal staff of the Treasury Department, for instance, must litigate all challenges to its rulings before the tax court. It also must assist the Justice Department in preparing civil and criminal cases involving tax evasion. Such attorneys also handle many matters that never reach trial. They represent the government in bankruptcy proceedings in order to press the government's tax claims; they file claims before probate courts for payment of federal inheritance taxes. Similar services — though on a much smaller scale — are performed by the legal staffs of other departments. Attorneys working for regulatory commissions play a key role in carrying out their programs. They investigate violations of the regulatory statutes, they conduct hearings before the commissions, and they prepare to defend the commissions' decisions when appeals are brought to the courts.

Most attorneys working for the government are civil servants who win a position through competitive examinations. Many make government work their career. Like most other federal civil servants, they may not participate in overt political activity. In the Justice Department, however, many attorneys are political appointees. This is true not only of the key policymaking officials in the department but also of the principal trial lawyers, the U.S. Attorneys.

The United States Attorneys are presidential political appointees. Each serves for a term of four years, although he may be asked to resign earlier. The term of office often coincides with the President's term, so that each President may appoint his own United States Attorneys. The post is one of the few patronage positions still available to the President for rewarding his political supporters. Consequently, those appointed are often lawyers

---

[3] U.S. Bureau of the Census, *Statistical Abstract of the United States, 1977* (Washington, D.C.: Government Printing Office, 1977), table 324, p. 186.

[4] Even though somewhat dated, the best discussion of government lawyers is still in Esther L. Brown, *Lawyers, Law Schools and the Public Service* (New York: Russell Sage Foundation, 1948), pp. 43–90.

who have been active in their party's political affairs. The office allows its incumbent to become prominent on the local political scene; it is sometimes used as a stepping-stone to a congressional seat, a judgeship, or a high state office. Few attorneys serve more than two terms before returning to private practice or proceeding to a higher public office.[5]

Although United States Attorneys resemble prosecuting attorneys, they normally enjoy much less independence.[6] The local prosecutor is usually an elected official operating without direct supervision, whereas the United States Attorney is part of the Justice Department's bureaucracy and has to carry out the orders he receives from Washington. In most instances Washington gives him considerable latitude in dealing with the ordinary cases that constitute most of his business. He apparently has as much latitude in dealing with a bank robber as the local prosecutor would have if the person had robbed a supermarket. But those cases to which Washington attaches special importance are prosecuted according to instructions. When a prominent union leader is on trial or when a major industrial firm is accused of violating the antitrust statutes, the United States Attorney operates under the close supervision of the Justice Department, which maintains specialists in Washington to assist United States Attorneys with their difficult cases. When a particularly important case arises, the department often sends a specialist to the trial court to help prosecute the case. Supervising such cases allows the Attorney General to use his field staff of United States Attorneys to promote particular policies through litigation. This is particularly important to the Attorney General, because some administration policies can only be promoted through litigation. The federal government, for instance, had few other means of assisting blacks in their attempts to register to vote in the South.

---

[5] Based on comparison of names listed in U.S. Civil Service Commission, *Official Register of the United States* (Washington, D.C.: Government Printing Office, 1944–59). The most comprehensive study of U.S. Attorneys is James Eisenstein, *Counsel for the United States: U.S. Attorneys in the Political and Legal Systems* (Baltimore: Johns Hopkins University Press, 1978).

[6] *United States Department of Justice, A Brief Account of Its Organization and Activities* (Washington D.C., 1954; mimeo.), p. 4.

Litigation is also the principal means of enforcing antitrust policies.[7]

Moreover, control over the prosecution of a case is important in order to lay the proper groundwork for an appeal. Controversial policy issues are rarely settled at a trial; they are usually appealed to a Court of Appeals and to the Supreme Court. To win a favorable ruling, the government must be careful to raise the right questions during the trial so that an appellate court can later rule on them. It must avoid mistakes that would raise irrelevant questions on appeal.

The Justice Department exerts a much tighter control over appeals than over original prosecutions. Most appeals must be approved by the proper division of the Justice Department and the Solicitor General.[8] Appeals are argued by a Justice Department lawyer from Washington rather than by the United States Attorney who originated the case. Still more centralized control is imposed on appeals to the Supreme Court. The Solicitor General passes on all such appeals. Although he is also a presidential appointee, he traditionally has remained somewhat independent of the Attorney General. He clears cases for appeal to the Supreme Court on the basis of his estimate of the government's chance of winning its case, the probable damage that would result if the government lost, and the work load of the court. As a political appointee, the Solicitor General also tries to advance Administration policy by controlling the flow of cases to the Supreme Court and by insuring that government briefs reflect the President's policy goals.

Appeals to the Supreme Court and to Courts of Appeals are handled by the specialized staff of the Justice Department in Washington. The Antitrust Division supervises litigation on re-

---

[7] The work of the antitrust division is described in Suzanne Weaver, *Decision to Prosecute* (Cambridge, Mass.: MIT Press, 1977).

[8] Jeffrey A. Burt and Irving Schloss, "Government Litigation in the Supreme Court: The Roles of the Solicitor General," *Yale Law Journal*, 78 (1969), 1442–81. Also see Leon I. Salomon, "The Government's Law Business: The Solicitor General and His Clients" (paper prepared for delivery at the 1962 annual meeting of the American Political Science Association, Washington, D.C., September 1962); the memoirs of former Solicitor General and Attorney General Francis Biddle, *In Brief Authority* (Garden City, N.Y.: Doubleday, 1962), pp. 97–151; Robert L. Stern, "The Solicitor General and Administrative Agency Litigation," *American Bar Association Journal*, 46 (1960), 154–58, 217–18.

straint-of-competition cases; the Civil Rights Division handles
cases involving civil rights; ordinary civil actions are usually prepared by members of the Civil Division. The other sections of
the department (Criminal Division, Internal Security Division,
Land and Natural Resources Division, and Tax Division) operate
similarly.[9]

One important consequence of these activities by the Department of Justice is that it operates with a higher level of expertise than most private litigants. Many of the Justice Department's Washington lawyers are career officials. They specialize
in a narrow range of conflicts and gain enormous experience with
the appellate courts before which they appear. The Solicitor General's office is not staffed quite so heavily by career employees.
It recruits top-ranking graduates from the leading law schools,
who serve for a few years before moving to other positions in
government or private practice. Although its lawyers are young,
they argue more cases before the Supreme Court than anyone
else. They learn through experience the personal proclivities of
the justices and are then better prepared for unexpected questions that the justices pose during an oral argument.[10]

Since the volume of government litigation is large, the Solicitor General can often choose to delay the appeal of an issue
to the Supreme Court until the right case or the right moment
comes. Most private litigants cannot do this, for they do not control a large enough volume of cases so that at any moment one
can be chosen to submit a question to the Supreme Court.

The Justice Department's control over appellate cases has
been used to advantage. It has gained the gratitude of the Supreme Court by helping the Court restrict its work load. While
private requests for Supreme Court rulings (in the form of requests for a writ of certiorari) doubled between 1930 and 1960,
the government's requests declined.[11] Although the Supreme
Court grants certiorari in less than 10 percent of all cases, it accepts more than two-thirds of the cases supported by the Solicitor
General.[12]

[9] Detailed descriptions of the various divisions' work can be found in *Annual
Report of the Attorney General of the U.S.*, issued for the fiscal year.
[10] Salomon, *op. cit.*, pp. 2–5.
[11] *Ibid.*, p. 13, note 23.
[12] Burt and Schloss, *op. cit.*, p. 1445.

The Solicitor General's control over government suits that are appealed to the Supreme Court gives the Justice Department considerable influence over the kinds of cases that the Supreme Court decides. If the time does not appear propitious, the Solicitor General may decide to accept a lower-court defeat that affects cases in only one circuit rather than to risk an unfavorable Supreme Court ruling that would affect the entire country. Not all cases, of course, are subject to review by the Solicitor General; private individuals may appeal their cases to the Supreme Court if they have lost in the lower courts, regardless of the Justice Department's desires. However, the Supreme Court accepts a much smaller proportion of such private appeals. In addition, since most policy issues involve the government, the Justice Department can either block review or oppose Supreme Court action on a private application for review. By restricting the flow of cases to the Court, the Justice Department influences the scope of judicial policymaking.

Moreover, the Justice Department can prevent judicial review of certain government actions by advising another agency to evade litigation. The Postal Service, for instance, sometimes stops the delivery of mail that it considers pornographic; when it does so, it acts as a censor. Its legal right to censor reading material is questionable under the First Amendment. Rather than risk judicial review of its policies, the service has often resumed the delivery of particular items as soon as it was sued in court. Such action renders the case moot and halts court action. Postal policy is not affected; the next shipment of pornographic literature may again be impounded.

In the same way that the Justice Department can block action by the courts, it can also promote judicial activity by initiating suits that will induce judicial declarations of policy. It may take the lead in forcing a judicial test of the constitutionality of a statute. It may support private test cases by submitting *amicus curiae* briefs.

Although litigation is a risky venture, the Justice Department's operations make it a more manageable tool of policy. Sometimes a President uses the department to enforce a particular policy, such as civil rights. On other occasions an administration may use litigation to suppress what it considers extremist opposition to its policies. Many observers gave this interpretation to the Nixon administration's decision to prosecute the Chicago Eight for allegedly crossing state lines to incite a riot at the 1968 Democratic National Convention in Chicago and to prosecute the "Berrigan Conspiracy," in which the Berrigan brothers and several others were accused of planning to kidnap presidential adviser Henry Kissinger and to blow up several heating tunnels in Washington to demonstrate their opposition to the Vietnam war.[13]

In summary, the federal government uses its lawyers for quite diverse purposes. It employs them to prosecute violations of federal laws and to defend the government in legal actions. The Justice Department also uses its staff to influence judicial policymaking by promoting the appeal of some cases while blocking the appeal of others. Such a use of government attorneys helps to make the federal court system a weapon in the political arsenal of a President.

Government Lawyers in the States

The states are also involved in important litigation. Their activities expose them to suits by citizens and suppliers. Their policies often require court action to become effective. They frequently employ the courts for ordinary administrative purposes, such as setting the price of land condemned for public use. Their laws constitute the major portion of American criminal law; when they are violated, the states need attorneys to prosecute the lawbreakers.

Like the federal government, the states have three sets of attorneys. Each state has an attorney general, who acts as the chief legal official of the state government and administers a miniature department of justice. Each state employs attorneys to assist operating agencies and local governments in carrying out their duties. Each state has a set of district attorneys who prosecute violators of state laws and advise some local governments.

---

[13] On the Chicago Eight, see Richard Harris, *Justice* (New York: Avon Books, 1969, 1970), pp. 169–70; on the Berrigan conspiracy, see *The New York Times,* Jan. 13, 1971, p. 1; Jan. 17, 1971, section 4, p. 1; Jan. 25, 1971, p. 20; Jan. 26, 1971, p. 13.

The attorney general of most states is elected on a partisan statewide ballot at the same time as the governor. In only six states does the governor appoint the attorney general; in one, he is selected by the state's supreme court.[14] In most states the office is a key elective position in state government. Most other elective offices, except the governor's, have only nominal duties; however, the attorney general can remain in the public eye through his actions in fighting crime and handing down legal rulings. Many aspiring politicians have used the office in recent years as a stepping-stone to the governorship.[15]

Although relatively important on the state scene, most state attorneys general do not have the prominence of their national counterpart. Their pay ranges from quite modest (Arkansas, $26,500) to very substantial (Tennessee, $73,000). Most receive a salary of $40,000 to $50,000.[16] In most states their office staffs are relatively small. They primarily handle the state's civil litigation — suits arising from contracts that the state has signed in the course of its many programs. Although state attorneys general rarely have direct authority to prosecute criminals, they sometimes play a prominent role in investigating criminal activities. Many possess small investigatory staffs, which, although not rivaling the FBI, are effective because they are free from local control. In some states the attorney general can initiate investigations to uncover crime and corruption. Although the attorney general's staff is relatively small, it often consists of highly expert civil servants who make a lifetime career of their work for the state. Such staff members sometimes know more than the elected attorney general; they frequently know more about the law than locally elected district attorneys. Consequently, the local attorneys often seek advice from the attorney general's office when they confront difficult cases. By offering such informal advice,

[14] *The Book of the States, 1982–1983* (Chicago: Council of State Governments, 1982), p. 176.

[15] That this is a trend is the conclusion of Joseph A. Schlesinger, *How They Became Governor* (East Lansing: Michigan State University Governmental Research Bureau, 1957), pp. 74–96. For a somewhat different view, see Samuel Krislov, "Constituency Versus Constitutionalism: The Desegregation Issue and Tensions and Aspirations of Southern Attorneys General," *Midwest Journal of Political Science*, 3 (1959), 88.

[16] *The Book of the States, 1982–1983*, p. 163.

the attorney general's office wins influence over cases with which by law they would have no right to interfere.[17]

Attorneys general in the states do not usually control appeals in the same manner that the United States Solicitor General does in federal courts. In many states the decision to appeal rests with the local agencies directly concerned with the original decision. Only when a state agency is involved or when a criminal case is being appealed by a defendant does the attorney general argue the case before his state's supreme court. Because most cases originate with local agencies, the attorney general usually does not control access to the state supreme court in the same way that the Justice Department does. Nor does his office exert the same degree of control over the kinds of cases that state appellate courts hear, for those courts are much more generous in granting appeals than is the United States Supreme Court.

Since the attorney general is usually an elected official, he sometimes is a political rival of the governor; in some instances he may even be a member of the opposite political party. Under such circumstances he may use his powers to argue appeals and bring original suits to a state supreme court to frustrate the governor's program. In Wisconsin, for instance, a Republican attorney general joined the Republican majority in the legislature in opposing a Democratic governor's appointments: the attorney general argued the legislature's case before the Wisconsin Supreme Court.[18] In Illinois in 1983, when the Republican governor proposed draconian budget cuts in medicaid and welfare programs to balance the state's budget, the attorney general (a recently elected Democrat) opposed the move in court action. In such instances the attorney general helps to bring political conflicts to the courts.

Attorneys general in the states also issue numerous advisory opinions to state and local agencies.[19] Such opinions are also

---

[17] For a description of their offices in selected states, see Richard A. Watson, *Office of Attorney General*, Missouri Studies No. 1 (Columbia: University of Missouri Research Center, 1962); "Office of Attorney General," *Florida Bar Journal*, 34 (1960), 14–21; R. L. Montague, "Office of Attorney General in Kentucky," *Kentucky Law Journal*, 49 (1960–1961), 194–224.

[18] *State ex rel. Thompson v. Gibson*, 22 Wis. 2d, 275.

[19] R. L. Larson, "The Importance and Value of Attorney General Opinions," *Iowa Law Review*, 41 (1956), 351–68; William L. Steude, *The Lawyer in Michigan State Government*, Papers in Public Administration No. 31 (Ann Arbor: University of Michigan Institute of Public Administration, 1959), pp. 34–37.

used by the United States Attorney General, but in the states advisory opinions play a more important role. Many state agencies lack their own legal staff and thus are forced to rely on the attorney general's opinions. In many states such opinions are binding on state and local agencies until a court overrules them. Most opinions interpret state laws not yet ruled on by the courts. The attorney general may be asked whether a particular method of tax collection is legal, whether certain procedures for annexing suburban areas are valid, or whether a local government is authorized to initiate a particular program. Such requests evoke opinions that indicate the interpretation given by the attorney general and his staff to the statute or constitutional provision in question. In some instances the attorney general endorses the view of the agency making the request; at other times he balks their intended action. The attorney general's advisory opinions give him an opportunity to make law and influence policy in the same fashion as appellate courts when they render decisions.

At the local level in most states each county has its own legal officer, the district attorney. Although he sometimes gives advice to local agencies and handles their civil litigation, his principal task is to prosecute violations of the state's criminal code. His functions involve the exercise of a high degree of discretion at every step. He alone controls the prosecution of alleged criminals in the county.

In most states the district attorney is elected on a partisan ballot at the same time as other local officials. His term of office is usually two or four years. Only in several eastern states — Connecticut, Delaware, Rhode Island, and New Jersey — is he appointed by the governor, the attorney general, or a court.[20] The fact that he is an elected official and controls the prosecution process places him in a powerful position in many counties. Moreover, he is often the most visible local official because his office produces most of the scandal and sensation on which the local press thrives. His cooperation with the press can be used to bring him favorable news coverage and more media exposure than any other public official receives. Consequently, ambitious lawyers use the office to advance their careers. For some it leads

[20] Duane P. Nedrud, "The Career Prosecutor," *Journal of Criminal Law, Criminology and Police Science*, 51 (1960–1961), 344.

to higher political office; for a few it leads to a career in the judiciary; for most it leads to a more lucrative private practice in law.

The character of the individuals who become district attorneys and the scope of their work vary considerably from state to state and from area to area within a state. For instance, in most rural areas the office is a part-time job: it allows the incumbent to engage in the private practice of law in addition to his public duties. Generally the office is very small, with one or two assistants at the most. In metropolitan centers, however, the office constitutes one of the largest law offices in the city. The Los Angeles district attorney, for instance, had more than four hundred assistants in 1972.[21]

Systematic studies of district attorneys throughout the nation are not available. However, by contrasting incumbents in Wisconsin, who served in both urban and rural communities, with their counterparts in New York County (Manhattan) one may obtain an impression of those who hold such positions. Using elections to select public officials often favors the recruitment of individuals who have deep roots in their community. In contrast to a civil service system that is open to all qualified applicants, elections stress localism. Long ties with a community assist a candidate in securing the nomination and in winning the election. In Wisconsin the elected district attorneys reflected this fact.[22] Five-sixths of the men who held the office between 1940 and 1963 were natives of Wisconsin; one-half had been born in the county that they served. Three-quarters attended college in the state; five-sixths went to one of the state's two law schools,

---

[21] Peter Greenwood et al., Prosecution of Adult Felony Defendants in Los Angeles County (Santa Monica, Calif.: Rand Corporation, 1973), p. 7. For earlier estimates, which include other cities, see John J. Meglio, "Comparative Study of District Attorneys' Offices of Los Angeles and Brooklyn," The Prosecutor, 5 (1969), 237; Robert S. Fertitta, "Comparative Study of Prosecutors' Offices: Baltimore and Houston," The Prosecutor, 5 (1969), 249.

[22] The following is based on Herbert Jacob, "Judicial Insulation — Elections, Direct Participation, and Public Attention to the Courts in Wisconsin," Wisconsin Law Review (1966), 801–19. The data are based on questionnaires sent to Wisconsin prosecuting attorneys who held office between 1940 and 1963; 81 percent of the questionnaires were returned. The findings are supported by a later study of Kentucky district attorneys in Richard L. Engstrom, "Political Ambitions and the Prosecutorial Office," Journal of Politics, 33 (1971), 190–94.

with most attending the University of Wisconsin Law School. Local education thus reinforced family ties. Since admission to the Wisconsin bar required a law degree, very few prosecutors lacked law school education; those who did were older men who had gained their legal training through an apprenticeship. The office of district attorney, however, did not attract those who did best in law school. Only 11 percent of the district attorneys served on their law school's law review or had been elected to the legal honor society, the Order of the Coif. However, in urban communities the office attracted twice the proportion of top-ranking students as in rural communities.

In Wisconsin, the district attorney rarely won his post immediately after graduation from law school, even in rural areas. Most prosecutors won their first election when they were over thirty years old. In rural areas, prosecutors in their late twenties were somewhat more common but still in a decided minority. For most, the position constituted their first elective office. Urban prosecutors were the only group that had considerable public experience before election: in almost half the cases they had served as assistant prosecutor before winning the chief position themselves.

The notion that the district attorney's office often leads the incumbent to higher public positions receives little support from the record of Wisconsin prosecutors. Almost half the men said that they had sought the position to obtain legal experience; an additional tenth had sought the office because it guaranteed a minimum income. Most retained their private practice while serving as prosecutor and retired from public office when their practice had become lucrative enough to allow them to do so. In most instances, building a practice required four to six years, so that most prosecutors served two or three terms.

Less than one-quarter retired as the result of defeat at an election. Only 16 percent left the office because they had been elected or appointed to a higher post. The remainder withdrew from the position for various personal reasons: their private practice had become lucrative; they were bored with the job; or the position had not lived up to their expectations and they needed to devote more time to building their own law practice. Less than 40 percent of the prosecutors held a subsequent elective office;

almost all those who did won minor local positions rather than more important state or national offices. Few prosecutors gained appointment to substantial state or national offices. A few of those who remained in public service won promotion to the judiciary. Ten (5 percent) became circuit or appellate judges; thirty-three (17 percent) won county or municipal judgeships.

A great many of these prosecuting attorneys returned to private practice. Public office was an interlude used to promote their careers but not to launch themselves into political life. Most district attorneys apparently had more lucrative practices after their tenure than before, because afterwards they practiced law more often in partnership than by themselves.

Urban and rural prosecutors in Wisconsin differed little in most of these characteristics. Even in Milwaukee, the district attorneyship had not become highly professionalized in the sense that the prosecutor made a career of the office. Although the average tenure of the Milwaukee prosecutor during this period was 7.3 years (or 2.4 years longer than the average in Wisconsin), seven other counties gave equally long tenure to their prosecutors. (The largest of these counties had only one-thirteenth of Milwaukee's population.) Thus, long tenures and professional careers as public prosecutor were rare in Wisconsin; when they occurred, they were not solely associated with large metropolitan centers.

Not all district attorneys are like those in Wisconsin. A study of the district attorney's office in New York County showed that it played a quite different role in the local and state political system.[23] Between 1938, when Thomas E. Dewey won the office, and 1974, it was held by only one other man, Frank Hogan. Dewey left the office to become governor and twice the presidential nominee. Hogan did not win promotion to another office, although he ran unsuccessfully for the United States Senate in 1958. Thus, the New York position was highly professionalized in that it held its incumbent for a long term, and yet it was used as a stepping-stone in attempts to reach more prominent positions in the state and nation.

[23] Richard Kuh, "Careers in Prosecution Offices," *Journal of Legal Education,* 14 (1961–1962), 175–90; Wallace S. Sayre and Herbert Kaufman, *Governing New York City* (New York: Russell Sage Foundation, 1960), pp. 237–38, 292–95.

At the same time, the office in New York was not enmeshed in local partisan politics. It is one of the larger legal offices in the nation, employing more than eighty assistants, each of whom is a lawyer. Although they are hired with little regard to their political affiliations, few make the office a career. In 1961 only twenty-three assistants had served in the office ten years or more; the remaining had shorter tenures. Twelve to fifteen assistants had resigned each year for better positions. In recent years, 54 percent of those who resigned went into private practice; 46 percent accepted other public positions. In most cases they obtained more lucrative positions. Even those going to other public offices earned from $1000 to $4250 more in their new jobs than as assistant district attorney.

In New York the *assistant* district attorney strikingly resembles the district attorney of most Wisconsin communities in that he uses the office to further his career, usually in private practice. However, the district attorneyship in New York occupies a much more prominent position. It attracts a career-oriented incumbent, who seeks to leave only on the condition of promotion to a higher office. Not all district attorneys in large cities enjoy such long tenure, for sometimes they meet with partisan or factional opposition. In Cook County (Chicago), the post is occasionally won by a Republican; in a city like New Orleans, it is a much-sought-after plum in the factional politics of that city.

District attorneys possess an advantage in seeking judgeships in areas where judges are elected. Aside from providing a relatively large share of elective judges, the office does not seem to be an effective springboard to higher office. American politics is too disjointed to make one office a prerequisite for winning another; no established career ladders surely lead an aspirant from lowly office to high office. Consequently, the district attorneys of the nation occupy a somewhat less important political position than most people suppose.

If the Wisconsin experience is typical for nonmetropolitan areas, the short term and elective nature of the position mean that the criminal-prosecution process is in the control of relatively inexpert lawyers who lack experience but who, like most politicians, possess some intuitive feel for the norms of their community. The elective nature of their job allows them to exercise their discretion, so that the prosecution process reflects the dominant community norms perhaps better than if a civil servant held the post.

Conclusions

The manner in which attorneys for the public are chosen in America gives officials who are selected under partisan conditions an opportunity to influence the judicial process directly. At the federal level, the Attorney General and the United States Attorneys are usually part of the President's team. He expects them to assist in promoting his policies; through their actions, the courts can be used as a tool of policymaking and policy execution. In the states no chief executive exercises this degree of control over the public attorneys. In most instances they are separately elected officials, responsive to their own electorate rather than to the governor's wishes. Yet they too respond to the challenges of the larger political arena and introduce cases that allow the courts to make law while enforcing norms and to participate in policymaking.

6
Judges

Although many officials work around courtrooms, none have the prominence and prestige of judges. The court is the judges' agency; they are responsible for its administration and its reputation for honesty and impartiality. When judges enter a courtroom, everyone rises. When they speak, others listen. Although judges may share the power to decide a case with a jury of laypeople, they alone interpret the rules that govern the proceedings.

Yet the work of judges is often misunderstood. They have many functions in addition to pronouncing judgment, and these must be recognized in order to evaluate appropriately the ways in which judges are selected and retired.

The Functions of a Judge

The conventional image of a judge is that of a black-robed man who passes judgment on criminals or between civil disputants. Although that duty remains a prominent function of judges, it occupies only a small portion of most judges' days. Judgment is the climax of the judicial process: many other activities lead up to it or divert from it. In addition, the stereotype of the black-robed man is giving way to women judges and judges who work in everyday clothing.

Judging has become a many-faceted role. The varied nature of trial judges' work is illustrated by Figure 6.1, which is based on a national survey of trial judges in 1977.[1] Almost half the judges in a typical work day presided over a jury trial, and an equal number presided over a bench trial. However, almost as many reported "wasting time" as a typical part of their day; and the vast majority spent some time on administrative work, reading case files, or keeping up with changes in the law. Promoting settlements, discussing pleas, and socializing with attorneys were also common activities. Almost a fifth of the judges surveyed spent part of their typical work day travelling to some distant courtroom. However, when trial work occurs, it occupies most of a judge's day; the other tasks rarely account for more than an hour each.[2]

Not all trial judges have the same responsibilities; their work varies with the kinds of assignments they are given. About three-fifths of the nation's judges have general assignments; that is, they handle any kind of case that happens to come before them. Another 13 percent are assigned to criminal courts, and twice that number are assigned to courts that hear only civil cases.[3] Moreover, some judges work alone, whereas others work in courts with dozens of other judges. Some judges work in small districts and go to the same courthouse each morning; others "ride circuit" and rotate among different locations on a daily or weekly basis.[4]

Many judges specialize. Some only preside over trials while others only do administrative tasks. Still others in many courts hear only the preliminary motions that settle procedural and evidentiary issues before the trial can begin. Unlike specialization in administrative agencies, however, such specialized assignments are only temporary. In most courts judges rotate their assignments as often as once a year.[5]

---

[1] John P. Ryan, Allan Ashman, Bruce D. Sales, and Sandra Shane-Dubow, *American Trial Judges* (New York: Free Press, 1980).

[2] *Ibid.*, pp. 34–36.

[3] *Ibid.*, p. 23.

[4] *Ibid.*, pp. 48, 53–55.

[5] *Ibid.*, p. 51.

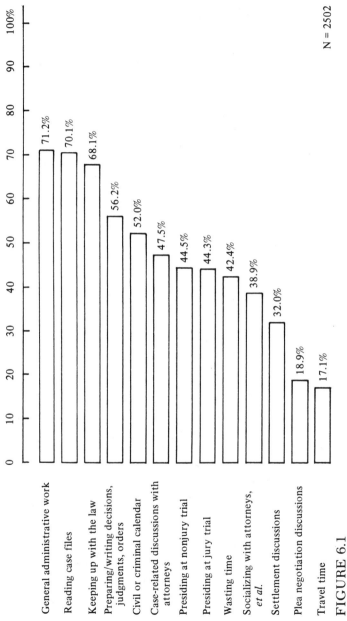

N = 2502

FIGURE 6.1
Proportion of Trial Judges Reporting Specific Tasks on Their Most Common Work Day

Source: John P. Ryan, Allan Ashman, Bruce D. Sales, and Sandra Shane-Dubow, *American Trial Judges* (New York: Free Press, 1980), p. 29. Reprinted by permission.

Thus, it is quite misleading to speak about judging in sweeping generalizations. The variety of functions and organizational contexts must be kept in mind as one examines judges' tasks.

The Administrative Function

Judges resemble high-level administrators in many of their duties. In most parts of the United States they are responsible for administering their own courts; they must appoint all clerical assistants, draw up the budget, and make certain that the physical facilities are adequate for the courts' operations.[6] Those judges assigned such administrative tasks discover that they must negotiate with the local governing body — the county board or city council — for whatever funds they need to operate their court. In making budget requests, judges must compete against the requests of other governmental agencies, because the sheriff or the county welfare department, for instance, may also have requisitioned the space they desire. Judges' pleas for additional clerical help must be justified in the same way as other requests, for they burden the local tax rate.

Such housekeeping tasks are ancillary to a judge's chief administrative problem of controlling the flow of cases in his court. Lawyers and litigants evaluate judges in large part by the manner in which they manage to keep up with the business that comes to their courts. Under normal circumstances, the more quickly judges dispose of cases, the happier plaintiffs will be. In part, managing the flow of cases simply involves establishing administrative procedures that ensure prompt attention for all litigation filed with the court.

Every case that is filed in court is entered on the records by the clerk. Once all preliminary papers are filed, the case is placed on a calendar that lists cases in the order in which they may be heard. Usually the listing is in chronological order, so that before any given case is heard, all those filed and ready for trial earlier are taken first. Most courts have several calendars, some having precedence over others. For instance, a court that hears commercial contract cases as well as personal injury cases may list

---

[6] A judge's housekeeping duties are described in Arthur T. Vanderbilt, *Minimum Standards of Judicial Administration* (New York: Law Center of New York University, 1949), pp. 32–64.

each type on a separate calendar and give preference to all cases on one calendar over those listed on the other.

If the flow of business were simply a function of the number of cases filed and of the order in which they were listed on the docket, a judge would have little influence over the speed with which he heard cases. However, it is not such a simple matter. Once cases are filed, many are settled out of court and withdrawn. Others, which should be ready for trial, may not be, because one side's lawyer is too busy with another case and remains unprepared.

Courts use a variety of procedures to control the movement of cases. Some use a master calendar, which sends cases to whatever judge happens to be free at a particular moment; others permit individual judges to control their own calendars. Much has been written advocating one or the other system, but efficient case management does not appear to be related to the kind of calendar used; rather, it seems to depend more on how well judges and attorneys communicate with each other and how well attorneys adjust their work styles to the courts' demands.[7] In some courts judges abdicate their control by waiting until lawyers certify their readiness; until then, the case remains inactive. Increasingly, however, judges take more vigorous measures to speed cases to their conclusion. They may do this by systematically calling their calendars: when a case is reached on the calendar, the attorneys must be prepared, or it will be dismissed. Another way is for the judge to be niggardly in granting delays and continuances. A third commonly used procedure is to limit the cases one attorney or firm may bring to a single court. This regulation seeks to eliminate the delay caused when a single attorney or firm handles so many of the court's cases that some are left unprepared.

[7] Ryan *et al.*, *op. cit.*, pp. 70–72. A careful analysis of the effects of several methods of expediting trials can be found in Maurice Rosenberg, *The Pre-Trial Conference and Effective Justice* (New York: Columbia University Press, 1964). See also Hans Zeisel, Harry Kalven, Jr., and Bernard Buchholz, *Delay in the Court* (Boston: Little, Brown, 1959), pp. 155–67; Proceedings of the Seminar on Practice and Procedure under the Federal Rules of Civil Procedure, Boulder, Colorado, 1960, 28 F.R.D. (1962); Seminar on Procedures for Effective Administration, 29 F.R.D. (1963); *Court Calendar Studies* (Chicago: American Bar Foundation, 1960).

Such rules are more than mechanical devices to expedite the handling of cases. When effectively applied, they mold the expectations of lawyers who contemplate taking a case to court. In a court where trials are held promptly, attorneys will prepare themselves on time; when they take their cases to such a court, they know they may expect prompt treatment. In other courts they may leave the case in their files until it has been passed over once or twice; if they have a choice, they take cases to such a court only when their clients are willing to accept a long delay.

Another point at which a judge can control the flow of litigation in court is in the handling of motions. Before a case goes to trial, lawyers on each side are likely to file preliminary motions raising points of law to undermine the opposition case, to clarify their own case, or to expedite taking depositions from witnesses. When they wish to undermine the opposition case, they may file a motion stating that the complaint is defective, that no legal remedy is available, that the allegations are obviously without basis of fact, or that the court lacks jurisdiction. In some instances these motions are made in earnest; in others they are dilatory tactics. If judges handle motions expeditiously and take a firm stand on motions that are filed only to achieve delay, the lawyers sense their impatience and accommodate themselves to the judges' preferences.[8] Of course, judges must gauge their actions carefully so that they do not let their impatience deter the filing of justified motions. This problem, however, is not unique to judges. All decision-making officials must establish procedures that efficiently process business without losing their sense of equity or their feel for the peculiarities of the matter. In a sense, judges face the same situation as tax agents who must handle a large number of returns but must also give enough attention to each so that every taxpayer is treated fairly. Judges must clear away procedural underbrush quickly and systematically without depriving litigants of their basic rights.

Promoting Settlements

Many cases are settled before a trial is scheduled. Many, indeed, proceed no further than the original complaint and an-

---

[8] See note 7; also Bernard Botein, *Trial Judge* (New York: Cornerstone Library, 1963), pp. 62–69.

swer. With these papers on the record, attorneys for both sides negotiate a settlement and withdraw their case from court. Increasingly, judges seek to promote such settlements — or, at the very least, expedite the later trial — by holding pretrial conferences. However, the mere fact that a judge holds pretrial hearings may not expedite settlements, for litigants may decide to delay settling their case until the judge calls both sides together. Since they know a conference will be called, they busy themselves with other matters until the judge takes the initiative and calls the pretrial hearing. A study of New York and New Jersey pretrial hearings by Zeisel, Kalven, and Buchholz suggests that this occurs. The hearings they studied showed only a slightly increased settlement ratio.[9] Nevertheless, their findings indicate that some judges are much better at promoting settlements than others and that some cases are more amenable to settlement at this stage than others.

What a judge does in chambers is apparently of crucial importance. Some judges use the conference simply to reach an agreement on evidence that will be presented at the trial; others use the conference to push litigants into a settlement. The latter course was often pursued by Judge Skelly Wright when he was presiding over the federal district court in New Orleans. He described his use of the pretrial conference:

> After we understand the issues, we have the lawyers ask each other any questions they want to about the case including, as I said, the witnesses and the documents. We make each side disgorge completely and absolutely everything about its case. There can't possibly be surprise, if the lawyers know what they are doing. And Federal lawyers usually know what they are doing, after a couple of cases.
>
> So then we set the case for trial . . . after we set the case for trial, we talk about settlement. I say "Well, have you exhausted the possibility of settlement?" And nobody says anything.
>
> Then I say to the plaintiff's lawyer: "You brought this suit, how much is it worth?" And they begin to talk; and then I actually find that they have discussed settlement, and they have reached a stand-off with reference to the offer of settlement: One having made an offer in X amount, the other having countered in Y amount.

[9] Zeisel *et al.*, *op. cit.*, pp. 141–54; see also Rosenberg, *op. cit.*

So, if it's a personal injury case, I look at the doctor's reports — just the last paragraph, where they show the extent of injury.

I tell them: "This case is worth $20,000 for the settlement," and, I tell them why; and I tell them further to go tell their clients that I said so.

And the funny thing is, the lawyers in my district want the judge to do that. They want to be able to go back to their clients and have some of the load taken off their shoulders. They say, "This is what I think, but the judge says this."

And by and large, these cases are settled.

Now in other types of cases, we are a little more tentative about the settlement discussion; we discuss the settlement, but we are much more tentative about it, because other issues may arise that you can't appraise at a pretrial conference very well and probably the trial of the case is required for resolution of such issues.[10]

Presiding over Trials

A very small proportion of all cases eventually come to trial. In these, the judge plays a varying role. When a jury hears the case, the judge plays the role of umpire. This is not entirely a passive role, for he must interpret and enforce the rules. In doing so, he must sometimes exert his influence strenuously to maintain the decorum of the courtroom and to prevent legal errors in the presentation of evidence. When all evidence has been presented, the judge must instruct the jury. In his instructions the judge may tell the jury which issues are irrelevant and should be disregarded. He may sum up the evidence and arrange the testimony so that it constitutes a more coherent story. In extreme cases he may even comment on the credibility of witnesses. The judge tells the jury which legal rules apply, how they should be interpreted, and what results the jury can reach. Although much evidence indicates that the judge's instructions are often misunderstood or ignored by juries, they are authoritative statements that at least on the surface appear to be influential. Consequently, attorneys make strenuous efforts to convince the judge to issue instructions favorable to their client.[11]

---

[10] 28 F.R.D. 144–45 (1962). For another judge's attitude toward pretrial conferences, see Botein, *op. cit.*, pp. 226-52.

[11] Vanderbilt, *op. cit.*, pp. 221 ff.

When there is no jury, the judge alone must make the decision. In this case the judge possesses a great deal of discretion and power. Few cases are brought to trial unless there is some doubt about their outcome; the decision can often go either way. The judge not only regulates the proceedings under which the evidence is presented but also makes the final ruling.

Even when juries make the final decision, American law increasingly gives the judge ancillary decision-making powers, which in the long run are almost as important as the jury's. In criminal cases, for instance, juries may determine innocence or guilt, but the judge usually decides what punishment will be inflicted on those found guilty. Studies of judicial sentencing behavior have shown that judges differ greatly in the severity of sentences; even the sentences of a single judge vary considerably over a period of years.[12] In a similar way, in some civil cases the jury may establish one party's fault and recommend the amount of damages to be paid, but the judge may reduce the amount. Thus, part of the ultimate decision remains in the judge's hands. A trial judge is by no means a passive observer who simply maintains order in the courtroom; rather, he possesses vital decision-making powers.

Appellate Judges' Functions

Appellate judges exercise a different kind of discretionary power. Courtroom procedure is rarely important in appellate cases, for little happens in open court. Appellate decisions are based principally on the record of the previous trial. Many appeals courts do not even permit oral argument; those that do limit it to a few minutes for every case.[13]

Moreover, most appellate courts in the country can exercise little control over the case load that comes before them.[14] A few, like the United States Supreme Court, can choose the cases they want to hear, but most are forced to hear every case that is appealed. However, when courts do have discretionary control of

[12] See Chap. 9.

[13] Vanderbilt, *op. cit.*, pp. 436–38.

[14] *Ibid.*, pp. 389–401. In the federal court system, the courts of appeals also must hear all final decisions from trial courts appealed to them. For details, see Chap. 11.

their dockets, this control vests considerable power in them. The Supreme Court, for instance, accepts about 10 percent of all cases that are brought to it. The most important criterion in the Court's selection of a case is whether it raises important policy issues.[15] Because this is a matter of opinion, the justices control the court's involvement in the political process by invoking their own standards rather than criteria imposed by law.

In all appellate courts the most important power that judges possess is that of making the decision. This power is never shared with a jury. Increasingly, however, it is being shared with staff attorneys, who draft decisions that the judges later sign. Such procedures are used only for "routine" cases, but the decision as to what constitutes a routine case is also often made by a staff attorney rather than by the judges.[16] In many other instances, a single judge considers the appeal and then submits his decision for approval to his colleagues, who generally agree and co-sign the decision.[17]

Appellate judges reach their decisions in the privacy of their chambers and conference rooms. In many cases the facts and the law are such that a ruling for either side can be justified. The only external limit to the exercise of discretion is that a higher court of appeals may overrule the decision. In practice this is not a very effective limit: with the Supreme Court there is no higher court, and the other appellate courts know that the Supreme Court accepts only a small portion of the appeals brought to it. The likelihood that a decision will be overruled is therefore relatively slight.

---

[15] Joseph Tanenhaus, Marvin Schick, Matthew Muraskin, and Daniel Rosen, "The Supreme Court's Certiorari Jurisdiction," in Glendon Schubert (ed.), *Judicial Decision-Making* (New York: Free Press of Glencoe, 1963), pp. 111–30.

[16] Thomas Y. Davies, "Affirmed: A Study of Criminal Appeals and Decision-Making Norms in a California Court of Appeal," *American Bar Foundation Research Journal* (1982), 632–36; J. Woodford Howard, Jr., *Courts of Appeals in the Federal Judicial System* (Princeton, N.J.: Princeton University Press, 1981), p. 198.

[17] Vanderbilt, *op. cit.*, pp. 385–453. The procedure of a federal court of appeals is well described in John P. Frank, "The Top U.S. Commercial Court," *Fortune*, 43 (Jan. 1951), 92–96; "The Second Circuit: Federal Judicial Administration in Microcosm," *Columbia Law Review*, 63 (1963), 874–908. The opportunity for corruption in one-man decisions is made evident in Joseph Borkin, *The Corrupt Judge* (New York: Clarkson N. Potter, 1962).

Appellate courts must make decisions based on ambiguities in the law; this gives judges discretionary power that has important implications for public policy. Appellate judges are frequently asked to interpret statutory or constitutional provisions in the light of public policy or community standards. Such decisions cannot be made on technical grounds alone; expertise in law does not give judges firm guidance in interpreting the public interest. In fact, judges in such cases must make a decision on the basis of their personal preference or of what they personally consider to be in the public interest.[18]

Other Functions of Judges

Because of their prestigious roles, judges also perform many nonjudicial functions. In New Jersey, the chief justice of the supreme court appoints six of the twenty-three members of the board of directors of the Prudential Insurance Company.[19] In Pennsylvania, judges appoint park commissioners in Philadelphia and scores of officials to other public agencies, such as the Board of Education and the Board of Revision of Taxes.[20] Moreover, judges control a vast reservoir of patronage positions that are associated with their judicial work. In some states, such as Connecticut, they appoint district attorneys;[21] in others, they appoint court clerks and other minor officials.[22] When judges probate wills, they must sometimes choose assessors. They also appoint guardians for the mentally infirm — often elderly people who have considerable estates that must be managed for a fee. Such positions have a potential for either influencing public policy or paying a salary or fee, and in some cities they provide the bulk of the patronage still available to political parties. At one

[18] Benjamin N. Cardozo, *The Nature of the Judicial Process* (New Haven, Conn.: Yale University Press, 1921), pp. 88–89, 113.

[19] *New York Times*, Feb. 24, 1962, p. 31.

[20] Sidney Schulman, *Toward Judicial Reform in Pennsylvania* (Philadelphia: University of Pennsylvania Law School Institute of Legal Research, 1962), pp. 59–67.

[21] David Mars, Fred Kort, and I. R. Davis, *Administration of Justice in Connecticut* (Storrs: University of Connecticut Institute of Public Service, 1963), pp. 35 passim.

[22] See, for instance, Wallace S. Sayre and Herbert Kaufman, *Governing New York City* (New York: Russell Sage Foundation, 1960), pp. 530–31; Schulman, *op. cit.*, pp. 65–67.

time in New York City, for example, there was scarcely a district leader of the Democratic party who was not a court-appointed official.[23] Some nonjudicial functions tarnish the courts with the suspicion of corruption. A Connecticut lawyer once complained of probate practices:

> In Connecticut probate courts, the system of estate appraisal is one of the most viciously corrupt systems ever distorted by the inventive minds of the greedy. By law, at least two appraisers are appointed for each estate; by rule-of-thumb, they are paid one-tenth of one per cent of the gross estate, each (or a minimum of $50.). By design, appraiser appointments are generally passed out to the judge's political cronies or to persons who can help his private practice; and by habit, the appraisers rarely earn their fees and very frequently simply sign their names to an appraisal inventory already prepared by the executing attorney.
>
> The corruption appears to be quite widespread and to be an established cornerstone in the post-election expectancies of both parties. One probate judge reformed the system in his own court and was rewarded by having his party turn him down for renomination. It appeared they wanted a good man but not one that good.[24]

Summary: The Judge's Functions

It is clear then that the judge exercises discretion at numerous points in the judicial process. Contrary to what Justice Roberts once asserted, the process does not consist of mechanically squaring the facts with the law and announcing the inevitable outcome. Rather, it consists of innumerable subjective decisions. Rules that affect the outcome must be formulated and applied; decisions must be reached. Although the judge is not the only participant in the decision-making process, he is at the center of it. Others may influence him, but he makes many of the decisions.

The judge occupies a vital position not only because of his role in the judicial process but also because of his control over lucrative patronage positions. Consequently, much attention has

---

[23] Sayre and Kaufman, *op. cit.,* p. 534.

[24] Howard A. Sackett, II, "Letter to the Editor," *American Bar Association Journal,* 49 (1963), 81.

been paid to the manner in which judges are chosen and to the sort of individuals who win positions on the bench.

The Recruitment of Judges

Unlike most countries, the United States has never possessed a group of career judges.[25] Would-be judges must possess no special training or qualifications. Since the nation's founding, judges in the United States have been selected from lawyers and occasionally from nonlawyers. Often they are selected to serve relatively short terms, although in practice most judges may serve for life if they want to hold their positions that long.

Three different procedures are used in the United States for initially selecting judges. The federal government and twenty-six states permit the chief executive to appoint judges. In the federal government and in most of these twenty-six states, such appointments are subject to confirmation or "election" by a legislative body. In sixteen states, the governor must appoint from a list of nominees that has been drafted by a commission of lawyers, laypeople, and an incumbent judge; the gubernatorial appointee is confirmed in his office by a plebiscite that is held after he has served for several years. This latter complex plan is variously called the Missouri Plan, merit selection, or the ABA Plan. Its adoption has been the objective of many reform efforts, and it has come into increasing use over the last decade.

The two other procedures for initially selecting judges involve fewer governmental bodies. One is partisan election, used by fifteen states. Candidates are nominated by partisan caucuses or primaries and then run on the party ballot at the usual November election. The third is nonpartisan election, used by sixteen states.[26] Candidates are generally selected by nonpartisan primaries and then run without party designation at a general election, usually held in the spring.

---

[25] For a brief review of judicial selection elsewhere see Henry J. Abraham, *The Judicial Process*, 3d ed. (New York: Oxford University Press, 1975), pp. 87–94.
[26] The count of states is derived from *Book of the States 1982–83* (Lexington, Ky.: Council of State Governments, 1982), pp. 254–55. The count exceeds fifty because some states use different procedures for selecting appellate and trial judges.

Each procedure gives access to different groups and establishes different sets of informal qualifications, resulting in somewhat different types of individuals being chosen for the bench.

Federal judges are appointed by the president after their nominations have been approved by the Senate.[27] The Constitution specifies this procedure only for Supreme Court justices, but Congress adopted it for other federal judges in the Judiciary Act of 1789. Because federal judges hold their office "during good behavior" — that is, for life — these appointments are extremely important: a President may leave the imprint of his administration on the country for a generation through his judicial appointees.

Although the formal process seems to give the President full power over the appointment of judges, senators have as much or even more influence in selecting district judges and, in some cases, judges of the courts of appeals. The President enjoys his full prerogatives only in the case of Supreme Court justices. The erosion of presidential influence in selecting judges has occurred as a result of senators using judicial appointments as patronage. Each senator, if the President belongs to the same party, expects to be consulted before a judicial appointment is made in his state. When the senator is a member of the opposition party, he usually recognizes the rules of the game, which give judicial appointments to the party in possession of the White House and leave him powerless.

Senatorial consultation means more than a simple conference. Most senators sponsor specific candidates for the bench and expect these candidates to receive the appointment unless grave misdemeanors cloud their pasts. Senators enforce their demands in various ways. Most important is the fact that the President needs the cooperation of individual senators, who may chair important committees, to gain adoption of his legislative program.

[27] An excellent description of the selection process for federal judges in recent years is Harold W. Chase, *The Appointing Process* (Minneapolis: University of Minnesota Press, 1972). See also Joel B. Grossman, *Lawyers and Judges: The A.B.A. and the Politics of Judicial Selection* (New York: John Wiley, 1965); John P. Schmidhauser, *The Supreme Court: Politics, Procedures, and Personalities* (New York: Holt, Rinehart and Winston, 1960), pp. 6–29; Joseph P. Harris, *The Advice and Consent of the Senate* (Berkeley: University of California Press, 1953), pp. 302–24.

If the President considers ignoring a senator's choice for a judgeship, he must weigh the importance of the judgeship against the importance of the legislation that he desires. Moreover, by custom, senators can enforce their wishes and block the appointment of anyone else to the post by invoking the rule of "senatorial courtesy." This unwritten rule states that, if a senator of the President's party declares that any appointee who is to serve in his home state is "personally obnoxious" to him, the Senate may refuse to confirm the nomination.[28] With very few exceptions (mostly when two senators of the same party and same state disagree), the rule is upheld. Therefore, senators possess a procedural weapon to reinforce the tactical consideration, and together these lead Presidents to favor the senators' choices for judicial positions.

Although the President's personal prestige is involved, the Attorney General handles all preliminaries in the appointment process.[29] As soon as it becomes evident that a vacancy will occur, the Attorney General's staff begins its search for a successor. It receives names from the senators of the state if they belong to the President's party, from local political organizations, from bar associations, and from other groups. Persons interested in a federal judgeship apparently mount vigorous campaigns to secure the appointment. They may apply directly; more frequently, however, they secure the endorsement of others who are influential. When the vacancy actually occurs, the Attorney General investigates the most likely candidates before recommending a single name to the President. In this search the Attorney General is limited by very few formal requirements. A district judge needs only to live in his state and district when he takes office, not before. A judge of the court of appeals needs only to live somewhere in the circuit. There are no residence requirements for Supreme Court justices. There are no educational or professional qualifications that must be met for any of the judgeships.

The ABA, however, places more severe restrictions on the Attorney General's search and the President's choice. For a long

[28] On recent changes in the application of senatorial courtesy, see Sheldon Goldman, "Carter's Judicial Appointments," *Judicature*, 64 (1981), 383.

[29] Much of the following is based on Grossman, *op. cit.*

time it has insisted that lawyers be consulted on judicial appointments, because they can best rate potential judges. As the leading national organization of lawyers, the association contends that it possesses the special technical competence necessary for the task. With considerable support from the press, it finally succeeded during the Eisenhower administration in winning the privilege to advise on and later to veto, judicial appointments. Since 1958 the Attorneys General have agreed to let the ABA's Committee on Judicial Selection make a preliminary inquiry into all candidates seriously considered for a lower federal judgeship. On the basis of this informal investigation, the ABA committee informs the Attorney General whether the candidate will receive a rating of "unqualified," "qualified," "well qualified," or "exceptionally well qualified" from the bar. Eisenhower instructed his Attorney General not to make appointments of men rated unqualified by the bar. As shown earlier in Chapter 4 (Figure 4.1), subsequent Presidents followed the ABA's advice almost as closely and appointed few judges who were initially rated unqualified. They continued to allow the ABA to make its ratings early in the appointment process and made its committee privy to developments concerning judicial appointments.[30]

The Justice Department and the President gain from the ABA's participation, for it provides them with information that they otherwise might not have. Neither is eager to appoint unqualified people to the bench. The President may also be happy to have an ally in warding off a senator's insistence that a particular friend be appointed. If the ABA rates a candidate unqualified with good reason, the President may be able to convince the senator to endorse another candidate.

In other cases, however, the ABA's activities restrict the President's choice in ways less desirable to him. There is no guarantee that the President's and the ABA's standards are the same. Under Eisenhower they usually were; under Kennedy, more frequently they were not. For example, Judge Harold Cox of Mississippi, rated by the ABA as "exceptionally well qualified" be-

---

[30] *Ibid.*, pp. 114–56; Elliot E. Slotnick, "The ABA Standing Committee on the Federal Judiciary," *Judicature*, 66 (1983), 348–62.

fore he was nominated by President Kennedy, became a dogged opponent of the Supreme Court's 1954 desegregation decision and used whatever means were at his command to delay decisions that might enfranchise blacks.[31] President Kennedy had made this appointment partly because no candidate with more liberal views could win the support of Mississippi's two senators but also because Judge Cox had won the unqualified support of the ABA. Another case involved the ABA rule that no one over sixty-four years old be appointed. President Kennedy wished to appoint a woman to the bench. His candidate was a very well-qualified woman who, however, was already sixty-four years old. The Justice Department argued with the ABA committee that women have a longer life expectancy than men and that the ABA rule should therefore be relaxed. The ABA refused to make an exception; the administration likewise refused to abandon the nomination — with the result that the administration appointed a judge rated unqualified by the bar.[32]

Other conflicts also occur: the ABA rates an individual's character, and, on this point, honest differences may arise. When the administration is politically liberal, it may differ from the committee simply because the ABA represents a rather conservative viewpoint. Such ideological conflicts rarely rise to the surface; most debate about judicial appointments focuses on the nominee's legal qualifications. Experience shows, however, that in some instances the assertion that a judge is unqualified is a cloak for opposing him because of differences in political judgment.[33] Since the ABA has now won formal status in the appointment process, the President sometimes finds himself confronted with opposition to judicial appointments that would not otherwise exist. Although the ABA is not strong enough to veto appointments that the President is committed to make, in borderline cases it has intervened successfully against a candidate who had some support among the President's advisors.[34]

[31] Judicial Performance in the Fifth Circuit," *Yale Law Journal*, 23 (1963), pp. 101–2, and note 71, p. 107.

[32] The incident is related by Grossman, *op. cit.*, pp. 150, 179–80.

[33] The best-known example was the opposition to Louis Brandeis when he was nominated by President Wilson as Supreme Court justice. For an account see A. L. Todd, *Justice on Trial* (New York: McGraw-Hill, 1964).

[34] Grossman, *op. cit.*, p. 153.

To provide himself with an independent check on a candidate's character and reputation, the Attorney General institutes an FBI investigation on those candidates seriously considered for appointment. Such investigations seek to uncover personal faults (such as heavy drinking), professional entanglements that might be undesirable, and financial embarrassments. If a candidate passes the FBI investigation, has the necessary political support, and meets the other political and merit requirements of the administration, that candidate's name is proposed to the Senate for confirmation.

In most instances the Senate makes only a perfunctory examination of the nominee. Senators are sent blue slips on which to record their endorsement or opposition. Only if a senator is eligible to invoke the rule of senatorial courtesy will opposition from a single senator be meaningful. The Senate Judiciary Committee holds a quick hearing — usually consisting of nothing more than friendly questioning by the appointee's senator sponsor. Even if the ABA opposes the candidate publicly or the candidate has aroused bitter opposition from other sources, the hearing rarely becomes a real inquiry. Opposition during the Judiciary Committee hearings has not prevented the approval of an overwhelming proportion of judicial appointees.[35]

Because senatorial courtesy does not extend to appointments to appellate courts and the ABA is not often consulted in the early stages when Supreme Court appointments are made, the President has much greater discretion in choosing higher-court judges. The Senate must still confirm such appointments, but opposition, when it arises, is grounded more on personal prejudices or policy matters than on patronage. The spectacular debates that eventually led to Senate rejection of President Nixon's nominations of Clement F. Haynsworth, Jr., and G. Harrold Carswell for the Supreme Court centered around policy disagreements between the nominees and many senators — as well as the desire of some senators to embarrass the President politically. Only a few years earlier, other senators had objected in vain to the appointment of Thurgood Marshall to the Supreme Court because of his role as chief counsel for the NAACP Legal

---

[35] *Ibid.*, pp. 156–95.

Defense Fund. Thus, personal attributes and policy commitments rather than patronage concerns become the central issue in the struggle over higher-court appointments.

A concern for such matters is illustrated by Theodore Roosevelt's attempt to learn Oliver Wendell Holmes's attitudes. He wrote Henry Cabot Lodge to inquire about Holmes:

> I should like to know that Judge Holmes was in entire sympathy with our views, that is with your views and mine and Judge Gray's, for instance, just as we know that ex-Attorney General Knolton is, before I would feel justified in appointing him. Judge Gray has been one of the most valuable members of the Court. I should hold myself as guilty of an irreparable wrong to the nation if I should put in his place any man who was not absolutely sane and sound on the great national policies for which we stand in public life.[36]

Despite this concern, Presidents have not always guessed correctly how their appointees would decide court cases. It is true that Grant predicted correctly that Justices Strong and Bradley would help form a new majority to reconsider the legal tender cases and reverse the original decision of the court (*Hepburn v. Griswold*).[37] Other Presidents were not so lucky. Woodrow Wilson, for instance, appointed not only the liberal Brandeis but also the reactionary McReynolds. Eisenhower's generally conservative preferences were not reflected by the activist and liberal stance of Earl Warren after Eisenhower appointed him Chief Justice, and Kennedy appointed the conservative Byron White.[38] However, Lyndon Johnson and Richard Nixon generally succeeded in appointing to the Supreme Court judges who reflected their own policy predilections, with Johnson appointing Abe Fortas and Thurgood Marshall, the first black to serve on the Court. Nixon was able to make the Court much more conservative with his appointments of Warren Burger, Harry Blackmun, Wil-

[36] Quoted in Walter Murphy and C. Herman Pritchett (eds.), *Courts, Judges and Politics* (New York: Random House, 1961), p. 83.

[37] Glendon Schubert, *Constitutional Politics* (New York: Holt, Rinehart and Winston, 1960), p. 53; 8 Wall. 603 (1870).

[38] It has also been difficult for Presidents to choose district court judges, especially in the South, who would uphold the Supreme Court's decisions. See Jack W. Peltason, *Fifty-Eight Lonely Men* (New York: Harcourt, Brace, 1961).

liam Rehnquist, and Lewis Powell, although Blackmun became more liberal over the years. President Reagan reinforced the conservative wing of the Court with his appointment of Sandra Day O'Connor, the first woman justice.

What have been the consequences of the appointment system for the federal courts? For the Supreme Court it has meant the appointment of high-status individuals. According to one study, 90 percent of all Supreme Court justices serving between 1789 and 1957 came from families of high social status and occupations.[39] Most were native-born Americans of West European ancestry.[40] A large majority were members of high-status Protestant denominations, although since the 1890s a few have been Catholics and Jews.[41] Most Supreme Court justices in this century have had an excellent undergraduate education and have gone to a high-ranking law school.[42] Without doubt, Supreme Court justices have come from the highest-ranking, most advantaged segments of American life. In addition, as the method of selection suggests, those who were active in politics won Supreme Court appointments much more frequently than the inactive. Slightly more than half the Supreme Court justices were primarily politicians; 99 percent held a public office before becoming a justice.[43]

Studies by Sheldon Goldman indicate that federal appeals judges and district court judges also come primarily from upper- and middle-class backgrounds.[44] For instance, the majority of judges appointed by Presidents Johnson, Nixon, Ford, and Reagan attended an Ivy League or private college and law school rather than public institutions. President Carter made a concerted effort to open the judiciary to new groups of applicants. He appointed many more women and members of minority

---

[39] John Schmidhauser, "The Supreme Court: A Collective Portrait," *Midwest Journal of Political Science*, 3 (1959), 7.

[40] *Ibid.*, pp. 17–18.

[41] *Ibid.*, pp. 19, 22.

[42] *Ibid.*, pp. 22–25.

[43] *Ibid.*, p. 37.

[44] This paragraph is largely based on Sheldon Goldman, "Judicial Backgrounds, Recruitment and the Party Variable: The Case of the Johnson and Nixon Appointees to the United States District and Appeals Courts," *Arizona State Law Journal* (1974), 211–22; Goldman, "Carter's Judicial Appointments," pp. 344–55; and Sheldon Goldman, "Reagan's Judicial Appointments at Mid-term," *Judicature*, 66 (1983), pp. 338–39.

groups. Many fewer of Carter's appointees were Protestant and more were politically active before becoming judges than had been true in the past. Nevertheless, more of Carter's appointees came from large law firms, and more had prior judicial or prosecutorial experience, than had been true of previous Democratic administrations. President Reagan especially favored Protestant male attorneys.

Another consequence of the federal appointment system with its life tenure has been that most sitting judges are relatively old. This is partly because federal judges do not usually win appointment until they are in their late forties or early fifties. Only 36.1 percent of federal district judges sitting in 1961 were appointed at an earlier age. Yet most judges stay on the bench until death or retirement at age seventy or over; life tenure means that they cannot be forced to retire earlier, although they may be given the status of senior judge and assigned only a limited caseload. For the Supreme Court, since 1917, the average retirement age has been over seventy-four. Until 1957, more Supreme Court justices had died in office than retired. Consequently, the average age of Supreme Court justices has ranged in the sixties.[45]

A final consequence of the appointment system is that most newly appointed judges are affiliated with the President's party. Even President Eisenhower, who professed a greater preference for a bipartisan judiciary than other recent Presidents, gave 94.4 percent of his appointments to Republicans. As a result, whenever one party wins the presidency repeatedly, the judiciary reflects this predominance. From 1865 to 1933, the judiciary was predominantly Republican; since Franklin Roosevelt's administration, it has been predominantly Democratic. Eisenhower's administration brought the partisan affiliation of judges to an almost even balance by his appointment of Republicans. President Kennedy once more made the judiciary predominantly Democratic: 93 percent of his 108 appointments went to fellow Democrats.[46] Presidents Johnson, Nixon, Carter, and Reagan followed

---

[45] Schubert, *op. cit.*, pp. 59–61; data for district judges from Kenneth Casanova, unpubl. paper.
[46] Richard J. Richardson and Kenneth N. Vines, *The Politics of Federal Courts* (Boston: Little, Brown, 1970), p. 68; "Report of the Standing Committee on the Federal Judiciary," *Reports of the American Bar Association*, 85 (1961), 455. See also Goldman, "Carter's Judicial Appointments," p. 348.

suit by giving more than 90 percent of their judicial appointments to members of their own party. Only President Ford broke this custom by appointing a substantial number of members of the opposite party to the judiciary.[47]

Partisan politics do not play as large a role in all states as in the federal judicial selection process. The degree of partisan influence and the routes through which it becomes effective vary greatly according to the formal selection procedure and political customs of each state.

In cases where judges are appointed, the formal procedure is much like that specified in federal statutes. However, no evidence shows that a custom similar to senatorial courtesy applies at the state level; governors appear to have more freedom than the President in selecting judges.[48] Most judges selected under an appointive system have served in the state legislature, where they become known and can impress others with their judicial potential.[49] Since many state legislatures (especially the branch that confirms appointments) have been predominantly Republican, regardless of the affiliation of the governor, governors have appointed more Republicans than Democrats as judges in all except the Southern states.[50]

In cases where judges are elected, party connections are most important when the election is partisan.[51] In fifteen states, judges are elected on the same kind of ballot as the governor, legislators, and county officials. To win a judgeship, a candidate must first

[47] Goldman, "Reagan's Judicial Appointments," p. 339.

[48] A unique account of a campaign to win gubernatorial appointment to a state judgeship is in John E. Crow, "Subterranean Politics: A Judge Is Chosen," *Journal of Public Law*, 12 (1963), 274–89.

[49] Much of the following comes from an analysis by the author of the backgrounds of state judges. For detailed tables and a discussion of the sources, see Herbert Jacob, "The Effect of Institutional Differences in the Recruitment Process: The Case of State Judges," *Journal of Public Law*, 13 (1964), 104–19. Bradley C. Canon, in "The Impact of Formal Selection Processes on the Characteristics of Judges — Reconsidered," *Law and Society Review*, 6 (1972), 579–89, places a greater emphasis on region when examining the selection of Supreme Court judges.

[50] Sayre and Kaufman describe the importance of partisan considerations in the appointment of New York City magistrates by the mayor, *op. cit.*, pp. 538–48.

[51] On judicial elections, see Philip L. Dubois, *From Ballot to Bench* (Austin: University of Texas Press, 1980).

win the party nomination and then campaign on the party ticket. Under these circumstances, former district attorneys seem to have the most success — more than three-fourths of the judges elected on a partisan ballot have served previously as district attorney.[52] In some states, such as New York, a place on the ballot requires a long apprenticeship in partisan politics as well as a considerable contribution to other campaigns. In Iowa, before the merit selection plan was adopted, prior political service was less important in winning a judicial post.[53] On the surface, the tenure of judges elected on a partisan ballot would seem to be tenuous and dependent on the shifting luck of the party in national and state politics. In fact, however, very few incumbent judges are defeated, even when they are selected by partisan ballot. In states like New York the high incumbency rate is the result of informal agreements not to oppose the other party's judicial incumbents;[54] in other states, the sitting judge simply has an advantage in bar support and public prominence that is very hard to overcome.[55]

In cases where nonpartisan elections are used, party influence is somewhat weaker. Almost half of the judges elected by such a system refuse to identify their party affiliation in directory biographies. However, party affiliation is not completely buried in nonpartisan elections. In Michigan, a place on the nonpartisan ballot can be won only by nomination at a party convention. In other states, party organizations make a fairly vigorous — al-

[52] This is also true for Texas; see Bancroft C. Henderson and T. C. Sinclair, *Judicial Selection in Texas: An Exploratory Study* (Houston: University of Houston Public Affairs Research Center, 1964), pp. 71–74.

[53] Thomas A. Ewers, "A Study of the Background of the Successful and Unsuccessful Candidates for the Iowa Supreme Court" (unpubl. master's thesis, State University of Iowa, 1959).

[54] Sayre and Kaufman, *op. cit.*, pp. 546–47.

[55] Cf. the experience of Florida and Louisiana: Emmett W. Bashful, *The Florida Supreme Court: A Study in Judicial Selection* (Tallahassee: Bureau of Governmental Research and Service, Florida State University, 1958), pp. 49–52; Kenneth N. Vines, "The Selection of Judges in Louisiana," in Kenneth N. Vines and Herbert Jacob, *Studies in Judicial Politics*, Tulane Studies in Political Science, Vol. 8 (New Orleans: Tulane University, 1963), pp. 113–18; for Minnesota, see Robert A. Heiberg, "Social Backgrounds of the Minnesota Supreme Court Justices, 1858–1958," *Minnesota Law Review*, 53 (1969), 903–7. Formal provisions of tenure are given for each of the states in *State Court Systems* (Lexington, Ky.: Council of State Governments, 1976).

though secret — effort to elect their candidate under the guise of nonpartisanship.[56] Precise measurements are unfortunately quite difficult because nonpartisan elections force party activity underground. It is fair to estimate, however, that in about half of the sixteen states that use nonpartisan judicial ballots, parties play some role in the selection of judges. Moreover, the governor often plays a major role in judicial selection in these states, for in most of them he fills vacancies on the bench by appointment. The appointee serves to the end of the regular term before running for the office as an incumbent rather than an aspirant, thus gaining an almost insurmountable advantage in the election. In many states with nonpartisan elections, judges often resign or retire before the end of the term, which gives the governor *de facto* appointment power. A study of state supreme court incumbents, for instance, showed that well over half those nominally elected by nonpartisan ballots were in fact originally appointed to the bench by the governor.[57]

Tenure presents no problem to most judges selected by nonpartisan elections.[58] In Wisconsin, for instance, only four incumbent supreme court justices were defeated between 1853 and 1949. In Minnesota only one supreme court justice was defeated for reelection between 1912 and 1941, and only four of eighty-four district judges were defeated in their reelection bids during that time.[59] Indeed, elected district court judges in Minnesota held office longer during that period than the life-term federal judges.[60]

In both partisan and nonpartisan elections, the bar seeks to influence the selection of judges. A generation ago, the Chicago bar began an attempt to control party nominations by staging a "bar primary," in which members of the bar association voted

[56] For an illustration in Minnesota see Malcolm C. Moos, "Judicial Elections and Partisan Endorsement of Judicial Candidates in Minnesota," *American Political Science Review*, 35 (1941), 69–75.

[57] James Herndon, "Appointment as a Means of Initial Accession to State Courts of Last Resort," *North Dakota Law Review*, 38 (1962), 60–73.

[58] Dubois, *op. cit.*, p. 109.

[59] For Wisconsin see Timothy G. Higgins, "The Justices of the Wisconsin Supreme Court," *Wisconsin Law Review* (1949), 754; for Minnesota see Heiberg, *op. cit.*, p. 903, and Moos, *op. cit.*, p. 69.

[60] Forrest Talbott and William Anderson, *Intergovernmental Relations and the Courts* (Minneapolis: University of Minnesota Press, 1950), p. 27.

on all candidates. Those who won a majority were endorsed and given campaign support by the association. About 70 percent of all elected judges between 1887 and 1934 had the bar's endorsement; the remainder were elected without bar support.[61] The use of a bar primary has been extended elsewhere, although it has not been completely successful in any city.[62] The bar also may try to influence elections through private channels. In Florida, leaders of the state bar association have succeeded in winning interim appointments to the state supreme court; when they ran for a full term on the court, they were supported by the bar association.[63] Elsewhere, informal consultation between party officials and leaders of the bar may occur. Mayor Wagner of New York established one such arrangement in 1961 with considerable fanfare. The result in New York, however, did not demonstrate a high degree of bar association influence: the same kinds of politically active individuals were appointed after the arrangement as were appointed before it.[64]

Bar associations find it difficult to win great influence in the choice of nominees for judicial elections, because the elections themselves are so obscure as to be almost invisible. When judges are chosen in a general election, they occupy last place on a long ballot, and few voters know much about the candidates.[65] When judges are selected at special elections, the voter turnout is usually very low. In both cases the bar has difficulty making its weight felt.

To overcome such handicaps, the ABA has long advocated changing the selection procedure. It has succeeded in convinc-

[61] Edward M. Martin, *The Role of the Bar in Electing the Bench in Chicago* (Chicago: University of Chicago Press, 1936), p. 176.

[62] Ben R. Miller, "The Role and Responsibility of Local Bar Associations in the Selection of Judicial Candidates," *Louisiana Bar Journal*, 7 (1959), 171. Its use in Texas is noted by Henderson and Sinclair, *op. cit.*, pp. 33–36.

[63] Bashful, *op. cit.*, pp. 153–67. Also, Joel H. Goldstein, "Bar Poll Ratings as the Leading Influence in a Non-Partisan Judicial Election," *Judicature*, 63 (1980), 376–84.

[64] *The New York Times*, Feb. 18, 1962, p. 1; June 12, 1962, p. 25. Another unsuccessful attempt of the bar to win influence occurred in Pennsylvania; see Schulman, *op. cit.*, pp. 31–38.

[65] Claude J. Davis, *Judicial Selection in West Virginia* (Morgantown: Bureau of Government Research, West Virginia University, 1959), pp. 26–30; Martin, *op. cit.*, chap. 20.

ing a growing number of states to adopt a hybrid appointment-election system, called a *merit selection* plan. This plan provides for gubernatorial appointment from a panel of nominees initially selected by a commission composed of lawyers and laypeople. The appointee serves for one year or until the next election and then faces the electorate in a plebiscite, in which the voters are asked, "Shall Judge —— be retained in office?" If a majority votes "yes," the incumbent serves the full term and then faces another such "election." If a majority votes "no," the incumbent loses his seat, and another appointee is chosen under the same procedure. Although the merit plan seems to ensure continued incumbency, under unusual circumstances voters may reject a sitting judge.[66] Because short incumbency is not a problem in states using other selection systems, the improvement resulting from the merit plan on this count is not very important. However, the plan has had other results. It has given bar associations an official place in the selection process: normally, their representatives constitute half the nominating commission. Because the governor must appoint someone who has gained the approval of the commission, the bar has won a veto power over prospective judges. Bar politics have thus partially replaced partisan politics in those states using the merit plan. The plan has also been successful in removing judgeships from the ordinary career ladder of politicians.[67] Not only do an overwhelming majority of the judges chosen by the merit selection plan deny party affiliation, but most of them have never served in another public office. This contrasts sharply with the background of most judges selected according to other procedures. Even nonpartisan elections have not been as successful in eliminating party influence over judicial selection as the merit plan.[68]

The use of one selection system or another also influences other characteristics of the individuals selected for the bench. Some systems recruit homegrown talent; others are less exclusive. Judges selected by the merit plan or elected on a partisan

---

[66] Robert A. Leflar, "The Quality of Judges," *Indiana Law Journal*, 35 (1959–60), 293.

[67] See Jacob, *op. cit.*, pp. 109–13.

[68] Richard W. Watson and Rondal G. Downing, *The Politics of the Bench and the Bar* (New York: John Wiley, 1969); Jacob, *op. cit.*

ballot frequently were born in the district in which they serve; those selected by other systems more frequently come from outside the district or the state. Judges elected by a nonpartisan election or chosen by a legislature generally have a better educational background than those chosen by the other systems.

Other characteristics remain uniform for judges of major state trial and appellate courts. Most judges are selected for the state bench during their forties — about ten years earlier than federal judges. All are lawyers; almost all have attended a law school. Finally, regardless of the selection system, more judges are Republicans than Democrats in non-Southern states. This is not entirely a reflection of Republican predominance in northern states, for even in heavily Democratic districts less than half the judges are Democrats.

The Removal of Judges

One earmark of a democratic government is that its policymaking officials are elective or removable by some kind of popular action. Although judges are not normally considered politicians, they too make policy. Within each selection system some provisions for removal exist.

In states where judges are elected or subject to the plebiscite typical of the merit plan, the most obvious means of removing a judge is by defeating him at the polls. Such an opportunity, however, occurs less frequently than with other elected officials, for judicial terms are longer. In only eleven states is the trial judge's term as short as four years — the ordinary term of an elective official in the United States. In the rest of the states trial judges serve for longer terms, ranging from seven years to life.[69] Thus, even if electoral defeat can oust a judge, the opportunity for it arises infrequently. Appellate judges serve still longer terms, on the average. In every state, the terms are six years or longer. For elective judges on an appellate court, New York provides the longest term — fourteen years for its highest appeals court — and the shortest term — five years for its intermediate appellate court.[70] All available information indicates that elected judges are rarely defeated at the polls.

[69] *Book of the States 1982–83, op. cit.,* pp. 254–55.
[70] *Ibid.*

Some states make it possible to recall judges. The judicial recall requires petitions and a referendum: the same as the recall for other officials. The recall was applied to judges early in the twentieth century upon the agitation of union leaders who sought a way to unseat those they called "injunction judges" because they issued injunctions halting strikes. Although the judicial recall was adopted in several states, it had little success against judges. Its utility against the judiciary has remained nominal, as it has with other public officials.[71]

In a few other states, judges have occasionally been removed through legislative address, which involves a vote by the legislature on a resolution to remove a judge from office. It was employed with success early in the nineteenth century against a few judges in Kentucky; since then, although it remains available, it has rarely been invoked.[72]

Both the federal and state constitutions include provisions for impeaching judges. To warrant impeachment, a judge must be accused of "misbehavior," a term referring in law to criminal conduct. Impeachment proceedings take place in the legislature and usually require a two-thirds vote of one house for conviction. On rare occasions, state and federal judges have been impeached, but the threat of impeachment has been more effective than its use: faced with the threat, judges often resign.[73] Impeachment itself is an awkward proceeding, requiring a great deal of time from a busy legislature and necessitating a high degree of cohesion to win conviction. In practice, impeachment has remained an empty threat against both state and federal judges.[74]

A more effective weapon than impeachment is trial of an aberrant judge by a special panel of his fellow judges or a commission on judicial fitness. Such a procedure now exists in forty-one

[71] Frederick C. Bird and Frances M. Ryan, *The Recall of Public Officers* (New York: Macmillan, 1930), pp. 15, 293–97; James D. Barrett, *The Operation of the Initiative, Referendum and Recall in Oregon* (New York: Macmillan, 1915).

[72] William S. Carpenter, *Judicial Tenure in the U.S.* (New Haven, Conn.: Yale University Press, 1918), pp. 128–30; Francis R. Aumann, *The Changing American Legal System* (Columbus: Ohio State University Press, 1940), p. 172.

[73] Borkin, *op. cit.*

[74] The difficulties are well illustrated by Carl D. McMurray's account of an unsuccessful attempt: *The Impeachment of Circuit Judge Kelly* (Tallahassee: Institute of Governmental Research, Florida State University, 1964).

states.[75] In California, for instance, the panel has usually succeeded in forcing the retirement of a judge when investigation showed that evidence supported the allegations made against him.[76] The informal pressure of a judge's colleagues and the threat of bringing public proceedings apparently suffice to force him off the bench. In New York, a special tribunal has been convened several times in recent years to hear charges of corruption and bribery against state judges. Only the most serious cases are brought to the tribunal: in two recent instances, the court unseated judges by finding them guilty of wrongdoing. In both California and New York, the method of unseating judges involves no other agencies of government, but in many states the supreme court exercises the final authority. However, no charges are made to the legislature, where the proceedings could be confused by partisan alignments; nor is the public consulted through a referendum.

Abolishing the court on which an unpopular judge sits offers another way to remove such jurists. If the judge enjoys life tenure, it may be necessary to pay him his salary for the remainder of his life; however, he may no longer decide cases or exercise the powers of a judge. Jefferson and the Federalist party used this method for removing judges appointed by Adams in the last hours of his administration to the new circuit judgeships that Congress had voted. Some states have also employed this weapon.[77]

Despite the variety of procedures available to unseat them, judges are conspicuously more secure in their positions than are other public officials. Although it is true that many must seek reelection, which has occasionally distracted them from their judicial duties, only in the case of minor judgeships does the record indicate a relatively high turnover among judges, and such turnover is more the result of voluntary retirement or of promotion to higher office than the consequence of electoral defeat.[78] Re-

---

[75] Details are summarized in *Book of the States, 1982–83, op. cit.,* pp. 262–68.

[76] Jack E. Frankel, "Removal of Judges, California Tackles an Old Problem," *American Bar Association Journal,* 49 (1963), 166–71. Also see special issue on misconduct commissions: *Judicature,* 63 (Nov. 1979).

[77] Carpenter, *op. cit.,* pp. 113–14.

[78] For New York, see Sayre and Kaufman, *op. cit.,* pp. 534–35.

gardless of the statutory or constitutional provisions concerning judicial tenure, most judges in the United States enjoy tenure for life or until they reach the statutory retirement age.

The Impact of Selection Procedures

The manner in which judges are chosen and sometimes removed has important consequences for the judicial process. All of the selection schemes establish political routes of access to the bench. When partisan elections pave the way to a judgeship, the prospective jurist must often prove himself a loyal partisan before being considered for the bench. Moreover, in some places he is expected to make considerable donations to party funds. At one time New York judges were apparently expected to contribute up to $20,000 for the election of their party's ticket.[79]

When judges are not selected by a "merit" plan, political experience is often an unwritten prerequisite for the bench. Many judges in the United States are accustomed to partisan fights and understand at least a small part of the partisan political arena. When they ascend the bench, they are no strangers to public conflict. Often they have spent years of apprenticeship in policymaking positions in a legislature or an executive office. Leo Egan, late correspondent for *The New York Times*, wrote in 1962:

> Borough President John T. Clancy's decision last week to seek the Democratic nomination for Surrogate of Queens this year is drawing attention again to the peculiar role of the judiciary in Democratic politics in New York. . . . His desire to leave the vexing, often exasperating responsibilities of high administrative office for the comparative quiet and security of the bench illustrates the enormous attraction that judicial office has for top-flight lawyers in public life. . . . Among those in this category are such former legislators as Supreme Court Justices . . . McGiven of Manhattan . . . Crisona of Queens . . . Helman of the Bronx, Surrogates . . . DiFalco of Manhattan and . . . McGrath of the Bronx, General Sessions Judge . . . Davidson of New York County and County Judge . . . Farrell of Queens. Others include such former holders of administrative offices as Supreme Court Justices . . . McDonald of Brooklyn and . . . McNally of Manhattan.[80]

[79] *Ibid.*, p. 542.
[80] *The New York Times*, June 4, 1962, p. 21.

Such political ties are almost as common among judges selected through nonpartisan elections — as seen in the following sketch of a Wisconsin supreme court justice:

> From 1945 to 1950 he was a member and chairman of the Madison Housing Authority, and from 1956 to 1958 he was co-chairman of the mayor's metropolitan development committee. . . . In 1948, 1950, and 1952 he was defeated as a candidate for Congress from the Second district, but in 1956 and 1960 he was elected to the State Senate.[81]

Even federal judges often have significant political experience, as in the case of Governor Thomas Meskill of Connecticut, who was nominated by Richard Nixon to the judiciary over the bitter opposition of the ABA.[82] Judges are likely to bring to their role as policymakers some habits of decision making learned from their previous experience. Thus, the recruitment process links the judiciary with the other branches of government and with political conflicts.

The informal requirement of political experience for judgeships keeps many of the nation's elite lawyers off the bench.[83] Attorneys in large firms rarely engage in state or local politics and are rarely considered for judgeships. Moreover, judicial salaries are relatively modest. In most states, trial judges earn less than the median income for all lawyers.[84] Finally, in many states judicial candidates must live in the locale of the judgeships to be eligible for them. In metropolitan areas this requirement disqualifies many leading lawyers for city judgeships, because they live in the suburbs.

The backgrounds of judges, their personal experience, and the conditions of tenure combine with the demands of the judicial role to influence judicial decisions. For instance, during the early twentieth century certain judges were notorious for their hostility to labor unions and their friendship toward business enterprises. This, one might suppose, was a reflection of their prior contacts

[81]*Wisconsin State Journal*, December 16, 1962, sec. 4, p. 6.
[82] Sheldon Goldman and Thomas P. Jahnige, *The Federal Courts as a Political System*, 2d ed. (New York: Harper and Row, 1976), pp. 55–57.
[83] For the situation in Texas, see Henderson and Sinclair, *op. cit.*, p. 93.
[84] For trial judges' salaries, see *State Court Systems, op. cit.*, pp. 10–11; for income of attorneys, see Chap. 4.

with the business world. As Jerome Frank, himself a judge, wrote:

> When it comes to "finding" the "facts" in lawsuits where the oral testimony is in conflict, these obscure idiosyncrasies in the trial judge are bafflingly at work. The judge's sympathies and antipathies are likely to be active with respect to the witness. His own past may have created plus or minus reactions to women, or blonde women, or men with beards or Southerners, or Italians, or Englishmen, or plumbers, or ministers, or college-graduates or Democrats. A certain facial twitch or cough or gesture may start up memories, painful or pleasant. Those memories of the trial judge, while he is listening to a witness with such a facial twitch or cough or gesture, may affect the judge's initial hearing, or subsequent recollection, of what the witness said, or the weight of credibility which the judge will attach to the witness' testimony.[85]

Empirical examination of the relationship between judges' backgrounds and their propensity to decide one way or another has just begun. The results so far have been suggestive. For instance, Schmidhauser found that Supreme Court justices who had previously served on a lower court did not adhere to precedent more frequently than justices without prior judicial experience. Indeed, the opposite was true: justices with judicial experience were more willing to abandon precedent; they were also somewhat less likely to dissent.[86] Justices of humble family background were more likely to abandon precedent than those coming from upper-status families, and corporation lawyers were no more wedded to precedent than politician lawyers.[87] In another study, Schmidhauser found that during the sectional crisis from 1837 to 1860, leading to the Civil War, justices did indeed align themselves according to regional and party origins.[88] Once more, the justices who had judicial experience did not exhibit any more moderation than did those who came to the bench without such experience. Judicial experience apparently did not school these

[85] Jerome Frank, *Courts on Trial* (Princeton, N.J.: Princeton University Press, 1950), p. 151.

[86] John Schmidhauser, *Constitutional Law in the Political Process* (Chicago: Rand McNally, 1963), pp. 511–12.

[87] *Ibid.*, pp. 512–13.

[88] *Ibid.*, pp. 486–505.

judges in the conservative norms that are expected from a court. Rather, such experience gave the judges confidence to disregard such norms when that seemed necessary to reach a desired policy outcome.

A somewhat different line of inquiry, pursued by Stuart Nagel, indicates the importance of certain background factors in the decisional propensities of state supreme court justices. Examining state supreme courts that possessed acknowledged members of both political parties in 1955, Nagel found that Democrats were more likely to vote for the defense in criminal cases, for the administrative agency in business regulation cases, for the claimant in unemployment compensation cases, for a finding of constitutional violation in criminal cases, for the government in tax cases, for the tenant in landlord–tenant cases, for the consumer in sale-of-goods cases, for the injured in motor vehicle accident cases, and for the employee in employee injury cases.[89] These results certainly cannot be interpreted as showing that judges affiliated with one of the parties follow party doctrine, for American parties have no doctrine on most of the issues tested. However, the results are compatible with the general assessment of the Democratic party as liberal and especially concerned with the rights of the underprivileged, whereas Republicans are conservative and especially concerned with the prerogatives of the business community and property owners. Since Nagel's method eliminated one-party courts, he excluded Southern benches, where the characterization of the Democratic party as liberal would be incorrect.[90] In subsequent research, Dubois confirmed the importance of partisan identification in appellate decisions, although he found its strength varied from one state to another.[91]

Nagel was also able to indicate that other background factors play an important role in particular cases. When he examined

[89] Stuart Nagel, "Political Party Affiliation and Judges' Decisions," *American Political Science Review*, 55 (1961), 844. S. Sidney Ulmer, in "The Political Party Variable in the Michigan Supreme Court," *Journal of Public Law*, 11 (1962), 352–62, reports a similar distinction between Democratic and Republican judges in Michigan; Democrats were more lenient than Republicans to claimants in workmen's compensation cases.

[90] For evidence contrary to Nagel's conclusions, see David W. Adamany, "The Party Variable in Judges' Voting: Conceptual Notes and a Case Study," *American Political Science Review*, 63 (1969), 57–73.

[91] Dubois, *op. cit.*, pp. 178–241.

the criminal case decisions of state supreme courts, he discovered that former prosecutors voted for the defense less often than those lacking such experience, that members of the ABA were more prosecution-minded than nonmembers, and that Protestant judges were less likely to vote for the defense than Catholic judges. In addition, he found that the judges who scored high in "general liberalism" on an attitude questionnaire voted much more frequently for the defense than those who scored low.[92]

The background that judges bring with them to the courts also affects the acceptability of their decisions. If the public perceived judicial decisions as partisan, it might be less willing to accept them without demanding greater control over access to the bench. However, judges seem to be perceived as a quite different breed from other officials. Others are politicians; judges are guardians of the law. A judge's immunity to criticism crumbles only when he continually hands down decisions that are unpopular with part of the population. His qualifications are then called into question. For instance, extreme conservatives questioned the qualifications of Chief Justice Warren and liked to remind their audiences that Warren had not previously served on a court and had little legal experience before being appointed to the Supreme Court; he had been a politician. Yet the label "politician" does not easily stick with a judge, even when it is properly applied. Despite their political background, American judges do not suffer from the general disapproval accorded politicians. They are respected by most of the population and command more prestige than any other public official except the President.

The evidence is still quite fragmentary. Political scientists have isolated those factors that have proved convenient to measure, not those that might be, or have been proven to be, most important in affecting a judge's decision in a case. However, they provide some evidence for the proposition that judges, like other policymakers, reflect the training and background they bring to their position.

[92] Stuart Nagel, "Judicial Backgrounds and Criminal Cases," *Journal of Criminal Law, Criminology and Police Science*, 53 (1962), 335.

7
The Public in Court

Professionals dominate the judicial process. Judges and lawyers are not only the most conspicuous participants but also the most influential, and their power in the courts has increased in this century because of the tendency to restrict all spheres of decision making to the appropriate expert group. Yet their increase in power is not simply the result of a general trend. On the contrary, judges and lawyers have worked strenuously to restrict participation by amateurs, for the legal profession argues that lay participation distorts the administration of justice.

However, the courts are not a private reserve for professionals. They serve ordinary people who bring criminal complaints via the police and prosecutor's office or who come to court to rectify some alleged wrong. Those roles for the public will be described in Chapters 9 and 10. Here we wish to examine another form of public participation. Since the establishment of the colonies in America, the public has had a role in the judicial process, not only as litigant but also as spectator and participant. Trials have been open to the public so that they cannot be abused for political purposes. Members of the public have traditionally participated in civil and criminal trials as jurors.

Conditions in the twentieth century have not altered the public's desire to participate, but they have altered some consequences of such participation. Trials continue to be open, but only a few spectators witness them personally. Most of the public pay attention only to sensational trials that are brought to them by mass media. The electronic media — radio and television — can bring such trials directly to the home of all who tune in. Thus, in selected cases, courtroom proceedings have a far more direct impact on the population today than in previous centuries. At the same time, as more of the public become spectators, it becomes more difficult to justify the participation of the public as jurors in judicial decision making. The media make it more difficult to find jurors who remain free from bias; moreover, because cases have become more complex, untrained men and women find it difficult to decide them rationally.

The legitimacy of public participation in the judicial process is under heavier attack now than ever before. Many professionals seek to restrict both the use of juries and reporting by the media. Evaluation of these trends requires careful regard for the empirical consequences of public participation in the judicial process. To render a judgment, one must examine the extent of public participation and its apparent consequences for the administration of justice in America.

Juries

Juries are a relic of the medieval origins of our legal system. They originated in England during the Middle Ages to help the royal government enforce law and order. Originally, jurors were neither random representatives of the community nor unbiased outsiders, but witnesses who were compelled to testify. The use of jurors to give testimony gradually dwindled, and juries won the right to participate in making decisions. The Magna Charta guaranteed to noblemen the right to trial by their peers — that is, by jurors who were the social equals of those placed on trial. In this way, juries became instruments for limiting the arbitrary use of the courts against political opponents.

The right to trial by jury was part of the English heritage that the colonists brought with them to America and later included in the Constitution. The Sixth Amendment guarantees: "In all criminal prosecutions, the accused shall enjoy the right to a speedy and public trial, by an impartial jury of the State and district wherein the crime shall have been committed." The Seventh Amendment adds: "In suits at common law, where the value in controversy shall exceed twenty dollars, the right of trial by jury shall be preserved." Many state constitutions include similar guarantees of trial by jury.

Today, however, the use of juries varies a great deal from state to state. Different kinds of juries exist. The most common is the *petit jury*, a body of six to twelve citizens who hear trials and decide their outcome. In addition, some states use a *coroner's jury*, which hears evidence about deaths that take place under mysterious circumstances and rules whether they were natural, accidental, or occurred at the hands of persons known or unknown. Finally, some states still use the grand jury, a body usually composed of twenty-three citizens who hear allegations about crimes that may have been committed. It is the duty of the grand jury to vote indictments when the evidence indicates that a particular individual committed the crime. The indictment becomes the basis for further court action, often leading to a trial at which a petit jury rules on the guilt or innocence of the accused.[1]

Trial (petit) juries make the most important decisions, for their decisions culminate the judicial process. In most states a finding of innocence in criminal cases cannot be overturned by subsequent appeals, and a ruling of guilty can be overruled only with difficulty.

In cases where juries decide innocence or guilt, power in the courtroom is shifted from the judge to the men and women sitting in the jury box. How they decide depends to a considerable degree on who they are. Although they are composed of ordinary citizens, juries are not representative institutions in the same way that legislatures are. Jurors are not elected by their fellow citizens; they have no mandate from them. They are selected by chance to *serve* their community rather than to *represent* it.

[1] On the grand jury, see "The Grand Jury — Its Investigatory Powers," *Minnesota Law Review*, 37 (1953), 586–607; Robert Scigliano, "The Grand Jury, the Information, and the Judicial Inquiry," *Oregon Law Review*, 38 (1959), 303–15.

Jurors are appointed by a more or less random process. In theory, every citizen should have an equal chance to serve. In practice, however, both laws and customs make it impossible to select jurors randomly.[2] The statutes governing the selection of juries specify certain minimum qualifications. In most cases jurors must be electors — that is, registered to vote. As a consequence, all citizens who do not bother to register for voting or who are not qualified to vote are excluded. That qualification bars those who are transient or illiterate and at the same time disqualifies those convicted of a crime. In addition, statutes in most states specify a long list of occupational groups whose members cannot be called or may be excused upon request. Lawyers, ministers, teachers, doctors, nurses, policemen, and firemen are among those typically excused from jury service. The exclusion of some, such as doctors and firemen, is based on the need for their services even during trials, for they cannot be replaced without great public inconvenience and expense. Others, such as lawyers and policemen, are so intimately connected with the judicial process that they are not likely to be unbiased.

Common practice excludes still others from jury lists. In many communities juries are selected by jury commissioners, who must present the court with a list of names twice a year. They procure these names by asking their friends, civic clubs, and others to volunteer. In some instances jury service is used as a form of low-level patronage, for jurors are paid a nominal fee that constitutes a worthwhile remuneration only for people who are retired or unemployed. When jury selection depends on such procedures, only those known to the commissioners are likely to be called. In other communities, workingmen are systematically excluded from jury lists because they cannot afford to serve. An ordinary wage earner loses his wages while serving on a jury, and jury fees rarely equal what he would earn during his normal working day. This bar to jury service is slowly disappearing because some union contracts provide for compensation during jury service and many employers make it a matter of civic pride to

---

[2] For a review of various practices concerning the selection of jurors, see Arthur T. Vanderbilt, *Minimum Standards of Judicial Administration* (New York: Law Center of New York University, 1949), pp. 147–205.

continue paying their workers while they are serving on a jury.[3] However, when such arrangements do not exist, a prospective juror may ask to be excused because his family cannot subsist on the jury fee he would earn. Judges almost always honor such requests.

For all these reasons, jury panels are rarely a true cross section of the population. Studies in Los Angeles, Milwaukee, and Baltimore showed that professionals, managers, and proprietors are vastly overrepresented on juries, while working-class people are grossly underrepresented.[4] In Baltimore, for instance, professionals, managers, and proprietors constituted only 18.7 percent of the population but contributed 40.2 percent of the jurors in a federal court. At the same time, 41.4 percent of the population were working-class people, but only 13.4 percent of the jurors were blue-collar.[5] When conscious exclusionary practices lead to such discrimination, the jury's decision may be overturned by an appellate court, and a new trial may be held before a more "representative" jury. However, in most cases underrepresentation of working-class citizens is not the result of conscious attempts to exclude them.[6] Many working people are excused because they cannot afford to serve. Many more are never called for jury service because they fail to register to vote and are therefore excluded from the original listing used to procure a jury.

The same factors leading to exclusion or underrepresentation of working-class people also lessen the chances for blacks to serve on juries. Not only are most blacks in the working class, but many are not registered to vote. In the South blacks were deliberately excluded until decisions of the United States Supreme Court forced Southern courts to change their procedures so that they at least had a chance to serve.

---

[3] Robert L. Aronson, "Compensation of Industrial Workers for Jury Service," *Labor Law Journal*, 8 (1957), 95–104.

[4] W. S. Robinson, "Bias, Probability, and Trial by Jury," *American Sociological Review*, 15 (1950), 73–78; Edwin S. Mills, "Statistical Study of Occupations of Jurors in a U.S. District Court," *Maryland Law Review*, 32 (1962), 205–16; Marvin R. Summers, "Comparative Study of Qualifications of State and Federal Jurors," *Wisconsin Bar Bulletin*, 34 (1961), 35–39.

[5] Mills, *op. cit.*, p. 208.

[6] Hayward R. Alker, Carl Hosticka, and Michael Mitchell, "Jury Selection as a Biased Social Process," *Law and Society Review* 11 (1976), 9–42.

The law does permit the intentional exclusion of some individuals from jury service. Lawyers who try a case before a jury are allowed by law to reject prospective jurors on several grounds.[7] They usually question prospective jurors carefully to see if they have already made up their minds on the case or been influenced by press reports. Lawyers may usually reject an unlimited number of prospective jurors for good cause; they possess a handful of peremptory challenges, which they may use to bar a juror without giving any reason. Such considerations during the selection of a jury can make it extraordinarily difficult to choose juries in well-publicized cases. In December 1970, when Black Panthers Bobby Seale and Ericka Huggins were put on trial in New Haven in connection with the murder of a fellow Panther, lawyers questioned 1,035 prospective jurors over a four-month period before a jury was chosen. After their trial ended in a hung jury, the judge dismissed the charges against them because he thought it would be impossible to select another jury. In addition to rejecting jurors for unsuitability, some attorneys use the jury-selection process to secure the most favorable set of jurors available for their clients. This involves obtaining psychological profiles on prospective jurors and selecting only those likely to respond favorably to their client.[8]

Both the size of the jury and the rules by which it makes decisions may affect outcomes. The size of juries varies a good deal — in some states six constitute a jury for minor crimes and twelve for major ones, and in other states twelve are required for all juries. Large juries are more likely to result in deadlocks (hung juries) than are smaller ones.[9]

The procedures used by juries in reaching verdicts also vary. In most jurisdictions, conviction on a criminal charge requires a

---

[7] Vanderbilt, *op. cit.*, 197–200; for a caustic view of this process, called *voir dire* examination, see Jerome Frank, *Courts on Trial* (Princeton, N.J.: Princeton University Press, 1950), p. 121.

[8] Michael Fried, Kalman J. Kaplan, and Katherine W. Klein, "Juror Selection: An Analysis of Voir Dire," in Rita James Simon (ed.), *The Jury System in America* (Beverly Hills, Calif.: Sage Publications, 1975), pp. 49–66; Rita J. Simon, *The Jury: Its Role in American Society* (Lexington, Mass.: Lexington Books, 1980), pp. 29–47.

[9] Robert T. Roper, "Jury Size and Verdict Consistency," *Law and Society Review*, 14 (1980), 972–95; Simon, *The Jury*, pp. 73–106.

unanimous jury; in a few, it requires only a two-thirds or three-fourths vote. Civil decisions usually require less than unanimity. These variable provisions undoubtedly affect the outcome in some cases, but they do not seem to make it either easier or more difficult for the jury to reach a decision. When unanimous decisions are required in civil cases, hung juries occur only slightly more often than when unanimity is not required;[10] slightly greater propensity to convict, however, may have drastic consequences in criminal trials where the defendant's life or liberty hangs in balance.

The jury hears a case from beginning to end. Only while lawyers are arguing about the admissibility of evidence is the jury taken out of the courtroom. However, the jury observes passively; it may not ask witnesses direct questions. At the most a juror may pass a question to the judge, who may ask it or ignore it as he sees fit. In most instances jurors are also prohibited from taking notes during the trial. They must observe the evidence, listen to the testimony, and form their impressions as the trial progresses. At the end of the trial, lawyers for both sides sum up their case and seek to persuade the jury to decide in their favor. The judge closes the proceedings by instructing the jurors about the law as it applies to the case they have heard. He outlines to them the alternative decisions; for instance, in a murder trial they may find the defendant not guilty or guilty to first, second, or third degree murder. The judge explains what evidence is required for each kind of verdict. In some states he may comment on the evidence that has been presented, pointing out which seems reliable and which seems not. In most instances instructions to the jury are technical legal essays, which few jurors understand. In many states the instructions have been highly standardized to minimize the judges' chances of making mistakes: he merely reads the proper paragraphs from a handbook of instructions that covers the most common situations. After hearing the instructions, the jurors retire to their chambers to deliberate and to come to a decision.

The jury deliberates in complete privacy, behind locked doors. No outsider observes or participates in its debate. If the jury has

[10] D. W. Broeder, "University of Chicago Jury Project," *Nebraska Law Review*, 38 (1959), 746–47.

not reached its decision by nightfall, it retires to a hotel where it is isolated from all contact with the outside world; the next morning, it resumes its deliberations. It may request clarification of legal questions from the judge and look at items of evidence, but it may consult nothing else. When it has reached a decision by a vote of its members, it returns to the courtroom to announce its verdict. If the jury is hopelessly deadlocked, it may report that fact to the judge, in which case the judge may either insist that the jury continue its effort to reach a verdict or dismiss it and call for a new trial.

The extent to which juries are used varies considerably from case to case and region to region in the United States. Juries are most frequently used in auto accident damage suits; they are far less frequently used for complicated commercial contract cases.[11] In criminal trials that involve a felony, the defendant is entitled to a jury trial but may waive it with the prosecutor's or judge's consent, or sometimes without it. Although the frequency with which jury trials are waived varies from place to place, they are not used frequently in criminal cases anywhere in the United States. In 1972, for instance, only 9 percent of the felony defendants in Baltimore trial courtrooms and only 7 percent in Chicago and Detroit received jury trials.[12]

Although the jury's deliberations are secret, research with actual and mock juries provides some evidence of how juries reach their decision. Extensive research by a University of Chicago team has revealed that most juries do not make their decision after lengthy deliberations, at least in criminal cases. After interviewing the jurors in 213 different criminal cases in Brooklyn and Chicago, the researchers found that almost all juries took a vote as soon as they retired to their chambers. In 30 percent of the cases it took only one vote to reach a unanimous decision. In 90 percent of the remainder, the majority on the first ballot eventually won out, regardless of who sat on the jury or who constituted the majority and minority. Whether rich or poor, men

[11] For the federal courts, data on the use of jury trials is given in U.S. Bureau of the Census, *Statistical Abstract of the United States, 1981* (Washington, D.C.: Government Printing Office, 1981), table 321, p. 185.

[12] James Eisenstein and Herbert Jacob, *Felony Justice* (Boston: Little, Brown, 1977) p. 233.

or women, those in the majority carried the day after some de-
liberation; those in the minority could not convince their colleagues to switch over. Hung juries occurred only when a large
minority existed in the initial balloting. A single, stubborn juror
rarely caused a hung jury.[13]

Observation of simulated juries — men and women selected
from jury pools who heard tape-recorded trials in a courtroom
and were treated as if they were a real jury — also indicates some
dynamics of jury decision making.[14] For instance, it was found
that men talked a good deal more in jury deliberations than
women;[15] the better-educated also participated more frequently.[16] Most of the discussion in the jury room concerned the
procedure that the jury should follow, opinions about the trial,
and personal reminiscences that seemed appropriate to the problem. There was far less discussion about the testimony heard at
the trial, and little talk about the instructions that the judge had
given the jury.[17]

Who sat on the jury seemed to affect the likelihood of whether
a conviction or an acquittal would be secured. Jurors of German
and British background were more likely to favor conviction than
those of black or Slavic descent. In New York, those who qualified for blue-ribbon juries showed a higher propensity to convict
than those who did not qualify.[18] In a later Baltimore study, age,
sex, race, and education all were related (but in complicated
ways) to the likelihood that a juror would vote to convict.[19]

[13] Broeder, *op. cit.*, pp. 747–48.
[14] The researchers originally tape-recorded actual jury deliberations. When
this became known, it aroused the anger of many lawyers, judges, and congressmen. Congress subsequently passed a law prohibiting such observations of actual
jury deliberations even for research purposes. See Fred L. Strodtbeck, "Social
Process, the Law and Jury Functioning," in William M. Evan (ed.), *Law and
Sociology* (New York: Free Press of Glencoe, 1962), p. 145.
[15] Fred L. Strodtbeck, Rita M. James, and C. Hawkins, "Social Status in Jury
Deliberations," *American Sociological Review*, 22 (1957), 713–19; Fred L. Strodtbeck and Richard D. Mann, "Sex Role Differentiation in Jury Deliberations,"
Sociometry, 19 (1956), 3–11.
[16] Rita M. James, "Status and Competence of Jurors," *American Journal of
Sociology*, 64 (1959), 563–70.
[17] *Ibid.*
[18] Broeder, *op. cit.*, p. 748.
[19] Carol J. Mills and Wayne E. Bohannon, "Juror Characteristics: To What
Extent Are They Related to Jury Verdicts," *Judicature*, 64 (1980), 22–31; see also
Simon, *The Jury*, pp. 29–47.

The Chicago research also revealed that judges and juries frequently arrive at the same decision. When judges were asked to state how they would have decided jury cases over which they had presided, it was found that judge and jury agreed in 81 percent of the criminal cases. In 19 percent of the cases, judge and jury disagreed; on these cases the judges showed a marked tendency to convict where the juries had acquitted. Most disagreement occurred over statutory rape cases and first-offense cases. Judge and jury agreed in every narcotics case.[20]

The Chicago researchers also examined personal injury cases resulting from automobile accidents. Judge and jury agreed in 83 percent of the cases; in the 17 percent on which they disagreed, the judges would have ruled for the defendant 8 percent of the time and the juries, 9 percent.[21] Thus, little difference existed between judge and jury verdicts on the question of liability. However, judge and jury did differ somewhat when the type of defendant was taken into account. Juries decided in favor of the plaintiff more frequently than judges when the defendant was the government, a large corporation, or a railroad.[22] Thus, when the defendant appeared to be wealthy, the jury ruled against him more frequently than a judge would have done. Finally, it seems that jury awards differ significantly according to the region of the country and the location of the court.[23] On the east and west coasts, awards were substantially higher than in the Midwest or South. Moreover, urban juries awarded substantially higher judgments than did rural juries.

The manner in which juries reached a decision on the amount of damages that should be awarded confirms the suspicions of many lawyers. Even where an absolute liability rule applied, juries seemed to use comparative negligence standards. Plaintiffs who were not entirely blameless won lower awards, rather than no award at all. When the jury knew that the defendant was insured, the award tended to be higher than when it did not possess

---

[20] Broeder, *op. cit.*, pp. 749–50; see also Harry Kalven, Jr., and Hans Zeisel, *The American Jury* (Boston: Little, Brown, 1966), pp. 55–65.

[21] Broeder, *op. cit.*, p. 750; Kalven and Zeisel, *op. cit.*, pp. 55–65.

[22] Broeder, *op. cit.*, pp. 750–51. The same phenomenon has been observed in tax cases in several areas. See Robert H. Watson, "The Use of Juries in Federal Civil Income Tax Cases," *Taxes*, 39 (1961), 144–68.

[23] Broeder, *op. cit.*, pp. 748–49.

this knowledge. Moreover, juries reached their damage-award figures through a process of compromise. Some jurors suggested a high figure, often the one proposed by the plaintiff's lawyer; others suggested a lower figure. The final award was often just between the two, for the jury had apparently agreed to split the difference. The reputed size of a lawyer's fees also entered into a juror's calculations; in some cases the jurors attempted to calculate their award so that the plaintiff received what they thought he should after he had paid his lawyer.[24]

The evidence amassed by the Chicago Jury Project provides an empirical basis on which to examine criticism commonly made of juries. Some lawyers and judges have become increasingly critical of juries, because they seem so often to render arbitrary and groundless verdicts. The evidence that judges and jurors differ in less than one-fifth of the cases that come before them indicates that this criticism is unfounded and probably based on a small number of cases that are vividly remembered because of their spectacular nature.

The charge that jury trials — especially in civil cases — take longer than judge trials seems also to be exaggerated. Such trials appear to take longer because more complicated cases tend to go to a jury. When the nature of the case is taken into account, jury trials take little longer than trials before a judge alone.[25]

Another criticism of juries is that the complexities of much modern litigation make jury decisions hopelessly amateur. To critics, it seems anomalous in an age of growing professionalism to entrust important decisions to a group of randomly selected individuals, none of whom have any expert knowledge in the matter. At first glance, this criticism seems to be telling. Indeed, its exponents point to the growing number of cases that are decided without juries and the abolition of juries in civil cases in England. Apparently many litigants in civil matters and many defendants in criminal cases prefer to place their fate in the hands

[24] Strodtbeck, "Social Process, the Law and Jury Functioning," pp. 154–61.
[25] Broeder, *op. cit.*, p. 747. However, other members of the project have estimated that 40 percent of the trial time could be saved if auto accident personal injury suits were tried by a judge instead of a jury. See Hans Zeisel, Harry Kalven, Jr., and Bernard Buchholz, *Delay in the Court* (Boston: Little, Brown, 1959), pp. 71–81.

of a judge rather than a jury. Yet, once again, the evidence of the Chicago Jury Project that in four-fifths of the cases the judge and jury agreed must be taken into account. At least in those matters — none of which required a great deal of technical expertise — juries did not, in fact, often come to conclusions different from those of judges.

However, some cases undoubtedly do require a great deal of technical knowledge. Patent infringement suits require that judge or jury have an extensive knowledge of the technology of an industry to decide whether the patent was really of something new and whether it actually had been infringed. Antitrust suits require an extensive knowledge of the economics of an industry. Contract cases require detailed knowledge of business practices. In most such cases juries undoubtedly lack the knowledge to make expert decisions and cannot gain it at a trial; on the other hand, most judges also lack the necessary expertise. Judges are not expert in economic, scientific, or social matters; they are expert in legal matters. Nor do judges have much opportunity to specialize once on the bench. The courts are so constituted that each judge must decide all kinds of cases and preside over trials on an enormous range of matters. The fact is that the court system imposes amateur judgments on technical matters, regardless of whether the judge or a jury makes the decision. To obtain expert decisions, special courts or commissions would have to be established. In fact, this course of action has been followed in the establishment of the Court of Patent and Customs Appeals, the Interstate Commerce Commission, the Nuclear Regulatory Commission, and similar agencies.

Another criticism of jury actions is that they often disregard the law and decide on the basis of common-sense notions of fairness. For instance, in personal injury cases they improperly take into account whether the defendant is insured or wealthy. Instead of disallowing damages when the plaintiff is to a small degree at fault, they merely reduce his award. They arrive at the award by negotiating among themselves rather than by rationally calculating what the reimbursement for damages should actually be. All these charges are factually substantiated by the findings of the Chicago Jury Project.

The decision-making process in the jury's chambers no doubt appears irrational, but evidence suggests that trial judges take similar matters into account when they decide a case. In most instances they do not give opinions justifying their decisions; when they do, it is not certain that the opinion explains rather than rationalizes the decision. The most serious element of the criticism against juries, however, is that they arrogate to themselves the function of making law when they disregard judges' instructions and take theoretically irrelevant facts into account. To be sure, juries are not duly constituted legislative bodies; they have no mandate from the people. Yet the effect of their action is to ameliorate the impact of legislative as well as judge-made law in single cases, by applying their common-sense notions of what justice demands. To demand legislative correction of laws that are overly harsh in some circumstances is to ask too much from the legislative process. It is normally quite difficult to secure the passage of remedial legislation when uninfluential interests are involved. For this reason, judicial interpretation of statutes is tolerated; for the same reason, perhaps, the actions of juries can be tolerated.

Moreover, jury actions often force legal controversies to be simplified so that the laypeople sitting on juries can understand them. In part, the need for simplification is met by an increased use of the "special verdict." The jury does not return with a general judgment for or against the plaintiff; rather, it answers a specific series of factual questions. On the basis of the jury's answers, the judge decides which party in a civil suit is at fault. An alternative procedure, used in some other states, allows the jury to return a general verdict along with answers to certain questions (called "interrogatories"). These questions allow the judge to decide whether the jury was consistent in its logic. If it was, the verdict holds; if not, the judge either sends the jury back to eliminate the inconsistencies or orders a new trial.[26] Even when special verdicts and interrogatories are not used (and they are never used in criminal trials), juries force lawyers to present complex issues in understandable terms. Because the legitimacy of court actions depends in part on the ability of the public to

[26] Vanderbilt, *op. cit.*, pp. 237–43.

understand them, the juries reinforce the legitimacy of court decisions, despite the complaints they provoke from judges and lawyers.

Juries are also likely to increase popular acceptance of legal decisions because people realize that some of their neighbors had a part in making the decision. Juries give the courts an element of popular participation that is otherwise completely absent from the judicial process. Courts are generally more isolated from ordinary political processes than other agencies because of the absence or infrequency of elections for judgeships. Jury participation in judicial decision making, however, gives the judiciary some claim to the popular base of authority possessed by other governmental branches. Juries appear as a democratic attachment to an essentially nondemocratic branch of our government; they lend the judiciary a measure of legitimacy that it would otherwise lack.

Ordinary Americans, in fact, value the opportunity that juries provide for popular participation in the judicial process. Despite the alleged defects of jury trials, most Americans prefer trial by jury to trial by judge. A 1957 Gallup Poll reported that 58 percent of the respondents preferred a jury trial in automobile accident cases and 51 percent preferred a jury in serious criminal cases, whereas only 16 percent preferred trial by judge in the former cases and 35 percent in the latter.[27] In Wisconsin, a poll taken in 1963 indicated that 56 percent preferred trial by jury, compared to 16 percent who preferred trial by judge.[28]

However, those who have served on juries express mixed reactions to their experience. In New York, 75 percent of those who served and were asked whether they would like to serve again unconditionally said yes,[29] and in Wisconsin, most of those who had served also said they liked their work.[30] But in a later nationwide sample, only 42 percent of former jurors reacted fa-

---

[27] W. J. Flynn, Jr., "Public Preference for the Jury," *New York State Bar Bulletin*, 32 (1960), 105. Percentages in the text do not add up to 100 because some respondents either gave ambiguous answers or were undecided.

[28] Herbert Jacob, "Judicial Insulation — Elections, Direct Participation, and Public Attention to the Courts in Wisconsin," *Wisconsin Law Review* (1966), 814.

[29] Flynn, *op. cit.*, p. 103.

[30] Yankelovich, Skelly, and White, Inc., *The Public Image of Courts* (Williamsburg, Va: National Center for State Courts, 1978), p. 20.

vorably to their jury duty.[31] The Chicago Jury Project reported that, among the general population that had been sampled, only 36 percent said they would like to serve on a jury; but of those who had already served in recent years, 94 percent were willing to serve again.[32]

Although not everyone participates or is willing to participate, the possibility of having a jury trial apparently reassures a large part of the American public that the judicial process is fair. Many people overwhelmingly prefer jury to judge trials, because they distrust judges who act alone. In Missouri, for instance, the reasons given for preferring juries to judges were that "twelve heads are better than one," juries favor the defendant, judges are "too harsh," and judges are prejudiced or corrupt. Those who preferred a judge cited the judge's training, knowledge of the law, and impersonality; they also thought that judges could not be tricked as easily as juries and would not respond as readily to emotional appeals.[33] In general, those who favored juries distrusted judges. Those who preferred judge trials mentioned the expertise of the judge more frequently than the undesirable qualities of a jury. Laypeople apparently are more impressed by the dangers inherent in judge trials than by the disadvantages of jury trials.

Such confidence in jury trials exists even though only a small portion of the population participates in the judicial process by sitting on a jury. In Wisconsin, less than 6 percent of a statewide sample reported having served in five years prior to the survey; an additional 8 percent had been involved in court as litigant, defendant, or witness.[34] The remainder of the population participates indirectly through interest groups or vicariously through newspapers and television.

Interest Groups in the Judicial Process

Interest groups enter the courts to promote public policies that would favor their members.[35] Although individual members

[31] Jacob, op. cit.

[32] Broeder, op. cit., pp. 751–52.

[33] Missouri Bar Prentice-Hall Survey: A Motivational Study of Public Attitudes and Law Office Management (Missouri Bar, 1963), p. 175.

[34] Jacob, op. cit.

[35] For an excellent general statement of the role of interest groups in the judicial process, see David B. Truman, The Governmental Process (New York: Knopf, 1951), pp. 479–98.

of the group are the formal litigants in such cases, the group provides financial backing and psychological support to litigants. By doing so, interest groups enable some citizens to use the courts to settle public as well as private conflicts.

Not all groups use the courts to achieve their goals. Those who do are generally disadvantaged in the political system. For most groups, legislative or executive action is preferable to a judicial decision, because legislatures and executive agencies can obtain directly what courts can achieve only by indirection. Court action may be useful in protecting group members against harm, but it is rarely useful in procuring for them positive governmental action.

The courts are particularly attractive to disadvantaged groups because access to courts is more readily available. To be influential in legislatures, a group needs to occupy a strategic position in the economy or to claim the allegiance of a significant number of voters.[36] No such prerequisites are required in the courts. If a group has sufficient funds to hire legal counsel and has a statutory or constitutional claim, it may seek court action to protect the interests of its members. Environmental groups, for instance, although small and therefore weak in the electoral and legislative arenas, regularly use certain statutory provisions, which require an environmental impact statement for all public and private projects effecting the environment, as a tool to block construction projects through court action. Like environmental groups, minority groups are often among the most active lobbies in court. Although minorities usually lack the standing required for success elsewhere in the political system, they command sufficient resources to go to court. In 1970, the Supreme Court liberalized the rules that permit groups to bring litigation affecting their interests.[37] This liberalization increased the tendency of groups to seek redress of their grievances through court action. In addition, public interest law firms now provide legal counsel for groups too poor to hire their own attorneys. A new statute passed by Congress in 1976 permits these law firms to collect their fees from defendants when the firm is successful in pressing its claim.

[36] *Ibid.*, pp. 321–51.
[37] Karen Orren, "Standing to Sue: Interest Group Conflict in the Federal Courts," *American Political Science Review*, 70 (1976), 723–41.

In other words, weak interests need only find a public interest law firm that is willing to risk their case in order to bring a dispute to court.[38]

Interest groups ordinarily use quite different techniques to influence courts from those they use to lobby legislatures or executive agencies. The principal techniques are to bring conflicts to a court's attention by initiating test cases, to bring added information to the courts through *amicus curiae* briefs, and to communicate with judges indirectly by placing information favorable to the group's cause in legal and general periodicals.[39] Each of these techniques seizes on a characteristic of the judicial process and employs it for the group's purposes. By initiating test cases, groups provide judges with opportunities to make policy, by which judges overcome the otherwise passive nature of the judicial process. By supplying additional information through *amicus curiae* briefs, interest groups help judges to overcome the narrow confines of the adversary process. In such a brief, the group may provide information on circumstances similar to those in the case and help the judge to formulate a policy applicable to the general situation rather than to the particular case alone. By communicating with judges indirectly by articles in legal periodicals, interest groups respect the privacy of the decision-making process at the same time that they take advantage of the need of judges to buttress their opinions with scholarly citations.

The involvement of interest groups in litigation provides another means by which large parts of the general public may participate indirectly in the judicial process. By supporting groups whose views they endorse, interested citizens may take part in

[38] See also Joel F. Handler, "Public Interest Law: Problems and Prospects," in Murray L. Schwartz (ed.), *Law and the American Future* (New York: The American Assembly, 1976).

[39] Clement E. Vose, *Constitutional Change: Amendment of Politics and Supreme Court Litigation Since 1900* (Lexington, Mass.: Lexington Books, 1972), pp. 329–40; Clement E. Vose, "Litigation as a Form of Pressure Group Activity," *Annals of the American Academy of Political and Social Science*, 319 (1958), 20–31; Samuel Krislov, "The Amicus Curiae Brief: From Friendship to Advocacy," *Yale Law Journal*, 72 (1963), 694–721; Karen O'Connor and Lee Epstein, "Amicus Curiae Participation in U.S. Supreme Court Litigation: An Appraisal of Hakman's Folklore," *Law and Society Review*, 16 (1981–82), 311–20; Chester A. Newland, "Legal Periodicals and the United States Supreme Court," *Midwest Journal of Political Science*, 3 (1959), 58–74.

litigation that concerns them. Group activity not only broadens the participant base of the judicial process but also brings controversial issues to the courts. Recourse to the courts allows groups to challenge unfavorable decisions and to bring up many controversies of the day.

Although group activity in controversial litigation is conspicuous, it would be incorrect to credit it with changing the mind of the judge or with altering the outcome of important cases. There is no measure of the influence of such lobbying. Although a group's view is sometimes adopted by a court,[40] it is not known whether this occurred because the group carried a test case to the court or filed an *amicus curiae* brief, or whether the judges would have ruled in favor of the group's interests without such activity. On the other hand, it would also be wrong to declare such group activity harmful to the judicial process. No evidence indicates that it has undermined public confidence in the judiciary or that the courts have suffered any damage from it. For the moment, the only conclusion possible is that group activity before the courts provides them with information that they sometimes use. Group activity has thus become an integral part of the judiciary's policymaking process.

The Media and the Judicial Process

The press in the United States and many other countries devotes much attention to crime and spectacular criminal trials and encourages widespread vicarious participation in the judicial process. Scarcely a month passes without detailed accounts of criminal trials on the front pages of American newspapers. Moreover, several times each week, Americans can watch courtroom dramas unfold on television.

The degree to which Americans are exposed to news about crime and criminal proceedings has not been exaggerated. A study of the crime coverage of newspapers in nine major cities

---

[40] Benjamin Twiss, in *Lawyers and the Constitution* (Princeton, N.J.: Princeton University Press, 1942), alleges this to be the case with respect to the Supreme Court's adoption of the interpretation of the Fourteenth Amendment that protected private economic activity against government regulation. Although Twiss confuses group activity with group influence, he provides interesting details of the attempted use of briefs to influence judicial decisions. For a more careful assessment, see Krislov, *op. cit.*, p. 711.

over a thirty-one-year period showed that between one and two of every ten front page stories were about crime. Only rarely did the front page of those cities' newspapers not carry a crime story.[41] Local television devotes about the same percentage of attention to crime news.[42] In addition, the typical television viewer, by watching crime shows, is exposed to an average of thirty police officers, seven lawyers, and three judges a week.[43] Most of what viewers see is far removed from reality. In half of such shows, for example, the police solve 90 percent of the crimes by a successful arrest,[44] whereas in real life that occurs in only a fraction of such cases.

Press and television coverage of crime and criminal trials results in a clash of fundamental values. On the one hand, extensive press coverage often makes it difficult to obtain an impartial jury to try the defendants. On the other hand, limitation of press coverage restricts a basic American liberty, freedom of the press.

Until recently, American prosecutors and the media broadcast accusations and displayed evidence long before the trial was under way. The manner in which the evidence against Lee Harvey Oswald and Oswald himself were displayed by the media after the assassination of President Kennedy was an extreme example of what had become routine. On some occasions confessions were read on television, accused criminals were described as having already been found guilty, and inflammatory articles were both printed and discussed on the air. In addition, press photographers, television cameramen, and radio producers attempted to gain entry into courtrooms so that substantial parts of actual proceedings could be televised and brought to audiences in their homes.

Some of these types of activities make it difficult to obtain jurors who have not been exposed to a case, while others threaten to interfere with the trial itself. Widespread discussion of a court

[41] Duane Swank, Herbert Jacob, and Jack Moran, "Newspaper Attentiveness to Crime," in Herbert Jacob and Robert L. Lineberry, *Governmental Responses to Crime: Crime on Urban Agendas* (Washington, D.C.: National Institute of Justice, 1982), pp. 86–87.

[42] Doris Graber, *Crime News and the Public* (New York: Praeger, 1980), pp. 20–44.

[43] George Gerbner, "Trial by Television," *Judicature*, 63 (1980), 419–20.

[44] *Ibid.*

case and the display of evidence expose many members of a community to the alleged facts of the case in a biased manner; if they form an opinion on the case, they are disqualified from jury service. Fortunately, in most instances enough of the public remains indifferent to this kind of news (as well as to other kinds) that jurors can still be obtained, although with some difficulty. Yet the sensationalism of the press in extreme cases makes the selection of an unbiased jury extremely difficult. In the Dallas trial of Jack Ruby for the murder of Oswald, 96 percent of all prospective jurors had apparently watched the murder as it was screened "live" or replayed on television. Actual witnesses to the event could only with difficulty be thought of as unbiased jurors.

Since the reversal of Dr. Sam Sheppard's conviction in the slaying of his wife because prejudicial publicity had prevented his obtaining a fair trial, judges and bar associations have actively sought to prevent the leakage of pretrial publicity. Judges now routinely prohibit attorneys from revealing evidence to the press before the trial and, in some instances, from preliminary proceedings, where decisions about the admissability of evidence are made. A bar association disciplinary rule also prohibits disclosure of information not already on the public record. Both the threat of reversal of conviction and of disciplinary proceedings against attorneys have considerably reduced the flow of such publicity.[45]

Other legal remedies exist for defendants who are confronted with a possibly biased jury.[46] The defense counsel may use his challenges to disqualify biased jurors. A defendant may seek a change of venue to transfer his trial to another locality in the same state; he may also ask for a continuance to delay the trial until the public clamor has subsided. The jurors may be sequestered after selection so that further reporting of the trial does not affect them. In addition, careful instructions by the judge advising the jurors to ignore biasing material may be sought by the defense counsel. None of these mechanisms, however, promises complete relief from the impact of widespread press cov-

---

[45] *Sheppard v. Maxwell*, 384 U.S. 333 (1966); Disciplinary Rule 1–107.

[46] Ronald Goldfarb, "Public Information, Criminal Trials, and the Cause Célèbre," *New York University Law Review*, 36 (1961), 818–22.

erage of a criminal case. For instance, the number of challenges a lawyer may use is limited. The media are so broad in coverage that inflammatory articles printed in one locality are likely to be reprinted in the new locality when a trial is transferred or a postponed trial finally held. Because juries often do not take such instructions seriously during their deliberations, jury instructions as a safeguard against prejudice may be more illusory than real.[47] In recent years judges have limited press coverage even more by excluding the media from various stages of the proceedings or prohibiting their publication of certain particulars of the trial. Such orders have provoked sharp conflict between the press and the courts over conflicting priorities: the freedom of the press versus the defendant's right to a fair trial.[48] The conflict remains unresolved.

Experimental research indicates that jurors who are exposed to inflammatory news stories more frequently vote to convict.[49] Although this research is not definitive, it suggests that the danger that jurors' views will be contaminated by the media is real. Electronic communications have undoubtedly increased this danger; wire services and television networks bring news of spectacular crimes to even the most isolated corners of the country. As long as the public craves such news coverage, it will be difficult — though not impossible — to find jurors who have not been exposed to news stories.

The attempt of television and news photographers to enter the courtroom to record a trial raises different issues. Their presence would not bias jury selection, for jurors would already have been chosen. However, their presence might disturb the proceedings and cause lawyers, witnesses, and defendants to "play up" to the mass audience that is watching. Television and news photographers are permitted in most states, but they are not widely used. Federal courts prohibit them.[50] In a few states occasional

---

[47] Broeder, *op. cit.*, pp. 754–55; see also Alfred Friendly and Ronald Goldfarb, *Crime and Publicity: The Impact of News on the Administration of Justice* (New York: Vintage Books, 1967).

[48] The leading Supreme Court case on this issue is *Nebraska Press Association v. Stuart*, 427 U.S. 539 (1976).

[49] Alice M. Padawer-Singer and Allen H. Barton, "The Impact of Pretrial Publicity on Jurors' Verdicts," in Simon (ed.), *The Jury System*, pp. 125–39.

[50] *The New York Times* (Midwest ed.), March 9, 1983, p. 8.

trials have been televised.[51] The equipment necessary for televising a trial is no longer so bulky as to distract attention from the proceedings, nor are the proceedings apparently disturbed by grandstand plays to attract the television audience. A justice of the Colorado Supreme Court reported that in his state the experiment with televised trials had been entirely successful.[52] Such evidence has reinforced the media's determination to gain entry into courtrooms. Most judges and lawyers, however, have continued to oppose this entrance.

The question remains whether televising trials and sensationalizing them through the press serves or violates the constitutional injunction that trials be public. It was undoubtedly not the intention of the writers of that provision that trials provide public entertainment. In fact, few members of the public attend trials in person. Most courtrooms are empty of spectators except for those who follow trials as a hobby. The purpose of making trials public was to impose limits on judges and juries, for at open trials they work in full view of the public and can be held accountable for the outcome. Public display protects the defendant against arbitrary treatment, which would arouse unfavorable criticism of the courts. On the other hand, it undoubtedly intimidates potential witnesses.

The impact of the press is, however, highly selective. Most criminal trials go unnoticed by the public; almost all civil cases remain obscure. That the press *may* report a case structures the expectations and behavior of those making judicial decisions in somewhat the same way as if the press did report every case. It is difficult, however, to measure the precise impact of this phenomenon.

Appellate proceedings are even more rarely in the public limelight. The decisions of intermediate courts and most state supreme courts are often too complex and too removed from partisan affairs to be easily reported by the daily press. Rarely are issues outlined with the stark simplicity of a sensational criminal trial.

[51] Gerbner, *op. cit.*

[52] F. H. Hall, "Colorado's Six Years' Experience Without Canon 35," *American Bar Association Journal*, 48 (1962), 1120–22.

United States Supreme Court decisions receive fuller coverage than the lower courts, but reporters work under severe handicaps compared to those covering other Washington beats.[53] The Court itself provides little help to reporters. They do not receive the handouts and press releases provided by most of the administrative agencies. Since the administration of Chief Justice Burger, decisions have at least been released with headnotes summarizing major points; however, all background and human-interest information must still be supplied by the reporter himself. By reading briefs and attending oral arguments, reporters often keep track of litigation as the Court processes it so that when a case is decided they have notes to help them interpret the Court's decision. In addition, a legal news service attempts to preview important cases for media representatives. Traditionally, the court gives no warning that a particularly controversial decision is about to be announced. The decisions are given to reporters exactly as the justices prepared them, fully clothed in legal verbiage and often without any background material. Reporters must read the decisions for themselves in the few hours before their deadlines, even though many decisions are lengthy, extending over one hundred mimeographed pages.

The partial, sometimes distorted news that the media provide about Supreme Court decisions reflects these difficulties. In the 1962 school prayer decision (*Engel v. Vitale*), the Court's opinion went out of its way to state that its declaration concerning school prayers did not extend to other practices, such as the motto on coins ("In God We Trust") or the provision of chaplains for the armed forces.[54] Yet newspapers and television reports indicated that all public symbols with religious connotations might now be unconstitutional.[55]

Although the Supreme Court is splendidly isolated from the bustle of the Washington scene in comparison with Congress and the President, it too feels the impact of such press comment. It

---

[53] Chester A. Newland, "Press Coverage of the United States Supreme Court," *Western Political Quarterly*, 17 (1964), 16–23.

[54] *Engel v. Vitale*, 370 U.S. 435, note 21.

[55] James E. Clayton, *The Making of Justice* (New York: E. P. Dutton, 1964), pp. 15–23; William A. Hachten, "Journalism and the Prayer Decision," *Columbia Journalism Review*, 1 (1963), 4–9.

has been suggested that assignments to write Court opinions are sometimes made with a view toward press reception, and that the assignment is given to the justice voting with the majority who is most likely to win press support. For instance, in 1963 the generally conservative Justice Clark wrote the Court's opinion declaring unconstitutional the reading of the Lord's Prayer or verses from the Bible as class devotionals.[56] On rare occasions, the Court has retreated when a decision has met a burst of popular disapproval.[57]

Conclusions

The jury system, interest group activity, and media coverage of judicial proceedings have affected the administration of justice in the United States. Juries add a popular element to the judicial process, which otherwise remains isolated from the general public. Although public participation through jury service is limited to a few, it adds an element of popular legitimacy to the proceedings. Interest groups bring public controversies into the nation's courtrooms. Much of the public can only participate vicariously in the judicial process, through reports in newspapers and on television, and this vicarious participation does not weaken the position of courts in the public's eye.

Both the supporters and the detractors of juries, interest groups, and media coverage have been extravagant in their estimate of the impact of such public participation on the fairness of judicial proceedings. All available evidence indicates that juries, interest group activity, and the media do not, as many lawyers and judges claim, damage the judicial process. Instead, they have broadened the popular base of the judicial process and brought popular support to the judiciary.

[56] *Abington School District v. Schempp*, 374 U.S. 203 (1963). For the press reaction to these decisions see Clayton, *op. cit.*, pp. 274–80. On the matter of assigning justices to write court opinions, see David J. Danelski, "The Influence of the Chief Justice in the Decisional Process," in Walter F. Murphy and C. Herman Pritchett (eds.), *Courts, Judges and Politics* (New York: Random House, 1961), pp. 503–5.

[57] For instance, the court quickly reversed itself on the question of requiring children to salute the flag if they refused for religious reasons. See David R. Manwaring, *Render unto Caesar* (Chicago: University of Chicago Press, 1962).

IV
The Structure and Rules of the Judicial Process

8
The Organization of Courts in the United States

Two separate court systems — federal and state — operate side by side in the United States. The structure is decentralized, complicated, and largely archaic. Nevertheless, within this structure the complex conflicts generated by twentieth century life must be settled. To understand how judges, lawyers, and litigants operate, it is necessary to become acquainted with the labyrinthine environment in which they work.

The dual system of courts reaches into every section of the country, with trial as well as appellate tribunals. The most striking feature of the American judiciary, its dual structure, arose from the creation of a federal court system in 1789 to operate alongside existing state tribunals. The federal court system was one triumph of the Federalists in the Constitutional Convention of 1787 and the first Congress in 1789: having a court system of its own, the new national government would not have to depend entirely on the goodwill of state courts to enforce its law. That the states retained their own courts, however, attested to their continued strength.

161

The relationship between state and federal courts was complex from the beginning. The Constitution provided that state judges should swear allegiance to its provisions and obey them regardless of the constitution or laws of their own state. Section 25 of the Judiciary Act of 1789 gave the United States Supreme Court authority to review state court decisions that had ruled against a claim based on the federal Constitution, a treaty, or a federal statute. Moreover, the Supreme Court held that state courts were bound by Court decisions on these matters.[1] This ruling meant that state courts were bound by federal interpretations of state laws when the constitutionality of those laws was questioned.

Despite such provisions, which appeared to make state judges subordinate to the federal judiciary, state courts retained most of their autonomy. The vast majority of cases decided by the state courts did not involve federal questions, and state judges ruled on them according to their own traditions. Although the state courts were *de jure* subordinates to the Supreme Court in federal matters, they retained a great measure of *de facto* independence.[2]

To a certain extent, state courts became competitors of the federal judiciary. Competition between the two court systems ensued from their overlapping jurisdiction. Originally, state courts held exclusive jurisdiction over most cases, and Congress confined federal courts to admiralty, patent, and copyright matters; suits where citizens of two different states contested a claim ("diversity of citizenship" matters); and criminal charges resulting from a few federal statutes.[3] Only in the last half of the nineteenth century, when the nation's expanding economy broke through state and regional barriers, was the jurisdiction of the federal courts broadened. Congress then expanded federal court jurisdiction to all matters involving federal rights — a category of conflicts that previously had been tried in state courts and only

---

[1] *Martin v. Hunter's Lessee,* 1 Wheaton 304 (1816).

[2] The degree to which state courts have remained autonomous is indicated by the infrequency with which they cite Supreme Court decisions in their own rulings. Stuart Nagel, "Sociometric Relations Among American Courts," *Southwestern Social Science Quarterly,* 43 (1962), 136–42.

[3] Felix Frankfurter and James M. Landis, *The Business of the Supreme Court* (New York: Macmillan, 1927), pp. 12–13.

occasionally appealed to the United States Supreme Court. Congress also greatly expanded the scope of federal statutory law involving commerce, civil rights, taxation, and criminal law. Each new statute provided federal courts with new sources of litigation.[4] The state courts, in the meantime, also faced new problems as a result of state legislative activity and of growing industrialization, both of which provoked new legal conflicts.

At the end of the nineteenth and the beginning of the twentieth century, litigants increasingly had a choice between state and federal courts. Sometimes federal courts were chosen to escape disadvantageous state rules. For instance, for a brief period (1860–61) Wisconsin abandoned the fellow servant rule and made employers (principally railroads) liable for injuries resulting from accidents caused by the negligence of employees.[5] This decision led railroads to take such cases to the federal courts, thus avoiding Wisconsin's decision. At other times, state courts were chosen over federal courts to take advantage of the more favorable attitudes of state judges.[6] Over the long run, state courts gradually lost ground in the competition with federal courts. Cases involving important public policy tended to go to federal courts because they dealt with federal statutes or claims under the federal Constitution. Just as state governments in general became less important to national policymaking, so state courts, to a somewhat lesser degree, lost their preeminent position in the judicial system and increasingly concentrated on private law cases, which enforce existing norms and affect only the immediate parties to a case.[7]

[4] *Ibid.*, pp. 61–69.

[5] Carl Auerbach, Lloyd K. Garrison, Willard Hurst, and Samuel Mermin, *The Legal Process* (San Francisco: Chandler, 1961), pp. 149–61, especially p. 156. Such a reason for transferring a case to federal court no longer exists, for since *Erie R.R. v. Tompkins*, 305 U.S. 64 (1938), federal courts have been obliged to apply the common law as well as the statutes of the state in which a case arose as long as they do not conflict with federal law.

[6] Forrest Talbott and William Anderson, *Intergovernmental Relations and the Courts* (Minneapolis: University of Minnesota Press, 1950), pp. 78–82.

[7] The proportion of civil cases involving the U.S. government as a defendant (cases often concerning fundamental rights) increased 6.3 times between 1941 and 1971, while diversity cases (mostly personal injury suits) increased only by a factor of 3.4. During the same period, the total number of civil cases in the federal district courts increased by a factor of 2.4, from 38,477 to 93,396. See Jerry Goldman, "Jurisdictional Politics and the Federal Courts" (unpubl. Ph.D. dissertation, Johns Hopkins University, 1974), p. 26.

The Structure of American Courts

From the beginning both the states and the federal government have maintained trial courts throughout the country. The network of state courts, however, remains by far the more extensive.[8] Each state possesses many trial courts.

Some state courts handle minor criminal and civil matters, such as traffic fines, local ordinance violations, and suits involving small amounts of money. These courts often exist in every large town of a county. Until recently, the presiding official, called a justice of the peace, was an untrained layperson elected along with other county officials. Where the office still exists, the justice of the peace often remains in charge of these minor courts, but in some states these functions have been limited to still more minor matters, and a professional magistrate or judge has been installed to hear criminal and civil suits. In most states, courts of minor jurisdiction may not hold jury trials; all matters that come before them are settled by the judge alone. If a jury trial is desired and permitted by law, the case must be transferred to another court.

Another tier of trial courts hears more important matters, such as felony trials where the defendant may be sentenced to a long prison term and civil suits involving a greater sum of money, usually more than $1,000. Such courts are generally located only at the county seat. In some states several counties share a single court, which normally sits in one and visits the other counties of the circuit for short periods each year. Judges of these courts are always lawyers and normally serve for relatively long terms. All jury trials take place in these courts, although most cases are heard by the judge alone or are settled out of court.

Finally, many states have a set of specialized courts, which fit somewhere between the major and minor trial courts. Some of

[8] A statistical summary of state court organization may be found in *The Book of the States 1982–83* (Lexington, Ky.: Council of State Governments, 1982). Detailed descriptions of courts in individual states are available for Connecticut, Maryland, and California: Elbert M. Byrd, Jr., *The Judicial Process in Maryland* (College Park: University of Maryland, 1961); David Mars, Fred Kort, and I. R. Davis, *Administration of Justice in Connecticut* (Storrs: University of Connecticut, 1963); Beverly Blair Cook, *The Judicial Process in California* (Belmont, Calif.: Dickinson, 1967).

these — as in Ohio — deal with family matters, such as divorce and juvenile delinquency. Most larger cities have special traffic courts to handle the thousands of parking and driving violations that occur each year. Some cities also possess small-claims courts to handle monetary claims of less than $500; in these courts, a lawyer is unnecessary and sometimes is not even allowed. Finally, larger cities often have special probate courts to handle the administration of wills and estates; in other locales, the major or minor trial courts handle the probate matters in addition to their other business.

No two states possess identical court structures, nor is the division of work between the courts of any state as symmetrical as would appear from the foregoing description. The jurisdiction of lower and higher trial courts often overlaps; potential litigants are thus confronted with a maze of tribunals through which they and their lawyers must pass to attain their goals.

Federal trial courts are much more simply organized. For one thing, there are relatively few of them — ninety-two in the entire country. Each state has at least one. Called district courts, these normally operate over a large portion of a state. The court usually travels to the more important cities within its territory, visiting each for two weeks twice a year. Many district courts have several judges, each operating his own branch of the court. The court hears criminal matters involving the violation of a federal law, such as taking a stolen car across state boundaries or illegally dealing in narcotics. Civil matters heard in federal court range from large suits involving the citizens of two states to complicated antitrust complaints filed by the federal government.[9] A single judge presides over each case. Although the Constitution guarantees the right to a jury trial for all criminal prosecutions and for many civil cases involving more than $20, only criminal trials make extensive use of juries. When no jury sits, the judge decides the case alone. These courts are often called "constitutional" courts because their judges serve for life (during good behavior) as provided in Article III, Section 1 of the Constitution.

[9] The most comprehensive description of the work of federal district courts may be found in Robert A. Carp and C. K. Rowland, *Policy Making and Politics in the Federal District Courts* (Knoxville: University of Tennessee Press, 1983).

The federal government also maintains several specialized courts. Although some legal controversy exists over whether they have the same standing as constitutional courts, they operate like constitutional courts except that the jurisdiction is limited, they sit mostly in Washington, their judges serve for set terms instead of enjoying life tenure, and they are assigned some quasi-legislative functions. These courts exist for custom and patent appeals and for claims against the federal government. They usually hear appeals of administrative decisions, much as the regular courts of appeals hear appeals from many regulatory agencies. The Supreme Court treats their decisions like those by courts of appeals.

Another extraordinary federal court is the three-man district court, which is an *ad hoc* tribunal specially convened in exceptional circumstances. Litigants who wish to use this court must make a special application to the senior judge of the district court. If he agrees to their request, the chief judge of the circuit convenes the court. It consists of three judges: at least one must be a district judge, and at least one must be a judge of the court of appeals. The court hears arguments and renders its decision. If the losing party wishes to appeal (and it usually does), the appeal goes directly to the Supreme Court. These three-man courts are used to hear some of the most controversial issues reaching the judiciary; they are intended to dispatch them more quickly and more authoritatively than a trial before an ordinary district court.[10]

Trial courts settle most cases with finality, either by promoting out-of-court settlements or by a judgment resulting from a formal trial. Some litigants, however, wish to appeal the results of their trial, believing that the judge made prejudicial errors that robbed them of victory, or seek to win a change in policy through an appellate decision. For such appeals, special appellate tribunals exist in every state and in the federal court system. Thirty-two states have intermediate appellate courts as well as supreme courts;[11] the remainder have only supreme courts to hear ap-

[10] "The Three-Judge Court Reassessed: Changing Roles in Federal-State Relationships," *Yale Law Journal*, 72 (1963), 1646–61.
[11] *Book of the States 1982–83, op. cit.*

peals. The federal judiciary has twelve intermediate appellate courts as well as its Supreme Court.

Where intermediate appellate courts exist, appeals usually must be directed to them before being taken to the appropriate supreme court.[12] In almost every case the litigants have a *right* to one appeal if they file their case properly: the appellate court is obliged to consider it regardless of the legal merit of the appeal and the importance (or triviality) of the conflict. The intermediate appellate courts serve large portions of their state or, in the case of the federal courts of appeals, several states. Like federal district judges, the judges of appellate courts ordinarily visit several major cities of their area, although most of their business takes place at the headquarters city. Unlike trial courts, each appellate court operates with several judges. There is no jury; a panel of three or more judges decides. Unlike most trial judges, appellate judges often give reasons for their decisions in a written opinion, which may be published for future reference by lawyers and other judges.

Supreme courts[13] make the final decision in the judicial process. State supreme courts render the final verdict for all cases involving state law; the United States Supreme Court renders the final judicial decision on all matters involving federal law or the federal Constitution. Some state supreme courts must hear every case appealed to them; other courts exercise a great deal of discretion in selecting the appeals that they will decide.[14] The United States Supreme Court is the best-known example of the exercise of discretion. The Court receives requests to hear approximately 5000 cases each year but decides only about 150 with signed opinions.[15] Among the state courts, Virginia and Louisiana are almost as selective. Many other state supreme courts hear almost all cases brought before them.

[12] Arthur T. Vanderbilt, *Minimum Standards of Judicial Administration* (New York: Law Center of New York University, 1949), pp. 385–454.

[13] The term "supreme court" is used generically here. In some states the highest court has another name, such as court of appeals, supreme judicial court, or supreme court of errors. Confusion is likeliest in New York, where supreme courts are the major trial courts and the court of appeals is the highest appellate court.

[14] Vanderbilt, *op. cit.*, pp. 395–401.

[15] U.S. Bureau of the Census, *Statistical Abstract of the United States, 1981* (Washington, D.C.: Government Printing Office, 1981), table 319, p. 185.

Three or more justices staff each of the state supreme courts. They hear cases as a group, although in some states the court divides into panels in the same way as most federal courts of appeals. In a few states — Missouri is an especially conspicuous example — the court parcels cases out to "commissioners," who are appointed by the justices to act as their alternates. Although the decisions of commissioners do not become final until adopted by the court, in practice their decisions are seldom overruled.

The supreme courts sit at the capital or in another large city of the state. Unlike other courts, which go on circuit as a convenience for litigants, supreme courts demand that litigants come to them. As a result, the lawyers practicing before supreme courts often constitute a rather specialized group, who handle cases for their less experienced colleagues when an appeal is necessary.

The principal bridge between the state and federal courts is at the supreme court level. When a case involves federal statutes or rights under the federal Constitution, the decision of a state supreme court may be appealed to the United States Supreme Court. The federal Supreme Court either affirms the state's decision or reverses it. Reversals mean that the case is sent back to the state court system for the appropriate action — a dismissal, a rehearing, or a granting of the remedy that the litigant sought originally. Although constitutionally obliged to follow Supreme Court decisions, state courts in fact sometimes ignore them. They may simply react to the Court's decision with disbelief and interpret it away, or they may rehear the case and come to the same result as before, but on slightly different grounds.[16] It would therefore be a mistake to describe the relationship between the state courts and the Supreme Court as that of subordinate and superior. It is more accurate to characterize the Supreme Court's position as being first among equals. In ordinary cases the Supreme Court's judgment is respected. In highly controversial ones, its decision is sometimes evaded by legalisms; for example, the state court may distinguish between cases on the basis of highly specific fact situations.

[16] Walter Murphy and C. Herman Pritchett (eds.), *Courts, Judges, and Politics* (New York: Random House, 1961), pp. 602–17.

Consequences of the Dual Court System

The existence of the dual system of courts is not without substantive impact. The system supplies alternative tribunals to which cases may be brought. The Southern black, for instance, may litigate to protect his civil rights in either a state or a federal court. As long as Southern legislatures ignored the desires of black citizens and blacks could not vote for state judges, they were likely to prefer federal courts, which proved to be more receptive to their claims. Likewise, Southern whites were apt to go to a state court, where they were likely to have more influence.[17] In Chicago, Democrats usually bring election disputes to state courts, which they control; Republicans prefer the federal courts.

A second consequence of the dual court system is that the interpretation of legal doctrine differs from state to state. Although several states may have similar or identical statutes and most state courts operate in the same common-law tradition, none of them interprets the laws or their common-law heritage in exactly the same way. To some extent the resulting variation of law reflects different social conditions and different attitudes of the public toward similar problems. It may also represent experimentation by certain state courts in an effort to develop more effective ways of dealing with problems. Mostly, however, the diversity of legal doctrine is simply the consequence of a fragmented court system, representing neither conscious experimentation nor an explicit adaptation to peculiar social conditions. Consequently, it is impossible to summarize the state of the law in the United States in brief form. What the law says about a particular matter depends not only on the whims of fifty-one legislatures but also on the accidental development of judicial interpretation in fifty-one judicial systems.

The dual court structure also provides a weapon for both the federal and state governments in their struggle to expand or retain their functions. State governments use their courts to resist what they regard as federal encroachments by asking state courts

---

[17] Kenneth N. Vines, "Southern State Supreme Courts and Race Relations," *Western Political Quarterly*, 18 (1965), 5–18.

not to honor federal decisions. In turn, the federal government promotes litigation in its courts to extend the scope of its power. Thus in the 1950s and 1960s Southern courts were involved not only in the desegregation dispute but also in the larger issue of what powers each governmental level possessed. State courts in both the North and the South have on occasion sought to deny federal jurisdiction over a case to protect their state's sovereignty.[18]

The Administrative Organization of Courts

Another peculiarity of the American judiciary is that, within each state, courts are almost completely independent of each other. This is partly a consequence of the development of the judiciary as a separate branch of government, independent of the executive. In other nations, the judiciary is controlled by the ministry of justice or the ministry of interior, but in the United States, no executive department controls the courts at either the federal or the state level.

Until recently, each court in the nation governed itself.[19] Each one formulated the rules under which cases would be heard and hired its own auxiliary personnel; each judge determined independently the days and the hours to hold court. No one had responsibility for the operation of the court system as a whole, collected statistics to determine which courts were overburdened and which were left unused, or had the authority to transfer a judge from one court to another to alleviate delay in hearing trials. No organization existed through which judges could compare their experiences, exchange ideas, or learn of new developments in the conducting of court. The problem was well described by an observer of the Minnesota court system:

> It is important to know that constitutionally the legislature can do a great deal to reorganize the local courts, and that the state supreme court by overruling local court decisions can exercise pressure in the direction of statewide uniformity of decisions. It

---

[18] A good example is New York's effort to argue that federal courts should not grant a writ of habeas corpus to a prisoner in a state penitentiary who has not taken advantage of the opportunity to appeal his case in state courts. *Fay v. Noia*, 372 U.S. 391 (1962).

[19] Vanderbilt, *op. cit.*, pp. 29–90.

is also important to know, however, that neither the legislature by passing laws of statewide application, nor the supreme court through decisions in particular cases can actually bring about complete uniformity of court practices and decisions. Overruled in one decision a local judge may make just as unorthodox a decision in the next case. The higher courts can again overrule him and give him a verbal spanking, but they cannot otherwise discipline and they certainly cannot remove a lower judge just because his decisions are wrong. In this respect the state supreme court is in an even weaker position than, for example, the state tax commissioner in his efforts to bring about uniformity in the assessment of property for taxation.[20]

The description remains apt, not only for Minnesota but for most of the nation. The country possesses several groups of courts that remain administratively unrelated to each other.

Since 1922 the federal courts have operated under minimal administrative supervision. Although their authority comes from legislative enactments, judicial administrators work independently of the legislative or executive branches. In the federal court system an administrator of the courts, operating under the supervision of the Chief Justice of the United States, collects statistics and other information to guide the work of the courts.[21] Most authority, however, rests with the Supreme Court, which may promulgate rules for the entire federal court system, with conferences of judges, who meet at various levels, and with the chief judge of the court of appeals in each circuit, who has some authority over the transfer of judges from one district (or circuit) to another.[22] Compared to an administrative agency's budgetary, personnel, and policy controls, the supervision over federal courts is quite rudimentary.

All of the states have adopted similar managerial controls; in 1981, all but two had court administrative offices.[23] Most of these offices operated under the supervision of the state's supreme

---

[20] Talbott and Anderson, *op. cit.*, p. 2.

[21] These are published in the *Annual Report of the Director, Administrative Office of the United States Courts* (Washington, D.C.: Government Printing Office).

[22] Vanderbilt, *op. cit.*, pp. 64–69; Frankfurter and Landis, *op. cit.*, pp. 259–60, 273–80.

[23] *Book of the States 1982–83, op. cit.*, p. 269.

court or its chief justice; many of them were quite small and possessed only a skeletal staff. However, in a few states, the administrative office has become a sizeable agency: New York's office had a staff of 315 in 1981; its director was a well-paid official with an annual salary of $71,300.[24] Despite the growth of these offices, however, only a handful of states compile statistical reports containing enough information to be useful in supervising court operations. In a few states, effective administrative controls have been imposed over all the courts. In New Jersey, for instance, the chief justice is head of the judicial branch. Each judge is required to hold court during specified days and hours. He must submit weekly reports on the number of cases heard, the decisions rendered, and other pertinent matters. By rule of the supreme court, judges may not withhold a decision on a case for more than two weeks; if they do, they must justify their delay. When necessary, judges may be shifted from one court to another to help alleviate long delays or unusually burdened court dockets.[25] In New York, Maryland, Missouri, California, Louisiana, and Wisconsin, courts operate under somewhat less stringent administrative controls, but some manner of control exists.[26] In each court an administrator (the post has various titles) operates under the supervision of the supreme court to collect information and formulate administrative rules to govern the work of the courts. However, even vigorous chief judges and court administrators meet strong resistance from trial judges, who insist on their autonomy. In New York, where there has been a long and sometimes bitter conflict between administrative judges and judges hearing trials, one trial judge had this to say of the chief administrative judge and his assistant:

> Murtaugh and Vetrano are my colleagues, not my bosses. They have no right to question my findings on facts or why I impose what I think are fair fines and proper sentences.

[24] *Ibid.*

[25] Arthur T. Vanderbilt, *The Challenge of Law Reform* (Princeton, N.J.: Princeton University Press, 1955).

[26] Vanderbilt, *Minimum Standards*, pp. 57–64. Vanderbilt does not include Wisconsin and Louisiana on his list of states with effective controls; such controls were not adopted until after publication — in Wisconsin in 1959 and in Louisiana in 1952.

If they don't like what we do, then let them be the only two judges in the court and let them sit on every case and make the decisions.[27]

Several states also possess "judicial councils," which ordinarily consist of judges, lawyers, and laymen who meet to consider judicial reforms that require legislative action.[28] Once a council determines a course of action, it proposes a bill and lobbies for it before the legislature. In Wisconsin, the council was successful in convincing the legislature to restructure the entire court system so that most overlapping jurisdictions were eliminated. Quite typically, however, the Wisconsin council was not strong enough to counter the opposition of the justice of the peace lobby: its proposals to eliminate justices of the peace met defeat in the legislature. On the other hand, an increasing number of state supreme courts have asserted an inherent power to make rules for governing court proceedings. These rules do not require legislative approval, and they provide a higher degree of uniformity among the courts of a single state.

Most states, however, do not impose effective administrative controls over their courts. In most, each judge remains sovereign over his own courtroom. He is free to adopt his own local rules of procedure to supplement the standard ones for the state. He may hold court during any hours he pleases. He appoints his own assistants, thereby preserving in many localities, the greatest source of patronage remaining on the political scene. Moreover, each judge is responsible only for the cases arising in his jurisdiction. If a neighboring judge is overburdened, there is sometimes no way to temporarily transfer a judge from one area to another to assist him. In most states the judiciary represents an extreme case of the fragmentation and autonomy that in more moderate form is so characteristic of American government. Whereas cities, counties, and special districts must conform to administrative controls in many of their activities, courts are left more independent.

[27] *The New York Times*, Nov. 15, 1963, p. 24.
[28] Vanderbilt, *Minimum Standards*, pp. 65–91.

The Courts' Resistance to Change

The structure and organization of courts in America have changed little since the founding of the country. Their structural stability is typical of American political institutions. Although Americans have been inventive in mechanical arts and social arrangements, they have failed to adapt governmental structures to new conditions. Thus, local governments have difficulty in coping with problems in metropolitan areas; state governments are often unable to accommodate themselves to their increasingly urban populations; Congress and many federal executive departments find their hands tied by tradition and red tape. The courts share this structural inflexibility and are affected by it even more than most governmental agencies.

The courts' inability to adapt to contemporary conditions is reflected not only in their failure to develop effective managerial controls but also in their reluctance to specialize. Almost all other social organizations have responded to the complexities of modern life by some degree of specialization. Governmental executive agencies have become highly specialized; legislatures have bowed to the trend by delegating most preliminaries of the legislative process to specialized committees, so that in fact many decisions are made by specialized subunits of the entire body. Courts, by contrast, have specialized only to a minor degree. Tribunals for divorces, family affairs, juvenile delinquency, small claims, and traffic offenses exist in most states; federal courts have parceled out bankruptcy cases, customs, and patent appeals to specialized tribunals. All other matters are heard by courts that possess an expertise in legal procedure but not in the substance of the conflicts that come before them. In a single month, a judge may interpret simple commercial contracts, levy liability in an automobile accident case, hear a divorce proceeding, and preside over a criminal conspiracy trial.

Failure to specialize has become especially burdensome in metropolitan areas, where the volume of cases is usually high enough to justify establishing specialized tribunals. Litigants often must take their problems to courts whose judges may not understand the technical problems involved. A high volume of certain kinds of cases may lead to a delay in all cases. Personal injury suits resulting from automobile accidents are alleged to cause the long delay in trials for other matters. If personal injury suits were parceled out to a specialized court, it might be possible to settle them more quickly, and even their delay would not affect other cases. Another type of case suffering from lack of specialization is that which leads to committing an individual to a mental hospital. Although such cases involve the freedom of an individual in much the same way that criminal cases do, judges are too rushed by other business to learn enough about each situation to rule discriminately.[29] Too few mental cases arise in small communities to allow specialization, but their number is sizable enough in metropolitan areas. Even so, metropolitan courts are rarely more specialized than the tribunals of the smallest county of a state.[30] In an age of specialization, the judiciary has remained the bastion of the generalist, home of the jack-of-all-trades.

The structural inflexibility of the courts remains despite many efforts to reform certain aspects of court organization. Many of these efforts have been directed to one or another element of the trial. Many courts have experimented with various kinds of docket controls, pretrial negotiation, reform of bail so that fewer defendants would be unnecessarily jailed, speedy trial rules forcing prosecutors to bring charges to trial or lose their case, and the diversion of minor criminal cases to rehabilitation services and of small civil cases to mediation panels, called neighborhood justice centers. None of these reforms has won universal acceptance or changed the fundamentally fragmented character of American courts.[31]

[29] See Thomas J. Scheff, "Social Conditions for Rationality: How Urban and Rural Courts Deal with the Mentally Ill," *The American Behavioral Scientist*, 7 (March 1964), 21–24.

[30] Maxine Virtue, *Survey of Metropolitan Courts Detroit Area* (Ann Arbor: University of Michigan, 1950), pp. 14–30; Maxine Virtue, *Survey of Metropolitan Courts Final Report* (Ann Arbor: University of Michigan, 1962), pp. 48–75, 179–96. An excellent earlier study of metropolitan courts is in Albert Lepawsky, *The Judicial System of Metropolitan Chicago* (Chicago: University of Chicago Press, 1932). Both the early and the recent studies emphasize the inconvenience and inefficiency of the fragmented, overlapping judicial structure that exists in metropolitan areas.

[31] On reform of criminal courts, see Malcolm M. Feeley, *Court Reform on Trial* (New York: Basic Books, 1983). On neighborhood justice centers, see Roman Tomasic and Malcolm M. Feeley, *Neighborhood Justice* (New York: Longman, 1982).

One reason for the courts' inflexible structure is the inability of judicial reformers to generate enthusiasm for such changes. Even attorneys often disagree about whether changes should be made, because some of them benefit from existing arrangements. As one observer wrote, "Prior judicial practice is not arbitrary but reflects an accommodation of the interests of participants. In the abstract, this accommodation may not be ideal, but in context, it is at least acceptable to participants."[32]

Court reform rarely enjoys a high priority among politicians or the general public. On the contrary, existing structures are backed by powerful forces with high stakes in the status quo. Political organizations fear they will lose patronage under reforms; sitting judges fear they will lose their posts; many lawyers fear they will have to learn entirely new procedures.[33] The groups opposing reform are often better entrenched than those desiring it. Occasionally, court reform fails because it is associated with an unpopular political cause.

In the federal judiciary, two examples of unsuccessful court reforms clearly illustrate the difficulties that beset those who would alter the judiciary. After John Adams and his Federalist party lost the presidential and congressional elections of 1800, they passed a law during the lame-duck session preceding Jefferson's inauguration to relieve the justices of the Supreme Court of the burden of presiding over the circuit courts. The law corrected a structural fault that had already become apparent through the operation of the original Judiciary Act, for it was difficult to find qualified appointees to the Supreme Court who were willing to undertake strenuous circuit-riding duties in addition to their work in Washington. However, Adams's act also provided Federalists with important new positions just on the eve of their ouster from Washington. Adams's midnight appointments to the bench during the very last moments of his administration convinced Jefferson and the Republican party leaders in Congress that the new law was more an attempt to pack the

[32] Raymond T. Nimmer, *The Nature of System Change* (Chicago: American Bar Foundation, 1978), p. 176.
[33] A good case study of the political difficulties faced by judicial reforms is by Gilbert Y. Steiner and Samuel K. Gove, *Legislative Politics in Illinois* (Urbana: University of Illinois Press, 1962), pp. 165–98.

judiciary with partisan foes than an effort to remedy a technical flaw in the machinery of justice. Consequently, one of the first domestic acts of the new Jefferson administration was to win repeal of the Adams Judiciary Act and oust the new judges from their positions. What might have succeeded as a technical reform could only be passed as a partisan measure; as a partisan act of a dying party, it was doomed to eventual defeat.[34]

More than a century later, similar circumstances prevented the federal courts from embarking on a policy of specialization. Pressure to remove certain categories of cases from the district court dockets led to the establishment in 1909 of a commerce court to hear all cases resulting from Interstate Commerce Commission decisions. The move met strenuous objections in Congress and passed only after vigorous endorsement by President Taft. However, the court's work quickly became a partisan issue. Democrats charged that the court was favoring railroads and undermining the position of the Interstate Commerce Commission. Although more dispassionate examination of the issue a half century later indicates that the charges were untrue,[35] once the reform became a partisan issue, the court's life became subject to its sponsor's fate. When Taft lost the election of 1912, the court's doom was sealed. The subsequent impeachment of one of its judges for corruption corroborated the suspicions of its opponents. It was abolished in 1913.

Several successful changes in court structure are attributable to their intimate relationship with more powerful partisan or social movements. Judgeships became elective positions with relatively short tenure as a result of the Jacksonian movement's drive to make all governmental positions subject to popular election. This change altered the judiciary's relationship with other governmental bodies and partisan groups in a fundamental fashion. For half a century thereafter, judgeships were regarded as political plums to be dispensed by whatever party machine was

[34] Max Farrand, "The Judiciary Act of 1801," *American Historical Review*, 5 (1899–1900), 682–86; Frankfurter and Landis, *op. cit.*, pp. 14 ff.

[35] The most thorough discussion of the incident is by George E. Dix, "The Death of the Commerce Court: A Study in Institutional Weakness," *American Journal of Legal History*, 8 (1964), 238–60. See also Frankfurter and Landis, *op. cit.*, pp. 162–73; William S. Carpenter, *Judicial Tenure in the United States* (New Haven, Conn.: Yale University Press, 1918), pp. 142 ff.

dominant in the area.[36] Another change that came to fruition as a result of a social movement was the establishment of juvenile courts for handling criminal hearings for young children. The rise of these courts reflected the increasing influence of social-welfare reformers in the early years of the twentieth century.[37]

Changes in court organization that developed apart from popular movements were successful only under two conditions: if they were advocated by extraordinarily persuasive and successful judges, or if they were limited to what seemed to be minor adaptations rather than basic changes. Many administrative reforms that have modernized the American judiciary in the twentieth century can be attributed to the efforts of two men: Chief Justice Taft of the United States Supreme Court and Chief Justice Vanderbilt of the New Jersey Supreme Court.[38] Taft brought to the court his unique experience as President. Vanderbilt spent much of his spare time in bar association politics to further his reform proposals. Taft's legacy includes the power of the Supreme Court to formulate procedural rules for the federal courts, the Supreme Court's discretionary power to reject cases, and the administrative mechanism by which judges can be transferred from one court to another for temporary duty. Vanderbilt was instrumental in establishing strong administrative controls over New Jersey courts and making judges throughout the country more receptive to their administrative responsibilities. Both men possessed capabilities rarely found in judges, for the bench does not usually attract individuals with administrative drive or with a desire to reform their environment. Entrepreneurial talent in the legal profession is much more likely to remain in private practice or to be siphoned off to executive offices in government — careers that offer greater opportunities for creative minds. The

[36] See my earlier discussion of this in Kenneth N. Vines and Herbert Jacob, *Studies in Judicial Politics*, Tulane University Studies in Political Science, Vol. 8 (New Orleans: Tulane University, 1963), pp. 18–21.

[37] Margaret K. Rosenheim (ed.), *Justice for the Child* (New York: Free Press of Glencoe, 1962), pp. 1–10; Ellen Ryerson, *The Best Laid Plans: America's Juvenile Court Experiment* (New York: Hill and Wang, 1978), pp. 16–34.

[38] Walter F. Murphy, "Chief Justice Taft and the Lower Court Bureaucracy," *Journal of Politics*, 24 (1962), 453–59. For Vanderbilt's contributions see his own *Challenge of Law Reform*, cited earlier.

changes that Taft and Vanderbilt successfully promoted were adopted in utter calm.

The success of Taft and Vanderbilt rested on more than their outstanding ability to persuade legislators and lawyers. They shrewdly limited their proposals to what appeared to be minor and often superficial changes in court structure and procedure. These incremental changes did not arouse the fierce opposition that often greets proposals for fundamental changes in the structure of the judiciary. A good example of failure by court reformers is the recent proposal supported by Chief Justice Warren Burger to establish a new federal appeals court that would make final decisions in most cases and thereby relieve the Supreme Court of the burden of most of its present docket. Although supported by several of the associate justices and many elite lawyers, the proposal has not been adopted out of fear that interests that can now obtain a Supreme Court hearing would be barred from making such appeals. Lacking popular appeal and the thrust of effective leadership, this proposal, like many others, gathers dust in law reviews.

The Traditional Independence of the Courts

The judiciary's resistance to innovation, although not complete and not unique in American politics, is the product of yet another set of forces. The courts' traditional place in government has been a step removed from the helter-skelter struggles of pressure groups and the intrigue of politicians. Constitutionally, the courts are the third branch of government, coequal with the legislative and executive branches. This constitutional position enables them to stand aside from the partisan struggles that characterize executive and legislative politics. In the eyes of the public and of political leaders, they are somewhat apart from the operations of other governmental agencies. Moreover, the independence of the judiciary has even deeper roots than the constitutional provision for the separation of powers. Judicial independence has long been thought necessary to prevent tyrannical government. To an unusual extent, Americans have viewed the courts as a bastion *against* governmental intrusion rather than as an instrument of the government itself.

As a consequence of their aloof and independent position, the courts often do not possess very good access to executive or legislative decision makers.[39] When judges request remedial legislation to correct faults in court operations, they lack contacts with political leaders and a medium of exchange through which to procure the desired legislation. Whereas governors can appoint friends of legislators to sinecure positions or reciprocate legislative favors in some other legal way, judges are usually unable to do so legitimately. Consequently, judicial reforms often fail for lack of interest on the part of the legislature and the governor.

In some states, the judiciary became isolated from the political process in which legislators and governors are immersed, even though the courts had accumulated a large number of extrajudicial functions and controlled many patronage appointments that could be used as currency in the political game. In Pennsylvania, for instance, judges appoint the boards of dozens of charitable institutions and control the election boards.[40] In New York, judges are nominated through party caucuses (although primary elections are held) largely on the basis of their past service to the party; the judges control the largest pool of patronage positions remaining in New York politics.[41] Unlike the governor, however, who can singly control all patronage positions, judges possess no central dispensary of patronage. Each judge makes his own appointments. Therefore, individual judges can play the game of politics by using patronage appointments to pay off political debts, but the judiciary as a whole is left without patronage or other political resources to advance its cause in the legislature.

Although judicial independence is costly to judges when they seek to innovate, most judges and lawyers cultivate it because it protects the judiciary from the partisan attacks that plague legislators and governors. As long as other participants in the political game believe in the myth of judicial independence, the

[39] A description of the limits of judicial lobbying in the states is given by Henry Robert Glick, "Policy-Making and State Supreme Courts: The Judiciary as an Interest Group," *Law and Society Review*, 5 (1970), 271–91.

[40] Sidney Schulman, *Toward Judicial Reform in Pennsylvania* (Philadelphia: University of Pennsylvania Law School, 1962), pp. 59–73, 250–55.

[41] Wallace Sayre and Herbert Kaufman, *Governing New York City* (New York: Russell Sage Foundation, 1960), pp. 530–34.

courts remain free from outside investigation and outside interference. Independence also permits judges to hinder unconstitutional acts by other officials. Consequently, judges and lawyers
remain ambivalent about the proposition that basic changes in
the judiciary are necessary to promote more efficient dispensa-
tion of justice. They desire some reforms, but they also want to
remain free from outside interference. In their effort to have the
best of both worlds, judges possibly reap only the worst.

9
Criminal Trials and Plea Bargains

Americans have two conflicting images of criminal proceedings. The dominant one pictures trials featuring dramatic confrontations between the prosecutor and defense attorney before a jury and judge. This is the image nurtured by television dramas and by press coverage of spectacular events like the Patty Hearst trial. This conception is also promoted by textbook insistence that the legal process is adversarial. A second image, however, is gaining currency. It emphasizes the collaborative character of many criminal proceedings. Some writers speak of assembly-line processes; others describe the criminal courts as if they were bureaucracies rather than courtrooms. Journalists occasionally report on the large number of guilty pleas and concede that guilty pleas rather than trials constitute the normal routine of criminal courtrooms.

Both images are founded in some fact, yet both seriously misconceive criminal proceedings. Jury trials and guilty pleas coexist and support each other; much that happens in courtrooms is a collaborative effort. But criminal proceedings do not resemble assembly lines, and courtrooms are not bureaucracies. Moreover, many courtrooms do not principally convict either by trial or by guilty plea; many specialize in dismissing cases. To understand this, it is necessary to examine the scope of the crime problem that the criminal courts face and the organizational context in which they work. Such a survey will also provide an understanding of the extent to which criminal courts treat blacks and whites, young and old, and men and women differently.

The Scope of the Problem

Criminal prosecutions involve many participants in a complicated sequence of steps, beginning with police apprehension of suspected offenders. Each year police throughout the United States arrest more than nine million people for assorted crimes; in 1980, more than two million of these arrests were for what the FBI terms "serious" crimes.[1] Nevertheless, these arrests cover only a small portion of crimes known to the police, and the crimes known to the police reflect only a portion of all crimes committed. Although almost all murders and most car thefts are reported to the police, less than half of all assaults are reported by their victims. The so-called victimless crimes, such as narcotics offenses, prostitution, and gambling, are almost never reported to the police. Active police work is required to uncover these illicit activities, and the police discover only a small portion of them. In addition, many crimes remain undetected or unpunished because the social status of the offender protects him from ordinary police surveillance. Cheating by retailers, sex and racial discrimination by employers, embezzlement by corporate officers, and bribe-taking by public officials are all activities that allegedly occur much more frequently than police records indicate.

Even when the police know about a crime, they usually cannot apprehend the criminal. Only when the victim has confronted the offender and can identify him are arrest and prosecution likely. Since most crimes are committed by stealth, few thieves or burglars are caught in the act. The police commonly estimate that, unless a burglar is caught within fifteen minutes of the burglary, there is almost no chance of apprehending him. Thus, it is fairly common to read in metropolitan newspapers of burglary

---

[1] U.S. Bureau of the Census, *Statistical Abstract of the United States, 1981* (Washington, D.C.: Government Printing Office, 1981), tables 309 and 310, p. 180.

rings that are broken up only after dozens of thefts totaling thousands of dollars have been committed; eventually, some of these rings are broken by a fluke or by a blunder made by one member. However, those actually arrested by the police represent only a small portion of the active criminal community at any one time.

In general, the discretion of each individual policeman and police department policy determine who will be arrested.[2] Individual policemen observe many illegal acts that they choose to ignore. These acts range from minor traffic violations, occurring when they are busy with more urgent business, to family assaults, which they either refer to welfare agencies or decide are matters more of keeping the peace than of enforcing the criminal law. Individual police departments place different premiums on maintaining order and enforcing the law. When, on a summer day in 1976, both the American Nazi Party and the Martin Luther King, Jr., League attempted to march through a racially tense neighborhood in Chicago, both sets of marchers were arrested to avoid a bloody confrontation, even though the arrests could be justified only on the basis of a technical violation of the city's parade ordinance. Such arrests rarely lead to prosecutions; in such cases the marchers are detained for an hour or two and released after the threat to the peace has dissipated. Police departments also place different emphases on making vice and narcotics arrests and on patrolling various neighborhoods. In those departments where their careers depend on their making vice arrests, the police will pursue such leads vigorously. Where their promotions depend simply on performing normal patrol duties well, they will pay much less attention to narcotics and vice and leave these offenses to specialized units.[3]

Even if all the preconditions are met — the victim complains, the police find the offender, and the crime falls within the cat-

[2] Michael K. Brown, *Working the Street* (New York: Russell Sage Foundation, 1981); Jonathan Rubenstein, *City Police* (New York: Farrar, Straus and Giroux, 1973); James Q. Wilson, *Varieties of Police Behavior* (Cambridge, Mass.: Harvard University Press, 1968).

[3] Rubenstein, *op. cit.*, pp. 51–54; John van Maanem, "Working the Street: A Developmental View of Police Behavior," in Herbert Jacob (ed.), *The Potential for Reform of Criminal Justice* (Beverly Hills, Calif.: Sage Publications, 1974), pp. 108–09.

egory that the police actively pursue — police officers still enjoy considerable discretion in making the arrest. Whether they arrest the offender depends not only on the seriousness of the crime but also on how threatening the behavior of the offender is toward the police. If the offender is deferential and if the victim does not insist on an arrest, the police may well let the offender go free with a warning.[4] In other cases the police officer may decide that the behavior in question is normal for the neighborhood and therefore not worth an arrest and the trouble that arrests require.[5] In cases where the offender can be brought to court with just a summons — requiring less paperwork and avoiding the trip back to the station house and all the red tape that booking necessitates — more people are charged with petty crimes.[6]

When arrests are made, it is often the police who select the charge on which the defendant is to be prosecuted.[7] For instance, they may choose between aggravated assault (a serious felony) or battery (a minor misdemeanor). These original charges become crucial benchmarks in all subsequent proceedings, often determining whether the offender is convicted and what his punishment will be. Even where prosecutors select the charge, they do so on the basis of what the police tell them happened. Thus the police, to a great extent, define the incident — by deciding whether the criminal process should be invoked at all, and if so, how seriously the incident should be considered.

The incidence of crime does not appear to be particularly responsive to policing, at least within the range of police work that occurs in the United States. More aggressive patrolling, more squad cars or more foot patrols, or an increase or decrease in

---

[4] Donald J. Black, "The Production of Crime Rates," *American Sociological Review*, 35 (1970), 733–47; see also Donald J. Black, *The Manners and Customs of the Police* (New York: Academic Press, 1980).

[5] Wayne R. LaFave, *Arrest: The Decision to Take a Suspect into Custody* (Boston: Little, Brown, 1965), pp. 110–14.

[6] *The Evanston Summons' Project* (Evanston, Ill.: Northwestern University Center for Urban Affairs, mimeo., n.d.).

[7] James Eisenstein and Herbert Jacob, *Felony Justice* (Boston: Little, Brown, 1977); Stephen R. Bing and S. Stephen Rosenfeld, *The Quality of Justice* (Boston: Lawyers Committee for Civil Rights Under Law, 1970), pp. 40–41.

police makes little difference in the incidence of crime.[8] Only when all police are removed — as occurred for a short time in Denmark during World War II — does crime increase markedly.[9]

However, the police do have a marked impact on the courts and the administration of criminal justice. The courts depend almost entirely on police work for their supply of cases. The quality of police work determines to a considerable extent what the courts can do with those whom the police arrest.

Criminal Prosecutions as an Organizational Process

Figure 9.1 shows how cases flow from one proceeding to another and from the misdemeanor courtroom to the felony courtroom. Less serious cases, misdemeanors, which generally are punishable by less than a year in jail, are handled by misdemeanor courts.[10] The courts in such minor cases set bail or revise the bail set by the police just after arrest;[11] at the arraignment they tell the defendant what charges he faces. A few days later the court either accepts his guilty plea or holds a trial. In most instances, such courtrooms can only hold bench trials, where the judge himself decides guilt or innocence; jury trials are usually reserved for felony courts. When a judge finds the defendant guilty, he sentences him to pay a fine, serve some time under the supervision of a probation officer, or spend some time in the local jail. Misdemeanor courts also dismiss many cases that the police bring to them.

In addition, misdemeanor courtrooms do the preliminary work for more serious cases, felonies, which are generally punishable by more than a year in prison. As with misdemeanors, the court sets or revises bail immediately after arrest and arraigns defend-

[8] George L. Kelling *et al.*, *The Kansas City Preventive Patrol Experiment: A Technical Report* (Washington, D.C.: The Police Foundation, 1974); James Q. Wilson and Barbara Boland, "The Effect of the Police on Crime," *Law and Society Review*, 12 (1978), 367–90; Herbert Jacob and Michael Rich, "The Effects of the Police on Crime: A Second Look," *Law and Society Review*, 15 (1981), 109–22, and rejoinders in *Law and Society Review*, 16 (1982).

[9] Johannes Andenaes, "The General Preventive Effects of Punishment," *University of Pennsylvania Law Review*, 114 (1969), 962.

[10] Malcolm M. Feeley, *The Process Is the Punishment* (New York: Russell Sage Foundation, 1979).

[11] Roy B. Flemming, *Punishment Before Trial* (New York: Longman, 1982), is the most comprehensive study of bail.

187

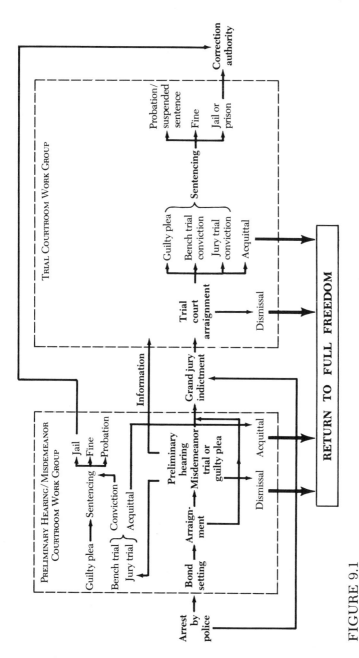

FIGURE 9.1
The Flow of Cases and Organizational Framework of Criminal Prosecutions

ants by telling them of the charges they face. These courtrooms may also hold a preliminary hearing, at which the prosecutor must show that there is "probable cause" to hold the defendant for further proceedings. At the preliminary hearing, the prosecutor must demonstrate that a crime has been committed and that the defendant was probably the perpetrator. Such hearings, however, are not universal. In some places, the defense may waive them to keep damaging testimony temporarily out of the official records, in the hope that by the time the trial occurs witnesses will have forgotten some things, become confused, or have disappeared.

In some jurisdictions cases may go directly to the grand jury, a body of twenty-three citizens that hears evidence presented by the prosecutor only and decides whether or not to issue an indictment. In other jurisdictions, cases go to the grand jury after a preliminary hearing has established probable cause. Most grand juries are controlled by prosecutors and return whatever indictments the prosecutor requests.[12] Where grand juries are not used, the prosecutor certifies probable cause by issuing an information against the defendant.

When an indictment or information has been drawn up, it is brought to a felony trial court, where another bond setting and arraignment takes place. In large cities, many courtrooms handle the trial proceedings. However, most defendants do not ask for trials; rather, they plead guilty or have their cases dismissed.[13] If they plead guilty or are convicted after a bench or jury trial, they are sentenced. As with misdemeanors, the sentence may be a fine, probation, or prison. American courts, however, rarely impose fines when an individual is convicted of a serious crime. Most convicts receive probation or are sentenced to prison.

Distinctive work groups staff courtrooms: prosecutors, defense counsel, and judges are the core personnel; court clerks and

[12] Robert A. Carp, "The Behavior of Grand Juries: Acquiescence or Justice," *Social Science Quarterly,* 55 (1975), 853–70.

[13] Donald M. McIntyre and David Lippman, "Prosecutors and Early Disposition of Felony Cases," *American Bar Association Journal,* 56 (1970), 1154–59. For Baltimore, Chicago, and Detroit in 1972, see Eisenstein and Jacob, *op. cit.,* p. 291; for New York, see Vera Institute of Justice, *Felony Arrests,* rev. ed. (New York: Longman, 1981).

sometimes bailiffs and police officers also play important roles.[14] In most courtrooms, the same small group of people work together for several months or years. The longer they work together, the more cohesive a work group they form. These people develop standard operating procedures for processing their common work load. They learn one another's preferences and habits and develop an understanding of the pressures each faces from his own environment. They become dependent on one another. As a consequence, decisions and case dispositions become collective products rather than the work of any single member of the courtroom work group.

The judge is the formal leader of these work groups. Judges have the greatest status and decision-making power; they also have often served the longest in the courtroom and have the most experience in criminal prosecutions.[15] Judges generally are in their mid-forties and often have served as assistant prosecutor or as defense attorney before winning a seat on the bench. They formally rule on motions that often determine whether a case must be dismissed or will lead to conviction; they order dismissals, determine guilt or innocence, and pass sentence. In recognition of their status, judges are accorded the highest respect — everyone must rise when they enter the courtroom. Those who do not or who disobey judges in other ways may be summarily punished by a short jail term or a fine. Judges also enjoy the best offices in the courtroom suite.

Judges, however, usually cannot translate their formal authority into complete domination. They do not select other members of the courtroom work group. In most instances, they lack detailed information about the cases that come before them. In the misdemeanor and preliminary-hearing courtrooms of large cities, each judge often sees fifty or more defendants every day; they know nothing about these people until the cases are called and the prosecutor presents some testimony. Judges also do not control the defendants. Because defendants possess important rights — including the right not to testify against themselves and

---

[14] Eisenstein and Jacob, *op. cit.*, pp. 67–171; Milton Heumann, *Plea Bargaining* (Chicago: University of Chicago Press, 1978).
[15] Eisenstein and Jacob, *op. cit.*, pp. 21 ff.

the right to insist on a jury trial — the course of proceedings cannot be determined by the judge alone.

Prosecutors control most of the information about the cases.[16] Their files contain the police reports; sometimes they have interviewed witnesses and know beforehand what these people will say. The prosecutor possesses the official police record of the defendant and knows what prior offenses he has been convicted of and how often he has been arrested for other alleged crimes. Consequently, the prosecutor is in the best position to determine what offense to charge the defendant with, what the most appropriate penalty is likely to be, and how the case should be disposed.[17] In addition to this information, the prosecutor possesses broad discretionary powers that neither judge nor defense counsel can ordinarily veto.[18] If the prosecutor does not wish to proceed against a defendant, it is difficult for anyone to force action: ordinarily, such cases are simply lost in the crowd of other cases. When prosecutors decide to proceed, they usually choose which charges to press; since they have more information about the case than anyone else, no one can ordinarily challenge their judgment. Selection of charges is very significant, because it usually determines both the maximum penalty and the actual penalty that is likely to be assessed. In addition, prosecutors have considerable influence over the timing of the proceedings. Until the prosecutor is ready, nothing can be done, although the judge and defense counsel may prod the prosecutor to speed up or slow down.

Small teams of prosecutors (usually two or three) staff each misdemeanor or felony courtroom. They are often permanently assigned to particular courts in a "zone" system, in which they handle all cases coming to the courtroom. (The alternative is for prosecutors to follow a case from beginning to end, regardless of the courtroom in which a proceeding takes place.) They work in the assigned courtroom for six months to a year. The assistant

---

[16] *Ibid.*, pp. 23 ff.; Lief Carter, *The Limits of Order* (Lexington, Mass.: Lexington Books, 1974), pp. 75–112.

[17] Albert W. Alschuler, "The Prosecutor's Role in Plea Bargaining," *University of Chicago Law Review*, 36 (1968), 50–112.

[18] "Prosecutor's Discretion," *University of Pennsylvania Law Review*, 103 (1955), 1057–81.

prosecutors are often young attorneys who are in the prosecutor's office to gain trial experience before striking out on their own in private practice. They usually work with relatively little supervision from their office; they enjoy considerable leeway in handling their cases and in adapting to the other members of the courtroom work groups. They typically spend more of their workday in the courtroom than in their offices; they interact more with other courtroom work group members than with other assistant prosecutors assigned elsewhere.[19]

Defense counsel are a more varied group.[20] Most large city felony trial courtrooms have public defenders who are as much a part of the daily courtroom work group as the assistant prosecutor or judge. Many misdemeanor courtrooms also have regular public defenders assigned to them. Public defenders represent indigent clients who cannot afford to retain their own private attorneys. These attorneys often are part of a team; other attorneys from the public defender office interview defendants after their arrest and help prepare the file for the courtroom attorney. Courtroom attorneys generally have little to go on besides sketchy accounts from their clients and the information that prosecutors share with them. Because public defender attorneys regularly work in the courtroom, they know the informal routines of the prosecutors and the judges; they know their motivations and their preferences. That knowledge — more than legal expertise — may enable them to obtain the optimum disposition for their clients.[21] While public defenders depend on prosecutors and judges for help in efficiently managing their case loads, the reverse is also true, for the public defender usually controls a larger portion of the judge's or prosecutor's case load than any other defense attorney. Public defenders who request a large number of hearings on motions or who insist on many bench or jury trials for their clients can drastically slow the production of

[19] Eisenstein and Jacob, *op. cit.*, pp. 86, 116–17, 151–54.

[20] Albert W. Alschuler, "The Defense Attorney's Role in Plea Bargaining," *Yale Law Journal*, 84 (1975), 1181–1206.

[21] Eisenstein and Jacob, *op. cit.*, pp. 119–20; Roberta R. Pieczenik, "Adjudication of Felony Cases in an Urban Criminal Court" (unpubl. Ph.D. dissertation, New York University, 1974), pp. 226 ff.; James P. Levine, "The Impact of *Gideon*: The Performance of Public and Private Criminal Defense Lawyers," *Polity*, 8 (1975), 215–40.

a courtroom and increase the uncertainty about outcomes for all other members. Consequently, public defenders have considerable influence on the daily operations of most courtrooms.

Private attorneys represent defendants who are not eligible for assistance by the public defender.[22] Private defense counsel are of two sorts: the "regulars" and the "occasionals."[23] The regulars specialize in criminal work and spend most of their day in and around the courthouse; many specialize in particular courtrooms and control a sizable portion of the private work load in them. They are as much a part of the courtroom team as the public defender, prosecutor, and judge; they know all the other regular participants and are privy to the informal arrangements that govern many proceedings. The occasionals, on the other hand, handle only a few criminal cases. They may be volunteer bar association attorneys who come from the large legal firms to handle their one *pro bono* case per month; often they are attorneys who are helping out a regular client by handling a case for one of his employees. Such occasional lawyers are rarely familiar with the informal routines of the courtroom. They are treated cautiously by the regular members of the work group, because no one knows what they will do or how they will respond to routine actions like a request for a continuance. Occasionals more frequently will send their client to trial because other members of the courtroom work group cannot readily negotiate with them; they are not around enough to be included in the informal workings of the court.

Court clerks, bailiffs, and police officers who are regularly assigned to particular courtrooms are also at times part of the regular courtroom work group. Clerks have their greatest potential influence in the arrangement of the daily docket call. In many courtrooms they determine when a particular case will be called — a very important consideration for private defense attorneys who need to be elsewhere later in the day. In some instances, this power degenerates into opportunities for petty graft. Attorneys ask for the case file and are expected to slip five dollars into it when they return it to the clerk; this contribution brings their

[22] Alschuler, "The Defense Attorney's Role."
[23] Eisenstein and Jacob, *op. cit.*, pp. 49–52.

case to the top of the pile. For favored attorneys, the clerk may accept a request for a continuance by telephone; otherwise, he may insist on the lawyer's personal appearance in the courtroom. Bailiffs can be helpful in obtaining clients for attorneys. They spread the word in the lockup about which lawyers are available and permit favored attorneys to enter early in the morning, before the court call begins, both to interview clients and to seek out new ones. Finally, court police officers present much of the crucial evidence on which the prosecutor depends for convictions in misdemeanor cases and for rulings of probable cause in preliminary hearings. During informal discussions before the cases are called, police officers can exercise considerable influence with their assessment of the strength of the evidence and their opinion of what the outcome should be. They are particularly likely to urge severe treatment for the defendant when police have been injured or are charged with misconduct; in such instances the courtroom usually obtains a conviction.

These regular members of courtroom work groups develop their own goals, normal operating procedures, and internal relationships, which taken together make each courtroom somewhat distinctive.[24] One of their goals is to see that justice is done, but justice is a vague term that each work group member interprets in his own way. More important are the instrumental goals of reducing uncertainty and of reaching the productivity levels of their sponsoring organizations and the outside world. While the concept of "doing justice" might lead courtroom members into conflict with one another, attempts to reduce uncertainty and meet production goals lead to collaboration and cooperation. Such shared goals lead to normal operating procedures, which in turn reduce conflict. Work group members share an understanding about the scheduling of cases. They rarely insist on hearing a case when one of the participants is not ready; they understand that private attorneys must collect their fees before disposing of their cases and will permit delays to allow prior payment. Defense counsel rarely would jeopardize a prosecutor's job when they might force him to lose a case on an embarrassing technicality. Prosecutors and defense attorneys alike will

[24] *Ibid.*, pp. 19–39.

normally accommodate themselves to the judge's schedule — for example, by avoiding potentially lengthy jury trials that might interfere with the judge's vacation.

One of the most important consequences of the development of the work group lies in its propensity to encourage plea bargaining. Plea bargains occur more frequently where these work groups are cohesive than where they are looser.[25] A comparison of work groups in Chicago with less-cohesive ones in Baltimore is revealing. Chicago felony work groups were well structured and highly cohesive.[26] Judges served for several years in the same courtroom; prosecutors and public defenders worked there for as long as a year, and the public defenders handled a large portion of the case load. Everyone in the work group — including some regular private counsel — was familiar with one another. The group regularly assembled in the judge's chambers before each day's court call to discuss cases informally. Over a period of several weeks or months negotiations occurred informally during these gatherings, as well as in the hallways and in the courtroom. When a case ripened for disposition, a formal conference was called in the judge's chambers, in which the judge participated. The prosecutor laid out his case and recommendation; the defense counsel countered with his client's story and his own recommendation. The judge then gave the attorneys his estimation of the "worth" of the case and promised a specific sentence in return for a guilty plea. The defense attorney took the offer to his client; if the client accepted, the participants moved into the courtroom for the formal ceremony, at which the guilty plea was offered by the defendant and accepted by the judge. Often the sentence was given at the same ceremony. If the bargain was rejected, further negotiations took place or a trial was scheduled. In Chicago all this worked smoothly; the participants worked in the context of dozens of prior pleas and in the expectation of continuing these arrangements for the indefinite future.

By contrast, in Baltimore no one knew which courtroom would process a case until the day it was scheduled for disposition.[27] The defense counsel did not know beforehand which judge his

---

[25] *Ibid.*, pp. 60–64; Pieczenik, *op. cit.*
[26] Eisenstein and Jacob, *op. cit.*, pp. 98–125.
[27] *Ibid.*, pp. 67–97.

client would face; even more important, he did not know which prosecutor would handle the case. At the last moment the case might be transferred to another courtroom, and a different prosecutor might pick it up. Prosecutors also did not know which cases they would handle on any particular day or who would be the opposing lawyer for the defense. Further, Baltimore had a higher turnover of prosecutors than Chicago, which meant not only that they were less experienced but also that they were less familiar with other members of the courtroom work group. Consequently, Baltimore work groups did not develop as strong a consensus on goals or as thorough an understanding of normal routines. They had fewer opportunities to reduce uncertainty by negotiating and fewer occasions to discuss their cases informally. As a result, there were fewer plea bargains and guilty pleas in Baltimore than in Chicago. However, to meet production goals, Baltimore courtrooms held a large number of bench trials, which might be characterized as "slow pleas"; with these, attorneys presented evidence quickly and relatively informally under the active prodding and supervision of the judge. The proceeding was more formal than the chamber conferences in Chicago but much less formal than a jury trial. Attorneys and judge exercised more control over these bench trials than they could exert over jury trials, because the judge was experienced in weighing evidence whereas jurors are not.

More courts resemble the work groups of Chicago than of Baltimore, but there is a great range in the way in which courtroom work groups are organized. Los Angeles, for instance, also utilizes a short bench trial proceeding in place of a heavy reliance on pleas.[28] Detroit has centralized plea bargaining in a special prosecutor's office so that it takes place before the case goes to a felony trial courtroom.[29] The courtroom work group there has much less influence on the decision of whether to plea or to go to trial, but another work group, consisting of the pretrial prosecutor and defense counsel, works out the bargain with full knowledge of who the judge will be.

---

[28] Lynn Mather, "The Outsider in the Courtroom," in Jacob (ed.), *op. cit.*, pp. 263–89; Peter W. Greenwood *et al.*, *Prosecution of Adult Felony Defendants: A Policy Perspective* (Santa Monica, Calif.: Rand Corporation, 1973), pp. 35–41.
[29] Eisenstein and Jacob, *op. cit.*, pp. 138, 145–54.

Across the nation, considerable variation exists both in the kind of plea bargaining that occurs and the degree to which judges participate in it. In some places, bargaining focuses on the potential sentences; in many others, it centers on the charges to be prosecuted, with an implicit understanding about what a reduction in charges would mean with respect to the likely sentence. Most judges only ratify the bargains already struck between prosecutor and defense counsel, but in larger cities and in states with more permissive rules, judges tend to be more active in plea bargaining.[30]

What Happens to Defendants?

Misdemeanor courtrooms handle a wide variety of minor offenses. Some of them are city ordinance violations that do not even count as misdemeanors, although they may result in similar punishments. The misdemeanors themselves may include charges of drunkenness, minor assaults, petty thefts and shoplifting, prostitution, or minor gambling charges. No national statistics about the volume of these cases or about their outcomes exist; indeed, we do not even have such information for most large cities. The most detailed account of these cases exists for New York, where in Manhattan 47 percent of the misdemeanor cases were dismissed, whereas 31 percent were disposed of by guilty pleas. Trials occurred in only 4 percent of the cases, with two-fifths of these leading to acquittals and the rest resulting in convictions.[31] In New Haven in 1974, only 38 percent of misdemeanor defendants had their cases dismissed, whereas 50 percent pleaded guilty. None went to trial.[32] In New York, the misdemeanor court process was slow, with the average case taking three months from arrest to disposition.[33] In New Haven, delay did not appear to be a major problem.[34]

[30] John Paul Ryan and James J. Alfini, "Trial Judges' Participation in Plea Bargaining: An Empirical Perspective," *Law and Society Review*, 13 (1979), 479–507. That issue of the *Law and Society Review* also has an extensive bibliography on plea bargaining.

[31] John B. Jennings, *The Flow of Adult Defendants Through the Manhattan Criminal Court in 1968 and 1969* (New York: The New York City Rand Institute, 1971), pp. 6–9.

[32] Feeley, *op. cit.*, p. 127.

[33] Jennings, *op. cit.*

[34] Feeley, *op. cit.*, pp. 174–75, 222–25.

Sentences for these misdemeanor courts are rarely reported. However, we do know that, in New Haven, most defendants who were found guilty were assessed a fine of $50 or less. The major penalty in these courts may well be the arrest, the time in jail before release on bond, and the indignities suffered by the defendants as they are processed in the courts.[35]

Our knowledge of dispositions of serious cases is more complete. As with misdemeanors, many people accused of serious crimes escape conviction because their cases are dismissed during early stages of the proceedings. For instance, in Chicago in 1972, two-thirds of those arrested by the police and brought to the preliminary-hearing courtroom eventually had all charges against them dismissed.[36] Only 25 percent of all those originally brought in by the police were convicted; only 15 percent were sent to prison. Some cities convict a larger proportion of those accused: during 1972, Baltimore convicted 44 percent and Detroit convicted 57 percent. But the proportion sent to prison remained small — 28 percent for Baltimore and 20 percent for Detroit. These proportions were approximately the same for New York, Washington, D.C., Los Angeles, and San Diego.[37] Thus, one principal function of the courtroom work groups may be characterized as a screening function; they decide which cases to process fully and which to ignore.

What are some of the reasons for a courtroom work group to dismiss a case? Many cases represent essentially private disputes and are brought to court only as part of a strategy by the complainant to collect a debt or settle a fight. When the offender has offered compensation or become reconciled with the complainant, the complainant drops the case. The prosecutor is then left without a complaining witness and must dismiss the charges. Such results are not necessarily undesirable, nor do they consume much court time. Often in such cases, offender and complainant must continue to live together or work together; their reconciliation, even though it is through the medium of the crim-

---

[35] *Ibid.*, p. 138.
[36] Eisenstein and Jacob, *op. cit.*, p. 191.
[37] *U.S. News and World Report*, May 10, 1976, p. 37; Vera Institute of Justice, *op. cit.*, p. 7.

inal courts, is usually preferable to the imprisonment of the offender.

Other dismissals occur for different reasons. In some cases, the prosecutor is unable to locate complaining witnesses. If the police ask the complainant for his name and address in front of the offender, the victim often gives false information to protect himself from harassment. Consequently, all the notices about court appearances fail to reach the complainant; without the victim, the case is dismissed for lack of evidence. In addition, complainants often must appear several times before the case is finally brought to a hearing. Each appearance takes many hours of the victims' time: they lose a day's work and are insulted by the apparent neglect with which their presence is greeted. They may sit on a hard bench most of a day while awaiting their case, only to learn that it has been postponed for another month. Many victims eventually decide that it is not worth their while to appear in court, and they stop coming. Although they are formally subpoenaed, their failure to appear is rarely prosecuted; rather, the prosecutor drops the case against the original offender. Finally, prosecutors dismiss some cases because the evidence is factually or legally insufficient: evidence may have been seized illegally, or a powder that looked like heroin may have turned out to be salt.

Property cases are the most likely to be dropped; many assaults — especially where the offender and victim were friends or relatives — are also dismissed. The most serious crimes — murder, rape, and armed robbery — survive the screening process much more frequently. If the case survives the initial screening, the defendant's chance for acquittal is small. Among defendants whose cases were sent to trial courtrooms in Baltimore in 1972, 68 percent were convicted; in Chicago the conviction rate was 76 percent, and in Detroit, 72 percent.[38] Thus, misdemeanor courtrooms that hold preliminary hearings largely screen cases; felony courtrooms mostly convict defendants. In most cities, with some exceptions, a majority of those convicted are sent to prison. For instance, in Baltimore, 63 percent of those convicted in the trial courtrooms went to prison; in Chicago, 88 percent went to

[38] Eisenstein and Jacob, *op. cit.*, p. 291.

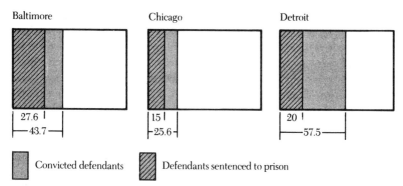

FIGURE 9.2
Proportion of Felony Defendants Convicted and Sentenced to Prison in Baltimore, Chicago, and Detroit in 1972

Source: James Eisenstein and Herbert Jacob, *Felony Justice* (Boston: Little, Brown, 1977), p. 293. Copyright © 1977 by James Eisenstein and Herbert Jacob. Used by permission.

prison; but in Detroit, a large proportion received probation, and only 35 percent were sent to prison.[39]

Despite these overall rates for conviction and sentencing, only a small minority of those arrested for serious crimes are incarcerated. Figure 9.2 shows the small proportion of those arrested in 1972 in Baltimore, Chicago, and Detroit who were sent to prison. This attrition rate is apparently quite representative of criminal justice in the United States. In Washington, D.C., during 1973, only one-third of the incidents in which an arrest was made led to a conviction for one or more of the offenders arrested; in two-thirds of the incidents, no one who was arrested was convicted.[40] Since most victimizations do not come to the attention of the police or lead to an arrest, the proportion of crimes that bring their offenders to prison is probably only half of what is represented in Figure 9.2.

Do these mass dismissals and selective convictions have any effect on the crime rate? We do not know. The deterrent effects

[39] *Ibid.*
[40] Kristen M. Williams, "System Flow Rates: Measuring Attrition in the Criminal Justice Process" (Washington, D.C.: Institute for Law and Social Research, November 1975, mimeo), table 6.

of sending offenders to prison have been studied in several ways.[41] These studies show that states with relatively high imprisonment rates compared to arrests or crimes have somewhat lower crime rates than states that send fewer offenders to prison. On the other hand, little relationship has been found between length of prison sentences and crime rates. These findings have been interpreted to mean that certainty of punishment has a closer relationship to deterrence than severity. However, these conclusions rest on very weak evidence and require many inferential leaps. Crimes known to the police and arrests are not counted in the same way as commitments to prison; thus, "certainty" of punishment is at best an attenuated measure, since it does not include punishment other than imprisonment. Severity of punishment as a measure is equally unsatisfactory, because it usually measures the length of the sentence currently being served in the state penitentiary rather than the length of the sentence as originally meted out (including nonpenitentiary sentences).

Another estimate of the effect of dismissals and selective convictions rests on an analysis of the incapacitative effect of imprisonment.[42] If offenders are in prison, they cannot commit further crimes against the general population. Clearly, the larger the number of offenders sent to prison, the greater the incapacitative effect, at least for the short run, although the costs of imprisonment may outweigh the benefits. Presently, researchers do not know how large the population of criminals is or how rapidly it would be replaced by new recruits if large numbers were kept in prison for long periods of time. If, for instance, new offenders rapidly took the place of those incarcerated, a policy of strict imprisonment would have little impact. Such a conse-

[41] Three extensive reviews of research on deterrence are Jack P. Gibbs, *Crime, Punishment and Deterrence* (New York: Elsevier Scientific Publishing, 1975), pp. 145–216; Charles R. Tittle and Charles H. Logan, "Sanctions and Deviance," *Law and Society Review,* 7 (1973), 371–92; Franklin E. Zimring and Gordon J. Hawkins, *Deterrence: The Legal Threat in Crime Control* (Chicago: University of Chicago Press, 1973).

[42] Contrast the different conclusions drawn by David F. Greenberg, "The Incapacitative Effects of Imprisonment: Some Estimates," *Law and Society Review,* 9 (1975), 541–80, and Raoul Shinnar and Shlomo Shinnar, "The Effects of the Criminal Justice System on the Control of Crime," *ibid.,* pp. 581–612.

quence is perhaps more likely for property crimes, where the incentive for committing them depends on opportunities and economic conditions, than for crimes of violence, which perhaps occur more frequently among individuals with psychological disorders.

Although the general social effects of selective screening and conviction are difficult to determine, their consequences for particular social strata are clearer. It is particularly easy to determine how they affect the poor, blacks, and women.

All the evidence available indicates that the criminal courts are fundamentally courts for prosecution of the poor. The crimes that attract the notice of the police are much more frequently those committed by poor people than those committed by the rich. Those few defendants who are not poor can often escape the worst consequences of their involvement, provided they are not caught in a spectacular crime. They can afford bail and thus avoid pretrial detention, and they can also obtain a private attorney who specializes in criminal work. They can usually obtain delays, which help weaken the prosecution case. They can compensate victims to help themselves escape punishment. They can enroll in diversion programs by seeking private psychiatric treatment or other medical assistance. They can keep their jobs and maintain their family relationships and, therefore, qualify as good probation risks. They can appeal their conviction (if, indeed, they are convicted) and delay serving their sentence. It is essential to note, however, that all these advantages accrue to only a tiny portion of all criminal defendants. Most defendants are welfare poor or working poor and cannot utilize this array of tactics.

The degree of discrimination against blacks is much less clear. Compared to poor white defendants who have similar criminal records and face similar charges, blacks are not severely discriminated against.[43] However, the degree of discrimination varies from almost none to a quite discernible amount.[44] It appears to

---

[43] John Hagen, "Extra-Legal Attributes and Criminal Sentencing: An Assessment of a Sociological Viewpoint," *Law and Society Review*, 8 (1974), 557–83; Eisenstein and Jacob, *op. cit.*, p. 284.

[44] Cassia Spohn, John Gruel, and Susan Welch, "Effect of Race on Sentencing: A Re-examination of an Unsettled Question," *Law and Society Review*, 16 (1981–82), 71–88.

be least apparent in large cities where substantial black populations exercise visible political power. For instance, blacks in
Detroit and Chicago play a formidable political role and are included among the judges, prosecutors, and defense counsel who
staff the courtroom work groups; larger numbers of blacks also
serve on juries. All of these factors tend to reduce the amount of
discrimination against black defendants.[45] Another study indicates that white judges discriminate against blacks, whereas
black judges discriminate in favor of blacks; hence, the citywide
averages show no discrimination.[46] However, in rural areas
where few blacks live, a California study suggests that substantial
discrimination still exists against them in the form of more severe
sentences.[47]

An increasing number of women are becoming offenders. During the decades between 1953 and 1972, the proportion of women
among all those arrested by the police rose from 11 percent to
15 percent; for serious crimes, it rose from 9 percent to 19 percent.[48] Almost all of the increase, however, has been in property
crimes rather than in crimes of violence.[49] The data on what
happens to women in court are scanty. In California, women are
generally convicted less frequently than men, although the difference rarely exceeds 10 percent for a particular offense.[50] For
property offenses, women are treated almost identically to men,
but when charged with violent crimes, women are more likely
to escape conviction.[51] When convicted, women are much less

[45] Eisenstein and Jacob, op. cit., pp. 121–22, 160–64.

[46] James C. Gibson, "Racial Discrimination in Criminal Courts: Some The-
oretical and Methodological Considerations" (Iowa City: University of Iowa Department of Political Science, 1975, mimeo.)

[47] Carl E. Pope, Sentencing of California Felony Offenders (Washington,
D.C.: Law Enforcement Assistance Administration, 1975).

[48] Rita James Simon, The Contemporary Woman and Crime (Washington,
D.C.: National Institute of Mental Health, Center for Studies of Crime and De-
linquency, 1975), p. 37; Ilene H. Nagel and John Hagan, "Gender and Crime:
Offense Patterns and Criminal Court Sanctions," in Norval Morris and Michael
Tonry (eds.), Crime and Justice: An Annual Review of Research, Vol. 4 (Chicago:
University of Chicago Press, 1983), pp. 91–144.

[49] Simon, op. cit., pp. 39–46.

[50] Ibid., p. 40.

[51] Ibid., p. 59; for similar findings in Washington, D.C., see Susan Katznelson,
"The Female Defendant in Washington, D.C." (Washington, D.C.: The Institute
for Law and Social Research, January 1976, mimeo); also Freda F. Solomon,
"Factors Affecting Differing Dispositions of Urban Felony Cases: Sex as a Critical
Variable" (unpubl. Ph.D. dissertation, Northwestern University, 1983).

likely to receive prison sentences.[52] Unlike blacks, with whom women's liberation leaders often compare themselves, women receive preferential treatment from criminal justice agencies. Although the number of women offenders is growing, they continue to receive somewhat more lenient treatment than their male counterparts.

The young are also treated in a special way. A very large portion of all crime is committed by young people between the ages of twelve and eighteen. Most of these offenders qualify for processing as juveniles and do not enter the regular criminal court system; rather, they are handled by special agencies, including juvenile courts.

Juvenile agencies, given responsibility for children for a variety of reasons, often become responsible for runaways or children who have committed pranks that do not in any way qualify as crimes.[53] Such children need greater supervision than their families provide and therefore become wards of the state, subject to the jurisdiction of juvenile authorities. Other children have been neglected by their parents and need foster care; they also may be sent to juvenile authorities in many states. Often, children who commit serious crimes, such as armed robbery or even murder, enter the same institutions as children in need of supervision and neglected children. They are processed much less formally than adult offenders and often receive little formal punishment. Many adult "first" offenders are, in fact, veterans of the juvenile courts and have long experience with probation officers, courts, and even corrections facilities. In general, it can be said that juveniles are treated more leniently than adults. They are the greatest beneficiaries of the process that dismisses or diverts many cases from trial courts and from prisons.

The Effects of Reform

Since 1953 many visible reforms have been made in the administration of criminal justice. Supreme Court decisions have reinterpreted the rights of defendants, making it mandatory to

[52] Simon, op. cit., p. 68.
[53] Cf. Aaron V. Cicourel, The Social Organization of Juvenile Justice (New York: John Wiley, 1968); Robert M. Emerson, Judging Delinquents (Chicago: Aldine, 1969); Malcolm W. Klein (ed.), The Juvenile Justice System (Beverly Hills, Calif.: Sage Publications, 1976).

warn them about self-incrimination, reminding them of their right to remain silent, and notifying them of their right to an attorney.[54] Every defendant who faces a jail sentence must now be provided with an attorney if he cannot afford to hire one himself.[55] Concurrently, many jurisdictions have initiated major bail reforms.[56] Rather than requiring a monetary bond, which usually had to be bought from a private entrepreneur, courts began to release defendants simply on their promise to reappear as long as it was established that they had firm roots in the community. This program, called *release on recognizance* (ROR), caused a sharp reduction in the jail population of many communities. Finally, a concerted effort has been made to quicken the pace of criminal prosecutions by placing firm deadlines on courtrooms. In the federal courts the case must be dismissed if action is not begun within six months; similar rules exist in some of the states.

The full effects of these reforms are not yet clear. The *Miranda* warnings on the right to counsel and on the right to remain silent stirred considerable opposition from the police who had to administer them. Despite dire warnings that the conviction rate would plunge without so-called voluntary confessions, conviction rates have remained about the same; many defendants still confess despite the *Miranda* warnings they are given.[57]

The right-to-counsel decisions increased the employment of lawyers. Public-defender systems spread, although they are not universally used; many smaller jurisdictions still use court-appointed attorneys. Defendants represented by public defenders and regular court-appointed attorneys appear to receive about the same treatment as defendants accused of similar crimes but represented by private attorneys.[58] This almost-equal treatment

---

[54] *Miranda v. Arizona*, 384 U.S. 436 (1966).

[55] *Gideon v. Wainwright*, 372 U.S. 335 (1963); *Argersinger v. Hamlin*, 407 U.S. 25 (1972).

[56] Patricia M. Wald, "The Right to Bail Revisited: A Decade of Promise without Fulfillment," in Stuart S. Nagel (ed.), *The Rights of the Accused* (Beverly Hills, Calif.: Sage Publications, 1972), pp. 177–205.

[57] O. John Rogge, "Confessions and Self-Incrimination," in Nagel (ed.), *op. cit.*, pp. 80–89.

[58] Eisenstein and Jacob, *op. cit.*, p. 285; Pieczenik, *op. cit.*, pp. 226 ff.; James P. Levine, "The Impact of *Gideon*: The Performance of Public and Private Criminal Defense Lawyers," *Polity*, 8 (1975), 215–40; Jean G. Taylor, "A Comparison of Counsel for Felony Defendants" (Arlington, Va.: Institute for Defense Analyses, 1972, mimeo).

occurs, not in spite of the fact that public defenders become part of the courtroom work group, but because of it. The public defenders learn the routines, do favors, and earn reciprocal accommodations; consequently, most defendants represented by the public defender receive as much consideration as if they were represented by their own private attorney. Defendants often do not think that they are being treated equally, however, because they lack the feeling of control that comes with hiring and paying their own attorney.[59]

Bail reform has had a visible impact on the processing of criminal defendants by reducing the size of jail populations and thereby saving the taxpayer thousands of dollars.[60] Even more significant, it has reduced the inherent unfairness of imprisoning some defendants before their conviction simply because they were poorer than others. Pretrial incarceration, however, has not been entirely eliminated, because many defendants still do not qualify for release on their own recognizance and do not have enough money to purchase monetary bonds. Such defendants are often those accused of the more serious crimes or those with long criminal records. They also stand the best chance of ultimate conviction, partly because the cases against them are strong and partly because they cannot withstand delay as well as defendants who are out on the street. For these reasons they have a stronger inclination to plead guilty.[61] On the negative side, society takes some risk in releasing defendants while they await trial; some commit new crimes while free — sometimes for the purpose of raising funds to pay for their attorney.[62]

Legislation to speed the criminal process has had less success. Courtroom work groups have considerable difficulty in controlling the pace of their work. The courtroom schedule depends not only on the group's own diligence but also on the willingness of civilian volunteers — the complainants and witnesses — to

[59] Levine, *op. cit.*; Jonathan Casper, *American Criminal Justice* (Englewood Cliffs, N.J.: Prentice-Hall, 1972).

[60] An evaluation of bail reform is given by Malcolm M. Feeley, *Court Reform on Trial* (New York: Basic Books, 1983), pp. 40–79.

[61] Eisenstein and Jacob, *op. cit.*, pp. 284–85.

[62] J. W. Locke *et al.*, "Compilation and Use of Criminal Court Data in Relation to Pretrial Release of Defendants," National Bureau of Standards Technical Note 535 (Washington, D.C.: Government Printing Office, 1970), p. 8.

appear. In some instances, a case does not mature rapidly because the victim must be given time to recuperate from wounds. Private attorneys also need time to collect their fees. Consequently, legislatively imposed time limits are commonly evaded by subterfuge. In Illinois, for instance, a trial must begin within 160 days of the arrest if the defendant is free on bail. In practice, those 160 days begin only when the defendant states that he is ready to proceed; if a delay occurs because the defendant asks for a continuance, the 160-day period is interrupted. Consequently, one of the common bargaining chips a defense attorney has to offer is a continuance "by agreement" in exchange for some other favor, thereby giving the prosecution more time to begin a trial or to secure a plea bargain. How often this occurs may be seen from the fact that, in 1972, the median case in Chicago took 267 days rather than the legislatively mandated 160.[63]

The elimination of plea bargaining is another reform that has attracted widespread attention. Proposals range from controlling it by requiring close adherence to prescribed procedures to simply forbidding it entirely.[64] In the latter circumstance, defendants can still plead guilty but can not be given any assurances about their sentence; moreover, they would have to plead to the charges originally placed against them, instead of to agreed-upon reduced charges. Widespread adoption of such reforms, however, is quite unlikely.[65] If they were to lead to even a 10 percent increase in jury trials, twice as many judges, prosecutors, defense counsel, and courtrooms would be needed, and, there is little enthusiasm for such expenditures. Moreover, the reason for plea bargaining lies in the structure of courtroom work groups. The desire of these groups to reduce uncertainty cannot be legislated away; only their ability to reduce uncertainty can be affected — for example, by employing procedures like those in Baltimore, which make it difficult for cohesive work groups to form. Even in Baltimore, however, quasi–plea bargaining occurred in the

[63] Eisenstein and Jacob, op. cit., p. 291.

[64] National Advisory Commission on Criminal Justice Standards and Goals, Courts (Washington, D.C.: Government Printing Office, 1973), pp. 42–65.

[65] One such attempt has been made in Alaska. See Michael J. Rubenstein and Teresa J. White, "Alaska's Ban on Plea Bargaining," Law and Society Review, 13 (1979), 367–83.

abbreviated bench trials that were the common procedure for handling felony cases. Although plea bargains violate the ideals of the adversary system, little evidence exists that they produce results that are less fair than bench or jury trials. When one controls for the type of case that is handled by each procedure, it can be seen that plea bargaining does not even produce more lenient sentences.[66]

Although critics focus on plea bargains, bench and jury trials continue to constitute an essential part of the criminal justice process. It is true that only a very small proportion of cases go to trial, and an especially small proportion go to a trial by jury. But the possibility of going to trial constrains the plea-bargaining process. No one has to accept a bargain that is worse than the decision that could be obtained from a jury trial. Doubtful cases can be brought to a jury or bench trial, even when the prosecutor would rather close the case with a lenient bargain. At the same time, politically sensitive cases, in which the defendant is prominent or the crime is well publicized, are often brought to trial to protect the courtroom work group against charges of favoritism that would inevitably arise from whatever bargain was made. Indeed, such charges of favoritism quickly arose when former Vice President Spiro Agnew in 1973 pleaded *nolo contendere* rather than face a trial.

Finally, much attention has been directed toward alleged sentencing disparities.[67] Persons convicted of similar crimes often receive quite different sentences. Such differences exist not only between urban and rural areas but also between different judges in the same area or for the same judge over a period of time. These problems led many states during the 1970s to adopt new sentencing laws, which in many instances made minimum sentences mandatory. The new laws also often replaced indeterminate sentences, which had permitted judges to choose from a broad range of years between the minimum and maximum, with determinate (flat) sentences, which give judges little discretion. In addition, some states adopted laws directed particularly against drug and gun offenders. Thus, New York under Governor

---

[66] Eisenstein and Jacob, *op. cit.*, pp. 277, 283.

[67] Hagen, *op. cit.*; Anthony Partridge and William B. Eldridge, *The Second Circuit Sentencing Study* (Washington, D.C.: Federal Judicial Center, 1974).

Rockefeller enacted a very stiff sentencing law on narcotics offenses, and Massachusetts adopted a strict sentencing law for offenses involving guns.[68]

The impact of these new enactments was mixed. New York's law resulted in costly additions to the court system and little apparent reduction in drug trafficking. The Massachusetts law apparently had only a temporary effect in reducing armed robberies.[69] Across the nation, however, new sentencing laws and a general mood of toughness resulted in a very substantial increase in the number of persons imprisoned. In 1981 alone, 40,000 additional persons were in prison, the largest increase in the prison population since such data were first recorded in 1925.[70] The increase produced a new crisis for prison authorities; thirty-one states in 1982 received court orders to reduce prison overcrowding.

Conclusions

Unequal treatment of special groups of defendants — the poor, blacks, and women — is more an apparent problem than a real one. Recent research has demonstrated that discrimination against these groups is not rampant, although it does persist in some jurisdictions. Moreover, the criminal prosecution process continues to be directed mostly against the poor, who are also often black, because it focuses mainly on the property crimes and crimes of violence that the poor commit. White-collar crimes are not pursued as vigorously.

Real problems continue to dog the criminal prosecution process. Many people harbor lingering doubts about the legitimacy of plea bargaining and are confused about the proper objectives

---

[68] Feeley, *Court Reform on Trial*, pp. 114–55. See also Martin L. Forst (ed.), *Sentencing Reform: Experiments in Reducing Disparity* (Beverly Hills, Calif.: Sage Publications, 1982); Jonathan Casper, David Brereton, and David Neal, *The Implementation of the California Determinate Sentence Law* (Washington, D.C.: Government Printing Office, 1982).

[69] Feeley, *Court Reform on Trial*, pp. 114–55.

[70] Bureau of Justice Statistics, *Prisoners in 1981*, Bulletin NCJ-82262 (Washington, D.C.: U.S. Department of Justice, May 1982).

of imprisonment. Many experience a high degree of frustration and feel that policing, judging, and imprisoning have little impact on the incidence of crime. As long as these problems persist, the criminal-prosecution process will be viewed with suspicion by many elements of the American public.

10
Civil Justice and Economic Discrimination

Civil courts, unlike criminal courts, are not the habitations of the poor; they exude signs of respectability. These are the courtrooms of the "haves" rather than the "have-nots." Well-dressed people usually fill them, and large amounts of money are often discussed. The complexity of the proceedings themselves, the remedies available, the ways in which the legal profession interacts with its potential clients, and the characteristics of the poor all combine to discriminate against the poor in civil proceedings.

Civil proceedings range over the entire potential for conflict in American society. Almost every dispute that does not involve a violation of the criminal code may come to a civil courtroom. Every broken agreement, every sale that leaves a dissatisfied customer, every uncollected debt, every dispute with a government agency, every libel and slander, every accidental injury, every marital breakup, and every death may give rise to a civil proceeding. Whether in fact they do depends on many characteristics of the case and of the disputants. The potential volume of cases is much greater than the actual. There were, for instance,

210

24.1 million traffic accidents in 1980, in which 5.2 million people were injured and which involved an economic loss of $57 billion.[1] Only a small fraction of these accidents resulted in court cases, although personal injury suits constitute the largest part of the work load of most courts. In the same year, there were 1.1 million divorces, most of which were also processed by civil courts. Almost two million Americans died in 1980; if they left property, their estates had to be probated through court proceedings.[2] Even in good times many Americans fall behind in their debts, and settling these debts produces another very large source of the courts' business.

Not all these cases represent real disputes, nor do they constitute the judicial work that has the greatest potential impact on politics and society. Much of the courts' work — especially that of state courts — represents either routine registration of the outcome of disputes or the use of procedures to avoid conflict. Most divorces, for instance, are uncontested; even in those states that still require court action for divorce, the ceremony is an empty ritual with the result completely predetermined. Such proceedings also consume very little court time. For example, probating wills usually involves the submission of documents, with a token appearance by the estate's executor. Only in those rare cases where someone contests either a will or the work of the executor does the court become actively involved in conflict resolution. In nearly all other types of cases, a plaintiff brings a dispute to court to signal the defendant that he is serious, but everyone expects an out-of-court settlement to be reached, and it usually is.

As Table 10.1 illustrates, most cases brought to ordinary civil courtrooms involve debts, monetary disputes over broken contracts, and liens. Debt actions, mostly involving consumer credit, were the most frequent cases brought to the civil courtrooms in Baltimore, Cleveland, and Milwaukee. Personal-injury cases and divorces constituted only 21 percent of the case load of these courtrooms.

---

[1] U.S. Bureau of the Census, *Statistical Abstract of the United States, 1981* (Washington, D.C.: Government Printing Office, 1981), table 1081, p. 622.
[2] *Ibid.*, table 83, p. 58.

TABLE 10.1
Caseload of Civil Courts in
Baltimore, Cleveland, and
Milwaukee, 1965–1970

	%
Debt actions	25
Money damage contracts	19
Liens	16
Divorce	11
Personal injury and property damage	10
Foreclosures	4
Evictions	3
Administrative agency appeals	3
Habeas corpus petitions	2
Injunctions	2
Other	5
Total	100
Sample N =	7,732

Source: Adapted from Craig Wanner, "The Public Ordering of Private Relations," *Law and Society Review*, 8 (1974), p. 422. *Law and Society Review* is the official publication of the Law and Society Association, which holds copyright to the article. Reprinted by permission. Based on random sampling of cases in courts of first instance with general jurisdiction.

These routine cases have a great aggregate impact on American society and its economy. Billions of dollars are transferred from the losers of cases to the winners as a result of the millions of cases that courts decide, even though most individual cases involve only modest sums.

Another class of cases has a more direct impact on politics and society. Many of the most controversial issues of the day find their way into America's civil courtrooms. Whether schoolchildren should be bused to promote racial integration, whether IBM should be broken up because of its dominant position in the computer market, whether suburbs can impose zoning restrictions to keep out apartment buildings (and the minorities who might live in them), whether universities must favor women and minorities in their admissions and staffing actions, whether labor unions may strike against state and local governments — these are among the issues that come to civil courtrooms. None of these cases constitutes a large part of any court's docket, but the effect of a single decision in such controversies is enormous. It often involves the expenditure of millions of dollars or alters the way in which thousands of people live and work.

Both small and large cases come to civil courts. As we have already seen, these courts are usually the same organizations that handle criminal cases. Often the same judges preside, although the attorneys are generally different. In some jurisdictions, particular courtrooms are set aside for specific kinds of cases: some may handle only housing disputes; others specialize in divorce; others process personal injury claims; and still others handle only disputes involving public agencies. In other jurisdictions — the federal courts, for instance — each courtroom docket is a mixture of criminal, antitrust, government agency, personal injury, and miscellaneous cases. In practice, federal courts have attracted a larger share of the public law cases involving controversial policy disputes, whereas state courts attract a larger share of the private disputes.

The Flow of Cases in Civil Proceedings

Civil proceedings are complex and involve many choices of forum, procedure, timing, and possible outcomes. These choices rest in the hands of litigants and their lawyers and permit them to engage in complicated strategies.

A conflict reaches court when it is filed by the plaintiff's attorney. In many instances, the plaintiffs have a choice of which court to use. They may choose between a federal and a state court in cases in which the plaintiff and the defendant live in different states and the claim exceeds $10,000. At other times plaintiffs may have a choice between several state courts that exercise overlapping jurisdiction.

Among the factors that plaintiffs and their attorneys take into account in choosing courts are the quality and known biases of the judges. In some areas many lawyers feel that federal judges are better than state judges.[3] Although this is not a universally held belief, some lawyers prefer going to federal courts if all other matters are equal because they have more confidence in the professional qualifications of the judge. However, the known prejudices of the judge may also affect the choice of court. It is no accident, for instance, that almost all civil rights suits brought by blacks in the South in the 1950s and 1960s were taken to federal courts, while most suits by whites against blacks or black sympathizers were taken to state courts. State judges in the South are elected and during that period often ran on explicitly racist platforms. Black litigants knew they could find no justice in the state court; for the same reason, white litigants preferred to be there.[4]

The opportunity to choose a court because of the known predisposition of the judge occurs only rarely; in most cases, the biases of judges are not known with enough certainty to make a choice between them.

Frequently, the rules of procedure available in the state or federal court force the choice. Federal courts have far more liberal rules of prior disclosure than many state courts, and the rules of evidence are often somewhat simpler. Therefore, many lawyers prefer to operate in the federal court when they can. On the other hand, certain lawyers, especially in small towns, may be more familiar with the rules of their local state court and prefer to operate within the safety of the more familiar courtroom rather than venture into a strange arena.

Still another factor in choosing a court is the delay that may be anticipated before the case is heard. In the same city, one court may have a clogged docket that necessitates a wait of three to five years; another court may be almost current, so that a trial may be expected within six months. Since most plaintiffs are eager to win quickly, their attorneys will file in the speedy court, if all else is equal, whereas defendants may seek to have the case transferred to a court with a greatly delayed docket.

[3] Kristin Bumiller, "Choice of Forum in Diversity Cases," *Law and Society Review*, 15 (1980–81), 749–74; Marvin R. Summers, "Analysis of Factors That Influence Choice of Forum in Diversity Cases," *Iowa Law Review*, 47 (1962), 937.

[4] Kenneth N. Vines, "Southern State Supreme Courts and Race Relations," *Western Political Quarterly*, 18 (1965), 5–18.

Finally, the relative convenience of the location for litigants and their lawyers may be an important consideration in the choice of a court. State courts are scattered throughout the country. Most are as close as the nearest county seat. Federal courts are located in only the one or two major cities of a state, so litigants must either travel to the court or wait until it comes to their own or a nearby town during its circuit travels. Often the court comes to a litigant's locale only once or twice a year. Thus, the litigant must wait to go to federal court and may win a quicker hearing at a local court.[5]

We have little empirical evidence to show which of these factors is most important in the choice of a tribunal. The litigant generally has little voice in the matter; the decision rests with the attorney who handles the case. Choosing the right court in which to file a suit is clearly one of the most important decisions an attorney must make. The wrong choice may mean certain defeat or costly delay for the client.

A dispute is brought to court by the plaintiff in the form of a complaint that specifies certain allegations.[6] The plaintiff must not only allege that he has been done a wrong but also establish that the court has jurisdiction to rule on it and can provide a remedy. The complaint is then served on the defendant, who is given some time to answer the allegations. His attorney does so in the form of an answer denying the allegations made by the plaintiff; sometimes the defendant also alleges wrongdoing by the plaintiff.

When all complaints have drawn an answer and all pleadings have been filed, the issue is said to be joined. The attorneys for each side are likely to appear in court relatively soon thereafter to argue preliminary motions. The motions may request the judge to allow the plaintiff or the defendant to interrogate the other party and that party's witnesses, or they may allege that the court lacks jurisdiction and the case should be dismissed. After pre-

---

[5] For an extended discussion of how such factors were once used by some lawyers in Chicago, see Albert Lepawsky, *The Judicial System of Metropolitan Chicago* (Chicago: University of Chicago Press, 1932), pp. 43–65.

[6] A simplified description of civil procedures can be found in Lewis Mayers, *The American Legal System*, rev. ed. (New York: Harper & Row, 1964), pp. 225–88.

liminary motions have been heard, the case typically remains in a dormant state for several months while attorneys for each party prepare their cases. In many large cities the wait may last several years. Each week or month the court publishes a list indicating which cases will be heard if they are ready. If a case is called for trial but one attorney is not ready or is busy with another case, a continuance may be granted. Continuances may delay the case for months.

During the delay between completion of the pleadings and trial of the case, negotiations often take place. It is incumbent upon attorneys to attempt an out-of-court settlement. Indeed, many cases are filed with no intention of pressing them to trial. Filing a case only shows a litigant to be willing to go to trial as a last resort; the litigant usually expects to arrange a settlement much sooner. The courts are thus often used as a bluff to expedite private settlements of disputes. More than three-quarters of the cases that are filed do not get beyond the preliminary stages.[7]

An elaborate subculture, resembling the one that surrounds plea bargaining in the criminal process, governs the negotiating of settlements in civil suits. In personal injury cases, for instance, insurance adjusters are eager to settle; their companies judge them on the speed with which they close cases. Plaintiffs who are represented by attorneys generally win much larger settlements than those who handle their own negotiations. The amount of the settlement is not governed by strict legal standards; rather, adjusters and attorneys decide on settlements by generally accepted rules of thumb that provide the injured party with medical expenses, plus three to five times more money to compensate for pain and suffering. When the defendant is not clearly liable, the settlement is smaller.[8]

---

[7] In the federal courts during 1980, 43 percent of all terminated civil actions were settled without any court action; another 35 percent were settled before a pretrial conference was held; and 14 percent were settled at the pretrial conference. Only 7.7 percent of all cases reached trial. *Statistical Abstract, 1981, op. cit.*, table 323, p. 186. The record of state courts is comparable.

[8] H. Laurence Ross, *Settled Out of Court* (Chicago: Aldine, 1970), especially pp. 136–231.

In recent years many courts have tried to expedite the settlement of cases through pretrial conferences.[9] Before being scheduled for trial in these courts, the case is discussed at a conference between attorneys in the presence of a judge, often the trial judge. Such pretrial conferences have several objectives, one of which is to simplify the case so that it takes as little time as possible in the courtroom. For instance, many facts are not disputed by either side. Instead of calling witnesses, both sides stipulate the undisputed facts by agreement; these stipulations are then entered into the record. Judges also attempt to simplify the disputed issues at trial. To make their cases impressive to clients and the court and to ensure themselves against surprises, many attorneys pack their pleadings with extraneous legal issues. At pretrial conferences, judges try to clear away such underbrush by encouraging each attorney to strike from the case those issues that will not actually be raised. At these conferences, each attorney also acquires a feel for the other's case.

Finally, judges will ask whether the attorneys have tried to negotiate a settlement. Often judges will suggest a particular amount that they think is reasonable, based on their experience with similar cases that did go to trial. Such suggestions from the judge may be enough to bring about a settlement.

Both economic and practical considerations reinforce judges' pressure to settle. In many cases the plaintiffs' lawyers are compensated by contingency fees. If they win their cases, they receive from 25 to 40 percent of the award; if they lose, they receive nothing. The less time lawyers give to a case in preparation, the more advantageous it is for them to accept a settlement, as long as it is not absurdly low. If the difference between a settlement award and a trial award is only a few thousand dollars, it does not pay a lawyer to push the case to trial. Moreover, many lawyers are not accustomed to practice in court; most of their work is done in their offices. If forced to go to trial, these lawyers may find it necessary to retain a trial specialist. Attorneys avoid much

[9] See Maurice Rosenberg, *The Pre-Trial Conference and Effective Justice* (New York: Columbia University Press, 1964), for a description of the pretrial conference and an analysis of its impact. See also the discussion in Chap. 6.

trouble and expense when they convince their clients that a pre-trial settlement should be accepted.

If no settlement is reached, the case becomes one of the small proportion that go to trial. Although jury trials are constitutionally guaranteed for many cases in both federal and state courts, most litigants waive the jury trial and choose to have a judge alone hear the case. This is particularly true for complex commercial cases, in which the lawyers for both sides hesitate to entrust their affairs to jurors who know little or nothing about the business involved. In automobile accident cases, however, many plaintiffs prefer a jury trial, hoping that the jury will be more liberal than the judge. In neither case does the trial have much of the drama shown on television or the stage. Because in many courts civil procedure allows for a good deal of pretrial probing of the other side's position, few surprises occur. Also, with no jury, few occasions arise for histrionics or dramatic appeals.

When a jury is used, it usually decides the case in its entirety — that is, it determines not only whether one party or the other was wrong but also the amount of damages, if any, that should be awarded. When a judge hears the case without a jury, he makes both decisions.

Although there are some civil courts with simplified procedures for handling small claims, most civil proceedings (including many in small claims courts) are too complex for the ordinary person to manage by himself. Civil proceedings involve a maze of jurisdictions, procedures, and deadlines; they almost always require the assistance of a professional. Indeed, the decision of whether or not to go to court is one that the layperson often cannot make intelligently alone.

Who Sues?

The courts are theoretically available to everyone, but only a few use them. Most people settle their disputes without any reference to courts or perhaps even to law. Many real and imagined wrongs are simply accepted: one learns to live with a neighbor's fence that encroaches on one's property by six inches. One decides never again to use a repair shop that cheats its customers; accepting is often easier than suing. Rather than asking for a divorce, some spouses run away. Other disputes are settled in the barroom or in the alley with fisticuffs; still others are settled by elaborate private settlement procedures, such as those involved in labor contract negotiations or arbitration proceedings between businesses. Only a small residue of disputes comes to court.[10]

One important determinant of whether a case comes to court is whether the court offers an appropriate remedy. Can the court do something worthwhile for the plaintiff that he cannot obtain more readily otherwise? In some instances, such as adoptions, courts enjoy a monopoly over the remedy; they alone may certify the transfer of parental rights and obligations. One can have a child live at one's home and treat the child as one's own without a formal adoption, but if a dispute later arises the lack of a formal adoption proceeding will become important. Debt collections are a class of cases in which courts offer especially convenient remedies. Without a court order, creditors must rely on their own efforts to collect what is owed. With a court order, they can use the sheriff to seize the debtor's wages or property, and this remedy is an enormously attractive incentive for bringing bad-debt cases to court.

Appropriate remedies, however, are not always available, and when they are, they are sometimes too cumbersome or expensive to make them worthwhile for many litigants. Tenants, for instance, cannot readily force landlords to repair their apartments; the law is mostly on the side of landlords. The time and the expense involved in going to court make it easier for the tenant to carry out the repair himself or to move to another building. Consumers who refuse to pay their debts because they feel they have been defrauded by the merchant usually find it difficult to prove their case in court. Proof that a product was faulty or that promised services were not delivered has often disappeared by the time the dispute becomes serious enough for the consumer to consider court action. Sometimes the fraud is simply beyond the reach of a single consumer to uncover, as in cases where rigged bidding on repossessed property results in a low sales price, forcing the debtor to sell the property for less than the debt

---

[10] Leon H. Mayhew, "Institutions of Representation: Civil Justice and the Public," *Law and Society Review*, 9 (1975), 413.

and leaving a large balance still owed. If the fraud were proved, the consumer might wipe out the debt through court action; but without investing the expense and time of proving the fraud, no remedy is available. Indeed, consumers who cannot pay lawyer and court fees for a bankruptcy action cannot even take advantage of the bankruptcy laws to protect themselves against overwhelming debts.

Even if legal remedies exist, people must know about them and have the resources to use them. Few people have extensive legal information; the amount of legal knowledge is closely related to an individual's level of education. It is also associated with the information network into which the person happens to be linked. For instance, debtors who have contacts with attorneys or with other debtors because their wages have been seized through garnishments are more likely to know about personal bankruptcy as a remedy to their problem than are run-of-the-mill debtors struggling to make their payments on time.[11] In general, persons who consult attorneys already know more about legal remedies than those who do not. As we have seen in Chapter 4, such services are mostly available to the poor and to the middle and upper classes; working people who do not qualify for legal aid but do not have money to spare on lawyers are the least likely to avail themselves of legal assistance or to have information about possible court remedies.

Many potential disputes do not come to court because of the peculiar stance of the legal profession with regard to seeking out clients. The bar severely condemns active pursuit of litigation. Such behavior is considered "ambulance chasing" and is prohibited by the Code of Professional Responsibility. Unlike those in almost every other occupation or profession, attorneys must sit in their offices and wait for clients to come to them. This passive stance reinforces the information network that favors potential upper-middle-class clients and those who happen to know about legal aid.[12]

Attorneys are the gatekeepers to the courts in civil matters, and those who cannot obtain the services of lawyers usually can-

[11] Herbert Jacob, *Debtors in Court* (Chicago: Rand McNally, 1969), pp. 56–65.

[12] Mayhew, *op. cit.*, pp. 416–26.

not use the courts. Only small claims can be handled effectively without an attorney, and even with these it is often more advantageous to be represented by a lawyer than to attempt to handle the case by oneself.[13]

The distribution of some of these informational and attitudinal factors in Milwaukee is shown in Figure 10.1. In every instance, ghetto blacks felt greater barriers to use of the courts than whites; in turn, more poorly educated and lower-income whites — those in working-class neighborhoods — felt more inhibited than middle-class whites. Large numbers in each group perceived attorneys to be costly and felt these costs were an obstacle to litigation, even under otherwise favorable circumstances.

Whether or not someone brings a complaint to court is also determined by the plaintiff's relationship to the defendant. The closer and more enduring the relationship, the less likely it is that the courts will be used, or, if they are used, they are used only as a last resort. By bringing a case to court, the parties publicize their dispute and take established positions, making it much more difficult to reconcile differences and to continue their relationship after the dispute has been settled by court action. Moreover, court action tends to result in a winner-take-all decision rather than in a compromise, which also makes subsequent relationships more difficult. Consequently, many personal disputes do not come to court, even when the courts offer suitable remedies that the potential parties know about. Rather, most of the conflicts that come to court are between strangers or involve individuals and large companies. For instance, disputes about compensation for automobile accident injuries typically involve strangers who never saw each other before their cars collided and probably will never encounter each other again. Also involved is an insurance company, which has an enduring but impersonal relationship with only one of the parties. Suits brought to collect bad debts often involve an individual and a large firm.

---

[13] David Caplovitz, *Consumers in Trouble* (New York: Free Press, 1974), pp. 222–24. Barbara Yngvesson and Patricia Hennessey, "Small Claims, Complex Disputes: A Review of the Small Claims Literature," *Law and Society Review*, 9 (1975), 250–51; Ross, *op. cit.*, pp. 193–98, 205–30; Austin Sarat, "Alternatives in Dispute Processing: Litigation in a Small Claims Court," *Law and Society Review*, 10 (1976), 349–52.

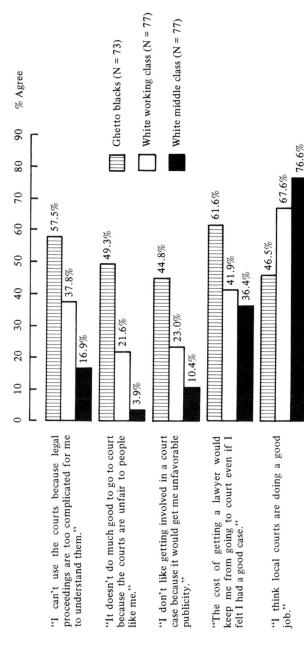

% Agree

Ghetto blacks (N = 73)

White working class (N = 77)

White middle class (N = 77)

"I can't use the courts because legal proceedings are too complicated for me to understand them."

57.5%
37.8%
16.9%

"It doesn't do much good to go to court because the courts are unfair to people like me."

49.3%
21.6%
3.9%

"I don't like getting involved in a court case because it would get me unfavorable publicity."

44.8%
23.0%
10.4%

"The cost of getting a lawyer would keep me from going to court even if I felt I had a good case."

61.6%
41.9%
36.4%

"I think local courts are doing a good job."

46.5%
67.6%
76.6%

FIGURE 10.1

Attitudes toward Courts and Litigation among Three Milwaukee Samples

Source: Random sample in three Milwaukee neighborhoods in 1969. For details, see Herbert Jacob, "Contact with Government Agencies: A Preliminary Analysis of the Distribution of Government Services," *Midwest Journal of Political Science,* 16 (1972), pp. 127–29.

When the creditor is a small business or a professional like a doctor, and if the creditor values the relationship with the debtor, the debt is typically sold to a collection agent, who interposes his impersonal presence and actually invokes the court process.[14]

These determinants working together produce a biased sample of disputes for court resolution; one cannot judge society's disputes from those that come to court. The sample is also biased in favor of large organizations and individuals with financial resources.[15] Thus, the courts, although theoretically open to everyone, are in fact more the instruments of the upper classes and the relatively strong than they are the bulwarks of the poor. In many instances, wealthy individuals and organizations use the courts against the poor; often they use the courts in disputes among themselves.

Legal aid has not thus far made the courts a resource of the poor to a significant degree. Most of the cases handled by legal aid are either family matters (the poor against the poor) or defense against claims by landlords, merchants, or government agencies. Even with legal aid, the poor rarely use the courts aggressively as plaintiffs to assert their claims. An important exception is when a legal aid organization takes on a case to establish a new principle of law that might assist many other poor clients. Particularly in the realm of consumer debts, legal aid groups have been successful in winning new requirements for hearings before repossession of goods bought on conditional sales contracts (for example, cars) and in limiting confession of judgment in sales contracts, a device by which the buyer surrenders all defenses against the creditor at the time the sale is made. Such decisions have made it easier for both the poor and consumers in general to defend themselves in collection cases, but they have not yet enabled poor people to become more aggressive users of court services.

Who Benefits from Civil Proceedings?

Courts dispense two kinds of benefits. The first results from systematic favoritism to one kind of litigant or another — some

---

[14] Jacob, *op. cit.*, p. 82.
[15] Craig Wanner, "The Public Ordering of Private Relations," *Law and Society Review*, 8 (1974), 423–25.

parties almost always win and others almost always lose. The second, more subtle, benefit comes from the ability of disputants to use a forum maintained at public expense to seek a settlement that allows them to maintain their ongoing relationship. The benefit here lies in the social and economic stability that may be fostered by the settlements that courts induce.

Systematic favoritism in the courts results from differential patterns of access to the courts. The poor are more often defendants than plaintiffs, and in the most numerous cases — those involving indebtedness — plaintiffs usually win.[16] The stakes for defendants are high. In housing courts, defendants stand to be evicted from their apartment for nonpayment of rent; in small claims courts they are threatened with loss of a substantial part of their wages or their property for nonpayment of a debt. Although the due-process rituals of the adversarial process should protect them against unscrupulous complaints, they rarely do so.

Many debtors never receive notice that a creditor has gone to court against them. Many of those who receive notice do not bother to go to court to file an answer; those who do are often discouraged by the court clerk from pursuing the matter. Most of those who file an answer find that their answer is inadequate, and they become subject to a default judgment. Trials are extremely rare: out of 308 cases studied in Chicago, seven went to trial; in Detroit three out of 387 probably went to trial; in New York, none of the 328 cases were tried within three years of filing. In each city the debtors lost their cases by default in 90 percent of the cases; 5 to 7 percent of the remainder were settled in other ways favorable to the creditor; the settlement that was probably favorable to the debtor occurred in only 4 to 5 percent of the cases.[17] Most of these debtors, of course, had no legal excuse for not paying their debts. However, about 20 percent claimed a reason for not paying that might have been upheld by a court, such as fraud, deception, or accounting mistakes by the creditor.[18] But these claims by defendants almost never reached a courtroom.

---

[16] Craig Wanner, "The Public Ordering of Private Relations, Part Two: Winning Civil Court Cases," *Law and Society Review*, 9 (1975), 295; Yngvesson and Hennessey, *op. cit.*, p. 243.

[17] Caplovitz, *op. cit.*, pp. 216–21.

[18] *Ibid.*, p. 53.

Such extreme biases do not exist in other types of civil court-room proceedings. Many cases produce no obvious set of winners or losers, but their social and economic significance is readily apparent. Some examples make that evident.

No industry is more important to the postindustrial development of the United States than the computer industry. For many years, it was dominated by International Business Machines, Inc. In the late 1960s and early 1970s, several of IBM's competitors and the federal government took it to court, alleging violations of the antitrust laws. These actions initiated a period of litigation that lasted more than a decade. The trial considering the federal government's charges alone took more than five years. Finally, in 1981, with a new conservative administration in the White House and after the trial had been finished (but no decision announced), the Justice Department dropped its case and, in effect, exonerated IBM. The company had also settled its other suits on generally favorable terms. Although the litigation was enormously expensive for IBM, the government, and the other parties, it provided an important means for clearing the air around the development of this essential industry. It siphoned the dispute from more partisan channels and eventually led to a "settlement" that permitted both IBM and its many competitors to put their relationship on a new footing.

In another case at about the same time, the Westinghouse Corporation found itself in a terrible predicament. To help it sell its nuclear reactors to electrical utilities, the company had contracted to sell enriched uranium fuel to the utilities at prices ranging from $6 to $8 a pound. However, after the Arab oil boycott of 1973, uranium prices skyrocketed. By the time they had reached $18, Westinghouse decided to try to weasel out of its contracts. The company had on hand only 15 million of the 80 million pounds of uranium it had contracted to sell. For every dollar that the price of uranium rose, Westinghouse stood to lose $65 million; if it bought the remainder at market prices, it might be forced into bankruptcy. The company therefore notified its customers that it was defaulting on its contracts on the ground of "commercial impracticability," an escape clause in the Uniform Commercial Code that had previously been applied to such things as acts of war but never to large price rises that a seller had failed to anticipate. The utilities naturally sued. The litigation that followed did not last as long as the IBM suits, and Westinghouse lost its bid to invoke "impracticability," but the courts managed to convince the utilities to negotiate a settlement with Westinghouse that would reimburse them for some of their losses but not destroy the company as a viable provider of electrical equipment. Westinghouse also discovered the existence of a uranium cartel, which was responsible for at least part of the price rise, and was able to negotiate a damage settlement from some of the cartel's members. The court cases did not settle the Westinghouse dispute but were an important ingredient in the negotiations that did.[19]

An even more complicated case involves the potential liability of asbestos manufacturers for the illnesses of users of asbestos materials. The fact that asbestos may cause cancer was not discovered until many years after it was first manufactured. By the early 1980s, hundreds of millions of dollars of law suits were being filed against asbestos manufacturers; no one knew what the total liability claims might be. Once more, the courts were called in. Several of the manufacturers decided to seek the protection of the courts in bankruptcy proceedings, even though they were technically solvent. Because the claims threatened them with actual bankruptcy, they sought to invoke bankruptcy to settle all the claims at once in the hope that they might then survive as commercial enterprises. The outcome of this case may well involve more partisan arenas; it may require legislative as well as judicial remedies for addressing the larger issue of who is to pay for "externalities" — the unintended byproducts of an industrial process.

It is difficult to pinpoint winners and losers in such litigation. From some perspectives, every party loses because of the high costs of conducting such cases. From another perspective, there are many winners, because the outcome typically involves compromise settlements rather than winner-take-all decisions. The principal winner, however, is usually the society at large. Conflicts that might otherwise fester or fundamentally disrupt nec-

[19] For a description of the IBM and Westinghouse litigations, see James B. Stewart, *The Partners* (New York: Simon and Schuster, 1983), pp. 53–113 and 152–200.

essary relationships are brought to a forum that commands respect and that manages to foster at least a temporary settlement.

The Impact of Reform on Civil Justice

As in the criminal justice system, the winds of reform are gently blowing through the civil courts. Reformers have mostly focused on changes in the substantive law rather than in alterations of court proceedings. Two changes have been particularly prominent: the institution of no-fault automobile insurance and the establishment of no-fault divorce.[20]

No-fault automobile insurance is designed to take out of court many of the personal injury cases that clogged the civil courts' dockets. Under no-fault laws, accidents leading to relatively minor injuries cannot be brought to court; rather, the injured party's own insurance company must provide compensation for medical expenses. The laws severely limit compensation for pain and suffering. Only when a major injury occurs may the victim go to court and sue the other driver if he was at fault. Because most accidents involve relatively small medical bills, such no-fault insurance eliminates many cases from court dockets and reduces the temptation of litigants and their lawyers to balloon claims on the basis of pain and suffering. The aim of this reform was both to make automobile insurance cheaper and to reduce litigation. Both objectives appear to be partially met in those states that have adopted no-fault insurance; however, the difference between no-fault states and those with the old liability system appears to be less significant than the proponents of no-fault had hoped.

Although divorce proceedings did not contribute to the clogged dockets of civil courts, they often gave rise to corruption and added painful conflict to the already difficult trauma involved in many divorce proceedings. Under traditional American law, divorce could only be obtained by one spouse proving that the other had committed some marriage-breaking act, such as adultery, mental cruelty, desertion, or one of the other misbehaviors specified by state law. If both parties had committed such

---

[20] Note that these reforms are analogous to proposals in the criminal arena to decriminalize certain offenses such as marijuana use.

acts, a divorce could be denied. As a consequence, most uncontested divorces rested on an agreed-upon script in which the husband usually accepted responsibility for having broken up the marriage and the wife appeared faultless in court. In New York, where divorce could only be obtained upon proof of adultery, hotel rendezvous with models clad in black undergarments were staged, with photographers on hand to provide the proof required by the court. In New York, the only alternative to such perjury was an expensive trip to a state like Nevada, where divorce was easy to obtain.[21]

No-fault divorce, or dissolution of the marriage, as it is often called, avoids these stratagems.[22] All that the law requires is that husband and wife show that the marriage is no longer viable; no particular misbehavior needs to be proven. It makes no difference who is at fault; indeed, the law recognizes that it may be impossible to blame one party or another for a process that probably took place over several months or years. If spouses do not contest the division of property or the custody of children, there is often no need to go before a judge. The entire proceeding is removed from the courts. With no-fault divorce, only contested issues are brought before the courts.

Less-publicized reforms of the civil courts have attempted to deal with congested dockets and court delay by altering court procedures. The greatest attention has been focused on increasing settlement rates by requiring pretrial conferences. This reform, however, has not substantially reduced the delay that many litigants face when they file their case in court. The delay in most jurisdictions is still more than a year, and in some it is more than three years. Such delays are particularly harmful to potential litigants who require swift remedies but whose cases cannot qualify for expedited action. For instance, the personal-injury victim who falls further and further into debt as he meets medical bills on credit lives with the constant anxiety that he will not be compensated adequately. By contrast, a litigant, generally a corporation or organization, seeking injunctive relief can generally obtain court action within ten days of filing by showing that

---

[21] Hubert J. O'Gorman, *Lawyers and Matrimonial Cases* (New York: Free Press of Glencoe, 1963), pp. 20–25, discusses an extreme case of these conditions.
[22] Michael Wheeler, *No Fault Divorce* (Boston: Beacon Press, 1974).

irremedial harm will be done if the court does not act at once. Thus, the cost of delay often falls hardest on those least able to bear it. For only a few is the delay an advantage.

Conclusions

Do civil proceedings benefit the rich more than the poor, or do they tend to equalize the economic and social differences that litigants bring to court with them? In debt collection and housing cases, civil proceedings do little to erase existing inequalities; one might even argue that they exacerbate them by providing landlords and creditors with powerful weapons to enforce unfair private agreements. The powers of the state are lent to landlords and creditors for their private purposes. The safeguards inherent in court proceedings are rarely invoked in these cases. On the other hand, civil courts do not discriminate against the poor in most other types of proceedings, and they sometimes provide unique opportunities to correct wrongs and induce settlements of important conflicts that are unreachable through other parts of the political process. The civil rights gains of blacks in the South in the 1960s and in northern cities in the 1970s were largely due to court interventions; the same policies could not be obtained through pressure on locally elected executives. Similarly, important changes in consumer law resulted from litigation brought on behalf of poor clients by legal aid attorneys. The conflicting claims of economic giants are also routinely processed in civil courts.

The major criticism of the work of civil courts is that access to them is restricted by distrust, ignorance, and cost. The "haves" know how to manipulate legal proceedings and have the resources to do so. The "have-nots" can rarely bring their case to trial, where they might benefit from the rules of due process; rather, they fall by the wayside in the preliminaries. The process begins when the poor sign contracts that are fundamentally disadvantageous to them and that often waive rights that might be significant in later litigation. Thus, discrimination against the poor in civil proceedings is caused as much by substantive law and prelitigation relationships as by prejudicial court procedures.

11
Appellate Proceedings

Appeals culminate the judicial process. They are the last decision point within the judiciary; they provide many legal doctrines and rules that ostensibly govern the courts and define the meaning of law. For a long time, appellate proceedings were the only portion of the judicial process that concerned law students and legal scholars. Most now recognize that appellate decisions have only a limited impact and that the law that affects most people is the law that results from bargaining and negotiation in and around trial courts. Nevertheless, appellate proceedings remain significant because legal doctrines and policy decisions are formulated there. Those doctrines and policies set the boundaries for informal negotiations. The impact of appellate decisions may be slow and indirect, but it is substantial.

Appellate proceedings differ from trials in many ways. They require additional resources, different rules apply, and different participants take part. Appellate courts hear cases usually after the completion of a trial; criminal cases compromised through bargains and civil cases settled out of court cannot ordinarily be appealed. In addition, appellate courts hear only some of the cases decided by trial, because many litigants become weary of the judicial process and accept the trial decision as final.

Consequently, cases brought to appellate courts are unrepresentative of the issues tried by trial courts. When cases come to an appeals court, the attorneys emphasize issues of legal policy rather than narrow fact.[1] The higher the court in the judicial hierarchy, the greater is the proportion of policy conflicts and the smaller the proportion of norm-enforcement cases.

Appellate courts do not all hear the same kinds of cases, nor do they all operate under the same rules. Gross differences are especially apparent between the operations of the federal courts of appeals, the state supreme courts, and the United States Supreme Court.

Federal Courts of Appeals

The twelve courts of appeals hear all appeals from federal district courts and from the decisions of certain administrative and regulatory agencies; in exceptional circumstances, they exercise original jurisdiction over a case. About one out of every four contested judgments by federal district courts goes to the courts of appeals.[2] In 1980, 19,259 cases from federal district courts as well as almost 3,000 appeals from administrative agencies were heard by the courts of appeals.[3] These statistics represent a sixfold increase in the work load of the appeals courts since 1960. Criminal appeals increased seven times and appeals in civil cases increased more than six times, producing severe stress on the appeals courts. The high level of appeals reflects both the Warren Court's broader interpretation of the rights of criminal defendants and the willingness of litigants in civil suits to spend the money necessary to pursue appeals.

[1] Richard J. Richardson and Kenneth N. Vines, "Review, Dissent and the Appellate Process: A Political Interpretation," in Herbert Jacob (ed.), *Law, Politics, and the Federal Courts* (Boston: Little, Brown, 1967), pp. 109–24.

[2] Jerry Goldman, "Federal District Courts and the Appellate Crisis," *Judicature*, 57 (1973), 211–12, and J. Woodford Howard, Jr., "The Flow of Litigation in the U.S. Courts of Appeals for the Second, Fifth, and District of Columbia Circuits" (Washington, D.C.: Federal Judicial Center, Research Report No. 3, n.d.), pp. 14–15.

[3] U.S. Bureau of the Census, *Statistical Abstract of the United States, 1981* (Washington, D.C.: Government Printing Office, 1981), table 320, p. 185.

The courts of appeals each operate with several judges. The largest court has twenty-three judges; the smallest has four. In some, the judges do not all reside in one city. For instance, in the Ninth Circuit Court of Appeals, which covers much of the West, some judges live in Honolulu and others in Alaska. Most reside in California, but some also live in Arizona, Oregon, and Washington. Although the judges are often widely dispersed, they meet in groups of three to hear cases; for, unlike trials, appeals are heard by panels of judges. There is never a jury in an appellate proceeding.

The courts of appeals must hear all appeals brought to them from district courts. Under federal law every litigant has the right to one appeal. The court has no power to refuse an appeal, even if the judges feel that it is unimportant or lacks all legal merit.

Although all federal litigants may appeal, the federal courts of appeals disproportionately hear cases involving the government. In three courts studied by J. Woodford Howard, the government was involved on one side or the other in half of the appeals outside of the District of Columbia, whereas in D.C. it was involved in more than 70 percent.[4]

Appeals are limited by the psychological and material costs associated with carrying a conflict to the appellate stage. Court fees are only an insignificant part of these costs, for they are quite nominal and may be waived for indigents. Other costs, however, limit the availability of appeals, even to those litigants who possess considerable resources.[5] Attorneys usually demand additional fees to carry a case to an appellate court. Often the trial attorney retires from the case, and a new lawyer must be retained. Appeals are argued on the basis of the trial record, so that a litigant who wishes to appeal must pay for the transcription of the record from the stenographer's notes and its reproduction for court use. Although it is no longer necessary to transcribe or print the whole record in federal courts of appeals, transcription and

[4] J. Woodford Howard, Jr., *Courts of Appeals in the Federal Judicial System* (Princeton, N.J.: Princeton University Press, 1981), p. 28.

[5] Bertram F. Willcox, Delmar Karlen, and Ruth Roemer, "Justice Lost — What Appellate Papers Cost," *New York University Law Review*, 33 (1958), 934–74; Arthur T. Vanderbilt, *Minimum Standards of Judicial Administration* (New York: Law Center of New York University, 1949), pp. 415–29.

reproduction of even part of the record of a trial can be expensive. In criminal appeals the cost of the transcript will be paid by the government for indigents. All other appellants must pay for the transcripts themselves or forego their right to appeal. In addition, the lawyer preparing an appeal must write a brief, in which he argues the merits of his case. This brief — often running to more than one hundred pages — must also be reproduced, usually by printing, for the use of the court.

The psychological strain attached to appealing a case may be as important as monetary cost. Appeals delay final decisions. A single appeal can add six to eighteen months to the total time required to hear a case. In many instances, even the losing party prefers the certain knowledge that he has lost to continued uncertainty about the outcome. By the time a trial has been held, many litigants suffer from "battle fatigue"; they are happy to conclude the case and go on to other matters. Consequently, even though an appeal is available, most litigants appeal only when the litigation concerns an issue that is vital to them.

Although the courts of appeal must receive all cases brought to them, they can no longer give all of them the complete attention they once received. Increasingly, the courts employ staff attorneys to prepare memoranda that help the judges screen some cases for full review and make decisions on others. These staff attorneys are anonymous civil servants; their work is supervised by the court, but the attorneys themselves are invisible to the general public. Many cases are disposed of summarily without oral argument and without full participation by the courts' judges.[6]

When cases are given the full treatment, they are considered by panels of three judges.[7] Unless the court has only three judges, judges are not permanently assigned to a particular panel. The chief judge of the court changes the composition of the panels frequently, with the result that permanent cliques within the court are less likely to emerge. Litigants have no way of knowing which judges will hear their appeal.

[6] Howard, *Courts of Appeals*, pp. 198, 278–79.
[7] *Ibid.*, p. 9; "The Second Circuit: Federal Judicial Administration in Microcosm," *Columbia Law Review*, 63 (1963), 874–908, provides a detailed description of the procedures of this court.

The judges work from the briefs, the record of the trial, and the oral arguments before the court. At the oral argument, each side is allotted time (as little as twenty minutes) to argue the case before the judges.[8] The time may be spent in a short speech by the attorney; more frequently, however, the judges will interrupt to ask questions to help them decide the case. After the oral argument the judges may confer briefly; if they are in agreement, they may announce their decision immediately. If they are not, they reserve decision until they meet in conference. In some courts of appeals the undecided cases are resolved only after all three judges have written memoranda stating their separate views. On the basis of these memoranda, the judges confer and reach an agreement. The decision is then announced, together with any dissent from the minority on the court. In some cases, the decision is accompanied by a written opinion explaining and justifying it. In an increasing number of cases, however, no opinion is written, or the opinion remains unpublished and may not be cited in future arguments.[9]

The court of appeals decision in most instances is final.[10] If, as is most common, the court affirms the trial court's decision, it orders the trial court to execute it. If it reverses the original decision, a new trial may have to be held. Only a few cases are carried forward to the United States Supreme Court.

The work of the courts of appeals serves several functions in the American judicial system. Since every litigant has the right to one appeal, the courts sometimes help to avert gross miscarriages of justice and ensure fair trials. Every trial court knows that its decision may be reviewed, even though in fact few are. Trial judges are proud of their record when few of their decisions have been reversed, and they are sensitive to the criticism implicit in frequent reversals of their judgments.[11] The success of trial judges in avoiding overrulings varies greatly. For instance,

---

[8] "The Second Circuit," op. cit., pp. 887–88. For details, see James E. Langner and Steven Flanders, "Comparative Report on Internal Operating Procedures of U.S. Courts of Appeal" (Washington, D.C.: Federal Judicial Center, July, 1973, mimeo).

[9] Howard, Courts of Appeals, pp. 279–80.

[10] Jerry Goldman, "Jurisdictional Politics and the Federal Courts" (unpubl. Ph.D. dissertation, Johns Hopkins University, 1974), pp. 47–49.

[11] Richardson and Vines, op cit.

Judge Hunter of the Western District of Louisiana was overruled in only 8.6% of the cases appealed to the Fifth Circuit between 1965 and 1967. At the same time, Judge Mize of the Southern District of Mississippi was overruled in 51.7% of his cases that were appealed.[12] The availability of appellate courts thus helps to procure fair trials for some litigants who might otherwise not receive them.

The courts of appeals also make the administration of justice and the interpretation of laws more uniform throughout the country. District courts are closely tied to the community in which they are located; their decisions sometimes reflect local biases. Appellate courts cover a whole region; their decisions are less likely to reflect local prejudices, as the action of the Fifth Circuit Court of Appeals in civil rights cases has dramatically demonstrated. Southern federal district judges working in the 1950s often ruled in favor of segregationist white litigants, who held the more popular views in their districts, even when Supreme Court rulings left little or no leeway for rulings adverse to black litigants, as in school desegregation cases. When such decisions were appealed to the Fifth Circuit, its decisions were more often in favor of the blacks.[13] Whereas 50 percent of the district court decisions in civil rights cases in the South were in favor of black litigants, 75 percent of the appellate court decisions in the South were in favor of blacks.[14]

In less controversial matters as well, the courts of appeals work to make the rulings of the several district courts more uniform. A judge in one district might interpret a federal tax statute one way; his neighboring judge in another district might interpret it in the opposite way. Few would dispute that justice should not depend on the location of the court. Appellate decisions reduce such differences in interpretation, because deviant decisions can usually be appealed and then reversed. In this way the courts of appeals play an important role in making the administration of

---

[12] Howard, *Courts of Appeals*, pp. 49–50.

[13] "Judicial Performance in the Fifth Circuit," *Yale Law Journal*, 73 (1963), 90–133.

[14] Kenneth N. Vines, "The Role of Circuit Courts of Appeals in the Federal Judicial Process: A Case Study," *Midwest Journal of Political Science*, 7 (1963), 310.

justice more uniform within a region. Nevertheless, the twelve courts of appeals may disagree with one another over the application of a norm or a policy. Such conflicts can be settled only by the United States Supreme Court.

State Appellate Courts

Much less is known about state appellate courts than about the federal courts of appeals or the United States Supreme Court. Available data indicate that many state appellate courts operate quite differently from federal appellate tribunals. In the thirty-two states with intermediate appellate courts, most appeals go to the intermediate court of appeals, which is manned by several judges, usually three, who hear the cases brought before them as a panel.[15] In the remaining states, appeals from trial courts go directly to the state supreme court.

All states possess a highest court of appeals, usually called a supreme court. Most state supreme courts have seven or nine justices; some have fewer (Delaware has only three).[16] Most courts sit *en banc*, with all justices participating, at least passively, in all cases.

The courts vary considerably in the choice that they have over cases to be heard.[17] Most states with intermediate courts of appeal limit the right to appeal to the intermediate court; if the supreme court wants to hear a case, it may do so as a matter of discretion, choosing its cases on the basis of its policy preferences. In the other states, the supreme court can exercise no choice. The judges must hear every case brought to them, whether they think it raises important issues or not, and whether it appears to have legal merit or not. In some states the jurisdiction of the supreme court is limited to appeals involving more

[15] For details on jurisdiction and organization see Marlin O. Osthus, *Intermediate Appellate Courts* (Chicago: American Judicature Society, 1976). For a description of two quite unusual state intermediate appellate courts, see Delmar Karlen, *Appellate Courts in the United States and England* (New York: New York University Press, 1963), pp. 11–29, and John B. Molinari, "The Decision-Making Conference of the California Court of Appeals," *California Law Review*, 57 (1969), 606 ff.

[16] *State Court Systems* (Chicago: Council of State Governments, 1976) provides organizational details of state supreme courts.

[17] Osthus, *op. cit.*, pp. 18–28.

than a minimum amount of money or to certain categories of cases.

Procedure before state supreme courts also varies.[18] Some courts require complete, printed transcripts of the trial and printed briefs. Some are satisfied with partial transcripts in typed form and typed briefs. Some have picayune rules for the form of the brief, its length, and even the size of the paper on which it is presented. Others have no such rules. Some use staff attorneys; others do not.

In most states, oral arguments resembling those of other appellate courts are held for many cases. A few states require a special request to the court before an oral argument will be permitted.[19] When arguments are not heard, the cases are decided on the briefs and the other documents that have been filed.

The principal procedural differences among state supreme courts are the ways in which the justices handle the cases. In some states each case comes to the attention of all of the supreme court judges: all read the briefs, participate in the oral arguments, and participate in the conference discussion of the case.[20] Only when the case has been decided by a vote of the justices is one justice assigned the task of writing the court's opinion. In other states — Michigan is one[21]— cases are given numbers when they are placed on the supreme court docket and assigned to a particular justice.[22] That justice alone is responsible for reading the briefs. Although other judges may participate in the oral argument, sometimes only the assigned justice does. After the argument, the justice assigned to the case writes a draft of the court's opinion; interested justices who disagree with the assigned justice may also draft an opinion. The drafts are then circulated to all of the justices; after a few days they confer on the drafts, hammer out one to which all (or a majority) can agree, and issue

[18] Vanderbilt, *op. cit.*, pp. 415–36.

[19] *Ibid.*, pp. 436–38.

[20] For instance, the New York Court of Appeals allows for participation by all the justices; Karlen, *op. cit.*, pp. 37–40.

[21] S. Sidney Ulmer, "Leadership in the Michigan Supreme Court," in Glendon Schubert (ed.), *Judicial Decision-Making* (New York: Free Press of Glencoe, 1963), pp. 16–17.

[22] For the other states and for evidence on the prevalence of one-man decisions by state supreme courts, see Vanderbilt, *op. cit.*, pp. 438–43.

it as the court's decision and opinion. Such a procedure, even though it permits participation by other justices, often promotes one-person decisions because the justices simply defer to the one who was assigned the case and wrote the opinion.

Cases are decided by majority vote of the justices. Those who disagree with the majority may simply note their dissent at the end of the case. They may also write a dissenting opinion in which they specify their reasons. Although the right to dissent is unquestioned in both the state and federal appellate courts, dissents are much less frequent on state supreme courts than on the federal Supreme Court.[23]

Brute voting force, however, is not the way decisions are made; persuasion and compromise dominate decision making. Only in Louisiana, of four states studied, was voting mentioned often as a means of reaching decisions.[24] The importance of personal interactions is further indicated by the characteristics that supreme court judges think important for colleagues to have. Pleasing personality, proper working habits, objectivity, and ethical personal conduct ranked ahead of scholarship.[25]

State supreme court judges usually cling more closely to established legal tradition and are less innovative than are federal Supreme Court justices. Except in New Jersey, of the four states examined, nonlegal factors are not considered "very important" by more than half the judges. More judges consider themselves law interpreters than lawmakers.[26]

It is therefore understandable that in recent years the most spectacular decisions have not been made by state supreme courts but by the United States Supreme Court. In addition to the innately conservative character of many state supreme courts, other forces have pushed them aside. Federal legislation has become more extensive, and more cases can be brought to the federal court system. Moreover, the Supreme Court has become in-

---

[23] Edward Ferguson III, "Some Comments on the Applicability of Bloc Analysis to State Appellate Courts" (paper delivered at the Midwest Conference of Political Scientists, 1961), pp. 12–13.

[24] Henry Robert Glick, *Supreme Courts in State Politics* (New York: Basic Books, 1971), p. 90. The others were New Jersey, Pennsylvania, and Massachusetts.

[25] *Ibid.*, p. 62.

[26] *Ibid.*, pp. 41, 83.

creasingly receptive to policy disputes that previously were settled by state supreme courts.

Nevertheless, state supreme courts play an important role in making policy decisions and participating in the state political system. On such matters as divorce law, personal injury litigation, and the powers of state and local officials (to name just a few), state supreme courts often make the final judicial decision. By doing so, such courts play a significant role in the policymaking process of their state.[27] Many other cases — perhaps most — involve the enforcement of norms and the gradual development of new law.

United States Supreme Court

No other court in the country matches the United States Supreme Court's prominence and political importance. It is the final adjudicatory body for all cases, whether they originate in state or federal courts. It also hears as the original tribunal a very small number of cases involving disputes between states. No judicial appeal is available beyond the Supreme Court.

Appellate cases may reach the Supreme Court by several routes.[28] They may be appealed from state courts, from federal courts of appeals, or from the special three-judge federal courts. Unlike most other appellate courts, the United States Supreme Court may choose the cases it wishes to hear. This is fortunate, because more than five thousand cases are filed with the Court every year. If the Court had to hear each of these, it could give careful attention to none.

In recent years, many Supreme Court justices have complained about the burden of their case load, which forces them to deal with many cases by summary procedures. Chief Justice Burger and other conservatives have suggested that these burdens are the consequence of the expansive interpretation of the Constitution by the Warren Court, especially with respect to civil

[27] Kenneth N. Vines, "Political Functions of a State Supreme Court," in Kenneth N. Vines and Herbert Jacob, *Studies in Judicial Politics*, Tulane Studies in Political Science, Vol. 8 (New Orleans: Tulane University, 1963), pp. 51–75.

[28] For a good discussion of the Supreme Court's jurisdiction and work load, see Stephen L. Wasby, *The Supreme Court in the Federal Judicial System* (New York: Holt, Rinehart and Winston, 1978), pp. 111–58.

liberties and the rights of defendants. However, the Court's own statistics show that, since Burger took office, criminal appeals have declined while appeals from private civil litigants have increased substantially.[29] Whatever the cause, Burger and other justices have suggested a variety of remedies, including establishing a new intermediary court to screen cases for the Supreme Court's consideration (thereby setting its agenda) or to hear cases in which several lower appellate courts have rendered conflicting decisions.

Because of its backbreaking potential workload, the Supreme Court selects its cases carefully.[30] Each request for a hearing, by petition for a writ of certiorari, a writ of appeal, or certification, goes to the office of the Chief Justice. Almost half the petitions come from paupers, usually prisoners in penitentiaries. These are investigated by the Chief Justice's law clerks, for the petitions are usually ill-prepared and cannot be evaluated on the basis of the evidence included in them. Other petitions come replete with the necessary records of previous court hearings, and these are circulated to the other eight justices. Each justice then examines (or has his law clerk examine) the petition. During a conference the justices vote on each petition for review. If four justices vote in favor of review, the case is docketed. If fewer justices favor review, the case is rejected, and the decision of the lower court stands.

When a case is accepted for review by the Supreme Court, the Court notifies the attorneys involved so that they can enter whatever additional briefs and materials they desire. Interest groups may also file briefs if they have the permission of the litigants or the Court. A few cases are scheduled for oral argument, but most are decided on the basis of the records that the attorneys supply without oral argument. The justices confer on the latter cases during their conferences and decide them with a very brief opinion. These are known as *per curiam* decisions. The opinion simply states the decision of the Court and cites other cases that supply some reasons for the Court's action.

Cases scheduled for oral argument are handled quite differently. The Court allows each side to speak for a specified period,

---

[29] The author is grateful to Thomas Y. Davies for pointing this out to him.
[30] Wasby, *op. cit.*

usually one hour but sometimes longer. Attorneys must be prepared to emphasize what they believe to be the strongest parts of their cases. They must also be prepared to answer whatever questions the justices may ask.[31] The questions seek to clarify difficult problems that bother particular justices in their contemplation of the case, and the attorney's answers sometimes directly affect the case's outcome. The importance of the oral argument is well illustrated by the decision in *Rathbun v. United States*, a case involving the power of the President to remove a member of the Federal Trade Commission. The government's attorney, Solicitor General Reed, was asked whether the logic of his argument would also allow the President to remove a judge of the court of claims. Solicitor General Reed agreed that it would. The decision in the case emphasized this point. Justice Sutherland, writing the opinion of the Court, stated:

> We are thus confronted with the serious question whether not only the members of these quasi-legislative and quasi-judicial bodies, but the *judges* of the legislative Court of Claims, exercising judicial power . . . continue in office only at the pleasure of the President.
>
> We think it plain under the Constitution that illimitable power of removal is not possessed by the President in respect to offices of the character of those just named.[32]

Various justices use oral arguments differently. Some — Justice Frankfurther was a notorious example — treat attorneys as if they were law-school students and bombard them with questions. Others rarely intrude on the attorney's argument.

After oral arguments have been heard, the Court reserves its decision until later. Periodically during its term the Court goes into conference to discuss the cases that it has heard argued. The conferences are attended only by the justices; no outsider is admitted. At the conferences the justices decide which new cases to hear and how to decide the argued cases.

---

[31] John P. Frank, *Marble Palace* (New York: Knopf, 1958), pp. 87–106; the flavor of oral arguments is well captured by James E. Clayton, *The Making of Justice* (New York: E. P. Dutton, 1964), *passim*.

[32] *Rathbun v. U.S.*, 295 U.S. 602 (1935), italics added; Glendon Schubert, *Constitutional Politics* (New York: Holt, Rinehart and Winston, 1960), p. 342.

The Chief Justice presides over the conference. His position enables him to exert great influence.[33] He speaks first in the discussion of each case and may therefore define the issues and set the tone for the debate. In addition, he calls for the vote when the discussion appears to have reached the decisive point. Some Chief Justices, such as Taft and Hughes, have used these powers skillfully to keep the discussion moving briskly without allowing acrimonious debate. Stone, on the other hand, was not as effective in leading the conference: while he was Chief Justice, conferences sometimes lasted several days. Discussion proceeds from the Chief Justice to the most junior justice according to seniority.

After a vote has been taken, the justices write opinions for those cases on which they have heard argument. The opinion for the Court (that is, for the majority) is assigned by the Chief Justice if he voted with the majority; otherwise, the most senior justice in the majority makes the assignment. Assigning opinions to the justices is very important. The opinion must be written so that the majority agrees with it after it has been written. Justices who write overly extreme opinions may find that their majority has melted away. Opinion-writing assignments must also be distributed so that every justice has a manageable work load. Because quite elderly justices often sit on the Court, sometimes fewer opinions can be assigned to them than to the younger justices. Moreover, justices become expert in certain fields of the law. Whenever possible, cases in a particular field will be assigned to the Court's expert. Finally, but not least important, the choice of the writer rests somewhat on the justice's reputation in the world at large. Justices who are particularly respected may be chosen to write opinions that the Court expects will stir controversy. Chief Justice Warren, for instance, often wrote the most controversial opinions of the Court, partly at least because he felt that the added prestige of the Chief Justiceship would help win acceptance of the decision.

[33] See Wasby, *The Supreme Court*, pp. 159–83, for an excellent summary of the decision-making process. See also Edwin McElwain, "The Business of the Supreme Court as Conducted by Chief Justice Hughes," *Harvard Law Review*, 63 (1949), 5–26; David J. Danelski, "The Influence of the Chief Justice in the Decisional Process," in Walter F. Murphy and C. Herman Pritchett (eds.), *Courts, Judges, and Politics* (New York: Random House, 1961), pp. 497–508.

Much bargaining accompanies the task of opinion writing.[34] Those who disagree with the majority on the Court may, if they wish, write dissenting opinions. They may circulate the dissent among all the members of the Court in the hope of winning votes away from the majority, so that what was originally a minority view may become the majority decision. Dissenters may also seek to persuade the majority to modify their opinion in exchange for not publishing quite as stinging a dissent or not publishing one at all. Such bargaining has occasionally led to the development of caucuslike meetings, which occur before the official conference; these meetings are attended by justices who think alike but want to be better prepared for the conference.[35] Unlike many legislative negotiations, no evidence of logrolling exists. Justices who often vote together may at times bitterly attack each other; justices who often oppose each other may be on warm personal terms.

Conference voting and the negotiations that ensue take place in complete privacy. When the opinions are completed and the justices are agreed on them, they are announced. Until a decision is announced from the Supreme Court bench, changes can be made.

Justices do not do all the work of the Supreme Court. Each justice has as many as four law clerks (the Chief Justice has more) to provide assistance.[36] These clerks are recent honor graduates of the nation's most prominent law schools. They serve for a year or two and do much of the preliminary research for a justice. Typically, a justice may draft an opinion with sketchy references to cases that he believes provide precedent or illumination for a particular case. The law clerks must then find the case in the court reports and check the accuracy of the justice's memory. In addition, law clerks prepare memoranda for the justice concern-

[34] Alexander M. Bickel (ed.), *The Unpublished Opinions of Mr. Justice Brandeis* (Cambridge, Mass.: Harvard University Press, 1957), *passim;* Walter F. Murphy, "Marshaling the Court: Leadership, Bargaining, and the Judicial Process," *University of Chicago Law Review,* 29 (1961–62), 640–72. For a controversial journalistic account, see Bob Woodward and Scott Armstrong, *The Brethren: Inside the Supreme Court* (New York: Simon and Schuster, 1979).

[35] Murphy, *op. cit.,* p. 670.

[36] J. Harvey Wilkinson III, *Serving Justice: A Supreme Court Clerk's View* (New York: Charterhouse, 1974), pp. 10–68.

ing the applications for review that must be voted on. They reduce the many pages of a brief to a few, so that the justice can quickly discern the main points of the case and decide whether it merits his and the Court's more careful attention.

The action of the United States Supreme Court is the final judicial decision on the points considered by the justices in the case, but it is not the final judicial action. Only when the Court affirms lower court action does the litigation cease, in which case the only further action required is to enforce the lower court decision. When the Supreme Court reverses a lower court action, further judicial action often follows. In a criminal case the prosecution may try the defendant again; in a civil case the trial may likewise be reheard. Litigants who win before the Supreme Court often lose in the rehearing of their case. They may win the affirmation of a principle but lose their case on the particular fact in dispute.

The procedures of the Supreme Court significantly affect its function in the judicial process and the political system. The manner in which it hears cases allows justices to focus on policy considerations not mentioned in the briefs. The hour-long oral argument with frequent questions by justices permits the Court to learn of the practices of other jurisdictions, the consequences of one decision or another, and the reasons for the litigants' positions. Although the Court deals with legal disputes, legal technicalities do not monopolize the justices' attention.

Policy considerations also win a hearing because the Court often reads the briefs and hears the arguments of those who act as "friends of the court." The federal government sometimes seeks permission to enter a case as *amicus curiae* when the Solicitor General feels that important public policies are at stake. Private groups appear as *amicus curiae* to argue the social implications as well as the legal significance of a case. Whereas trials and, to some extent, lower appellate court hearings focus more on legal technicalities, Supreme Court proceedings frequently consider social implications as well.

The Supreme Court's policy role is also the consequence of the justices' interpretation of their role in the judiciary. They have recognized that they cannot right every judicial wrong. The Court is not the last court of justice. Instead, it is the highest judicial tribunal for settling policy conflicts. In choosing cases to be heard, the Court consciously picks those that involve policy conflicts rather than those that appear to involve routine errors made in lower courts or insignificant private disputes. More than other courts, the Supreme Court behaves like a public governmental body dealing with public disputes. Whereas trial courts and most other appellate tribunals are equally open to both private and public disputes, the Supreme Court specializes in public policy conflicts.

This specialization does not mean that the Surpeme Court only hears cases brought by influential groups or by the government. Quite to the contrary, the Supreme Court's procedure allows penniless prisoners to appeal for review of their cases. Thousands of such petitions for review are received each year. Although an overwhelming proportion are rejected, a few are accepted and provide the Court an important opportunity to affirm individual rights in criminal proceedings. Such a case permitted the Court to review its earlier decisions regarding the availability of legal counsel to indigent defendants in criminal cases:[37] A poor handyman with a long criminal record had been tried in a Florida court without counsel, despite his request for an attorney. He was convicted, and his conviction was affirmed by the Florida Supreme Court. Writing on a sheet of prison stationery, the prisoner appealed for a review by the Supreme Court. The Court accepted, assigned a prominent lawyer to argue his case, and decided that all indigent defendants should be provided counsel if they request it; when this is not done, their conviction is unconstitutional. The prisoner obtained a new trial with counsel and was freed. For the judiciary and the political system, the new policy enunciated by the Court was more significant than the prisoner's release. That the Court makes appeals from paupers readily available does not necessarily reflect a special concern for the poor. Rather, the procedure guarantees the Court opportunities to hear a class of cases that would otherwise never be brought to its attention.

The form of the Supreme Court's opinions also has significance for the judicial process. Its opinions provide judges, law-

[37] A superb account of this case is Anthony Lewis, *Gideon's Trumpet* (New York: Random House, 1964).

yers, and the world at large with statements of the Court's reasoning and policy. At times the Court has used its opinions to invite further litigation so that it could reverse previous policies. For instance, in a flag salute case, the Court's opinion made it clear that a majority of justices was ready to reverse an earlier decision if a case involving an appropriate set of facts was appealed to it.[38] Likewise, dissenting opinions provide lawyers with clues that may help them to argue later cases more successfully.

Decisions announced without opinion also play a significant role in the judicial process. *Per curiam* decisions indicate that the Court feels that a matter is sufficiently well settled that the Court need not justify its decision at length. It merely refers to its past decisions and announces the results of the present case: affirmance or reversal of the lower court action. The Court often uses *per curiam* decisions to reverse obvious errors by lower courts. On the other hand, when it wishes to affirm a lower court without further proceedings, the Supreme Court may simply refuse to review the case, either by denying a writ of certiorari or by stating that the questions raised by the case about the federal Constitution are insufficiently significant. These summary decisions often have substantive significance. Although the Court never says so, some refusals to review seem to signify approval of the lower court action.[39]

What explains decision-making trends on the Supreme Court? Political scientists have devoted considerable attention to investigating this question. Most research has considered three related sets of factors.[40]

One set of scholars emphasizes the value premises of judges — their attitudes and the ideological positions they embrace. These scholars infer attitudinal and value positions from the justices' votes in cases where there is a disagreement on the Su-

---

[38] David R. Manwaring, *Render unto Caesar* (Chicago: University of Chicago Press, 1962), pp. 195–207.

[39] Glendon Schubert, *Quantitative Analysis of Judicial Behavior* (Glencoe, Ill.: Free Press of Glencoe, 1959), pp. 25–67.

[40] C. Herman Pritchett, "Public Law and Judicial Behavior," *Journal of Politics*, 30 (1968), especially pp. 496–509, gives a good bibliographic review of current research.

preme Court.[41] Through elaborate statistical analysis of voting patterns, Schubert characterizes justices as liberals, economic conservatives, or political conservatives; he finds they adhere differentially to liberal–conservative and pragmatic–dogmatic ideologies. Unfortunately, this research has a basic circularity, because the observer infers attitudes from votes in his attempt to explain voting patterns by attitudes. Although attitudes about fundamental political values are clearly revealed in selected cases, it is impossible to demonstrate that these particular attitudes caused the votes and subsequent decisions.

A second approach to Supreme Court decision making casts considerable doubt on the reliability of voting patterns as indicators of justices' attitudes. Working with private memoranda and office papers that justices have left in the archives, Bickel and Murphy showed that justices engage in considerable negotiation and bargaining and are sometimes willing to vote with the majority to win a colleague's vote in a later case or to gain an opportunity to modify the majority opinion, even when that opinion does not reflect the justice's own preferred values.[42] Decision making is analogous to a bargaining game and might be analyzed by game theory if data were available about all the justices' perceptions and preferences. Unfortunately, only scattered data are available. Many justices destroy their working papers when they leave the Court; others leave only a selection of their papers in the archives. Consequently, one cannot fully reconstruct Supreme Court decision making.

A third approach seeks to relate background characteristics of the justices to decision making. For instance, justices who previously served on lower courts have not been found more committed to precedent than justices who had never before served on a court before their appointment to the Supreme Court.[43] The

[41] See especially Glendon Schubert, *The Judicial Mind* (Evanston, Ill.: Northwestern University Press, 1965); Harold J. Spaeth, "Warren Court Attitudes Toward Business: The 'B' Scale," in Schubert (ed.), *Judicial Decision-Making*, pp. 79–108. A different approach is taken by John D. Sprague, *Voting Patterns of the United States Supreme Court* (Indianapolis, Ind.: Bobbs-Merrill, 1968).

[42] Bickel, *op. cit.;* Walter F. Murphy, *Elements of Judicial Strategy* (Princeton, N.J.: Princeton University Press, 1964).

[43] John R. Schmidhauser, "*Stare Decisis*, Dissent and the Background of the Justices of the Supreme Court of the United States," *University of Toronto Law Journal*, 14 (1962), 194–212.

propensity to dissent is somewhat related to the justice being Catholic, being from a rural area, coming to the court from a nonpolitical career, and having parents who were not engaged in politics.[44] However, in every case, background variables offer only a partial explanation.[45] It is clear that justices respond not only to experiences in the past but also to contemporary stimuli not measured by background variables.

All attempts to explain Supreme Court decision making stumble on the same barrier: the lack of data. The Supreme Court is extraordinarily secretive in its work. Its conference is closed; no outside observer may view its work. No records are kept or published of conference deliberations. The bargaining that occurs as opinions are drafted and circulated surfaces only many years after the event and only through accidental leaks in archives and memoirs. Consequently, scholars are driven to use the public indicators of decision making — votes and written opinions — even though those indicators are incomplete. Explanations of Supreme Court decision making will continue to be fragmentary until its methods become more open to public scrutiny.

Outcomes

Appellate courts mostly affirm the decisions made by lower court judges. In 1975, for instance, the United States courts of appeals reversed fewer than one of every five cases they decided.[46] The Supreme Court's reversal rate of argued cases is higher, but one must remember that the Court refuses to hear most of the cases brought to it, and for each such case the lower court decision stands. A great many of the appeals in the state courts also lead to affirmations rather than reversals.

The impact of appellate decisions varies considerably from case to case.[47] Many decisions — especially affirmations by in-

[44] S. Sidney Ulmer, "Dissent Behavior and the Social Background of Supreme Court Justices," *Journal of Politics*, 32 (1970), 580–89.

[45] David W. Adamany, "The Party Variable in Judges' Voting: Conceptual Notes and a Case Study," *American Political Science Review*, 62 (1969), 57–73; Joel B. Grossman, "Social Backgrounds and Judicial Decision-Making," *Harvard Law Review*, 79 (1966), 1551–64.

[46] Administrative Office of the U.S. Courts, *Annual Report of Director*, 1975 (Washington, D.C., 1975), pp. 11–21.

[47] Stephen L. Wasby, *The Impact of the United States Supreme Court* (Homewood, Ill.: Dorsey Press, 1970).

termediate appellate courts — affect only the litigants. The judges do not usually write opinions; or if they do, their opinions are not published and cannot be used in later cases as precedents. Many state supreme court decisions have an equally narrow impact, although most are published.

A few of the state supreme court decisions and most of the decisions by the United States Supreme Court for which opinions are written have a significant impact. They clarify the law for other litigants and often set guidelines that government agencies or private parties not directly involved in the litigation must follow. Thus, *Brown v. Board of Education* immediately affected every school board that ran segregated schools, and *Roe v. Wade* affected every state that had outlawed abortions as well as every medical facility that might perform them.

However, compliance with court decisions often takes a long time and is an uncertain process. More than a decade passed before overt segregation disappeared from the South; school segregation cases still came to the courts in the 1970s. By contrast, the abortion decision had an almost immediate impact. Within days hospitals were performing abortions throughout the country; within weeks clinics that handled nothing but abortion cases sprang up.

The reasons for variations in the speed and thoroughness of compliance are many. The clearer and less divided the courts' decisions, the more likely it is that they will have their intended impact. Although there were dissenting opinions, the abortion decision clearly specified when state regulation was permissible and when it was not; by contrast, the Court's statement that school desegregation should proceed with "all deliberate speed" was a confusing formulation. Equally important is the degree to which compliance is in the self-interest of the agencies responsible for carrying out the decision. School boards often had to face hostile parents and taxpayers when they began implementing desegregation plans. On the other hand, profits lured hospitals and clinics into quickly providing abortions. In some instances, those who evade a Supreme Court decision face swift retribution, whereas others can avoid such repercussions for a long time. Police departments, for instance, were quite unenthusiastic about providing warnings to defendants that they need not answer questions before conferring with their lawyer. However, failure to provide such a warning resulted in dismissal of charges against the defendant. Rather than seeing people they had arrested go free on this technicality, police departments generally complied and instructed their patrolmen to give such a warning to everyone they arrested.[48] Finally, the legal expertise available to those affected by Supreme Court decisions is important for their readiness to comply. Legal advisers can communicate such decisions to their clients; otherwise the client might remain unaware of his exact obligations. However, expert legal advice can also be used to discover ways to evade court decisions by finding loopholes or technicalities that might delay the impact or avoid it entirely.

The exact impact of appellate decisions is often difficult to predict. Some decisions have unanticipated consequences; others that seem important on the day of the decision eventually sink into obscurity. Many decisions require additional litigation or legislation before the original litigants achieve their policy goals.

Conclusions

Appellate proceedings give judges a more active role than lower court actions. The trial judge often is little more than a passive observer. Most cases do not even reach his courtroom, and those that do give him little scope, except when there is no jury. Appellate proceedings give the judge a far more central role. Very few cases are withdrawn; all remaining cases are decided by a judge. Appellate judges share their decision-making authority with no other body.

Although less out-of-court bargaining occurs in appellate proceedings than in trial courts, a considerable amount of bargaining and negotiation occurs among the judges who make the decisions.[49] Their personal values and preconceptions as well as the

[48] Neal Milner, *The Court and Local Law Enforcement* (Beverly Hills, Calif.: Sage Publications, 1971).

[49] Some appellate cases are brought to a negotiated settlement by a court-appointed arbitrator or by the parties themselves before the court has acted. See Jerry Goldman, *An Evaluation of the Civil Appeals Management Plan: An Experiment in Court Administration* (Washington, D.C.: Federal Judicial Center, 1977).

facts of the case play a significant role in the appellate decision. Several studies of the United States Supreme Court have tried to show that certain attitudes toward public affairs are central in the Court's decision making. Some justices favor less government control over business affairs than others; some stress individual rights more than others, particularly when these rights are challenged by the political action of the majority. The conditions under which such personal preferences come to the foreground and those under which they are repressed are not yet well understood; it is clear that appellate proceedings give greater scope to judgment, if only because fewer of the routine cases and more of the difficult ones come before the courts. The difficult cases lie on the frontier between accepted law and new policy; they require that judges evaluate the consequences of their decisions for the welfare of the society in which they live. Such explicit evaluations are much less frequently required of a trial judge, who usually enforces well-known norms on which agreement is more general.

An appellate court's preoccupation with public policy may occasionally lead to injustice in a particular case. This is especially true of the United States Supreme Court, which must of necessity refuse to review many cases where an injustice may have been perpetrated, in order to focus on those cases that have significance to more than the individual litigants involved. Therefore, the burden of assuring justice for the individual litigant rests on trial courts and the lower appellate courts, which have no power to refuse review of a case.

Because fewer studies of lower appellate court operations exist, it is more difficult to evaluate their performance. It is clear that the existence of appellate courts and the rules under which they operate give many litigants a second chance. In theory, at least, all litigants have the opportunity to appeal their case at least once. In fact, however, not all have an equal chance for a second hearing. Since an appeal requires additional financial and psychological resources, only those who can afford it will appeal.

Appellate proceedings have several latent functions. The secrecy in which appellate courts decide cases and the manner in which they announce decisions give their rulings added authority. Not only are appellate courts apparently removed from ordinary political strife, but they are also relatively insulated from the rougher atmosphere of a trial courtroom. Ritual reinforces dignity; remoteness strengthens the court's appearance of authority and legitimacy.

The opinions that appellate courts render also have an important latent function. They enable the courts to assume their policymaking role. Without published opinions, appellate courts could not make policy, for they would have no medium through which to inform the public about their actions. Each decision would be an isolated act with no further significance. By publishing their opinions, appellate courts not only give reasons for their actions but also inform others of the direction of their policy. Opinions justify decisions as well as pronounce general rules that govern other cases.

V
Conclusion

12
A Personal Assessment

How well do American courts perform their several functions as enforcers of commonly accepted norms, policymakers, and dispensers of equal justice to all? The data we have reviewed in the previous pages do not provide clear answers to such questions.

Millions of Americans go to court to obtain what they think is rightfully theirs or to complete procedures that are mandated by law to obtain their divorces or estates. These civil proceedings usually involve the successful invocation of widely held norms; through them, violators are punished or are forced to compensate their victims for losses sustained. The courts appear to be less successful in implementing criminal laws. Only a fraction of all violators are brought into court; the courts cannot send all violators to prison, even if it were appropriate, because the nation's penitentiaries cannot hold them. In many places, court proceedings are slow and uncertain and turn as much on a defense attorney's skill in bargaining as on the guilt of the defendant. The courts impose punishment for only a few crimes; they are almost powerless to provide compensation for victims, although victims of crime sometimes obtain partial compensation from insurance

255

companies or special government programs. These problems — not all of which are the fault of the courts themselves — dilute the effects of the sanctions that courts impose. The incomplete evidence we possess indicates that fear of punishment has relatively little effect on the crime rate.

The courts' policymaking role is even more difficult to evaluate. From the 1950s to the early 1970s, the courts played a very active role in formulating national policy. They concentrated on symbolic, emotion-laden issues that other policymakers avoided — racial desegregation, school busing to promote racial integration, regulation of the death penalty, legalization of abortion, and the provision of due process guarantees in criminal proceedings. In each of these instances, the original Supreme Court ruling was not the last word on the matter; rather, Supreme Court decisions set the agenda for legislators, administrators, and other judges to make further rulings and to continue the debate begun by the Supreme Court. In each of these areas, Supreme Court decisions have created substantially different conditions than existed before. The Supreme Court did not succeed in completely attaining the policy goals associated with each such decision, but it surely did not entirely fail.

Should such decisions have been made by courts? Did the courts neglect other significant areas? The answer to these questions depends on one's faith in purely democratic processes; it is clear that the courts are certainly less responsive to public opinion than are legislators and administrators. One can be certain that none of the decisions made by the Warren court would have been undertaken by Congress during the 1950s. These highly controversial decisions might eventually have become law through the legislative process, but only after long, bitter struggles. Legislatures are not well equipped to handle emotional issues or those that most severely affect small electoral minorities.

The author's personal conclusion is that the nation benefited from these judicially imposed policies. However, courts that at one time make wise policies may at another time make foolish ones; judges who are initially benevolent may in time become despotic. The fundamental safeguard in the American political process against such misfortunes lies in the fragmentation of the policymaking and policy-executing processes. The courts cannot impose their will singlehandedly upon the nation. They succeeded in imposing the Warren decisions because those policies represented the conscience and latent policy preferences of a large segment of the population. Opponents could not successfully mobilize the agencies of representative government against those policies.

Our evaluation, both of the courts' norm-enforcement functions and of their policymaking role, largely depends on the degree to which their decisions treat all segments of the population equally. If court rules or practices exclude certain classes of people or treat them unequally, the courts cannot perform their functions adequately. Although the evidence is once more not entirely clear, it appears that fewer biases exist now than five years ago. Systematic discrimination against the poor, blacks, and women seems to be considerably less evident as we approach the last decade of the twentieth century.

Blacks and the poor still constitute a much larger portion of criminal defendants than of the general population. This does not necessarily reflect bias in the courts. Rather, it reflects the enforcement of laws against personal violence and property theft and also the desperate economic circumstances of many young blacks, driven or enticed into criminal acts by their inability to find employment. Poor whites and members of other racial minorities also are the principal objects of criminal proceedings for the same economic and social reasons.

Once they are brought to court, however, the poor and the minorities find more equal treatment than they receive in most sectors of society. All courts now provide some kind of legal assistance to indigent defendants; in many instances, the assistance is as good as or better than the legal counsel that the rich can, and must, buy. Moreover, an increasing number of jurisdictions provide alternatives for bail bonds that must be bought from a bondsman; these programs enable many indigent defendants to remain free at minimal or no cost until convicted. When the offense, the prior criminal record, and the weight of the evidence are taken into account, the evidence shows that blacks and the poor do not suffer more severe treatment at the hands of the courts than others.

Nor do women suffer from the systematic discrimination of the past in criminal court proceedings. Women are much less likely to be excluded from juries. Rape victims now receive better treatment from the police and in court than they received in the past. Complaints made by women are taken more seriously. Also, although an increasing number of women participate in crime, they sometimes are treated more leniently than men.

Past inequalities in civil proceedings are also receding, owing to two significant developments that occurred within the last ten years. The first was the survival of widespread government-financed programs to provide legal services for the poor. These programs have survived the dismantlement of most other elements of the "War on Poverty" by the Nixon administration and the assault of the Reagan administration. Thus, many who cannot afford to pay a lawyer can obtain assistance in defending themselves against claims by landlords or by sellers of goods, or they can obtain help in seeking a divorce or in handling other matters involving family law.

The second development involved the alteration of substantive law to ease or erase disadvantages typically suffered by the poor and women. Thus, for instance, creditors may no longer repossess goods sold on conditional sales contracts without a court hearing. Confessions of judgment signed at the time something is bought are no longer universally valid. Third parties who buy credit paper now can be held responsible for the quality of the goods sold and the guarantees made by the seller. In many jurisdictions, landlord-tenant law now more clearly specifies the obligations of the landlord in ways that tenants can use to enforce their rights. These new remedies and procedures have become effective at the same time that legal assistance has made them realistically available to the poor. Nevertheless, the poor remain severely disadvantaged in many civil proceedings.

Additional serious problems confront the courts, of which three are particularly evident: the increase in litigation, the threats to the political independence of the judiciary, and the question of the courts' ability to cope with increasingly technical matters.

Civil litigation and criminal cases have been increasing over the last decades, and the trend shows no sign of abating. In part, the growth of litigation results from new rights and privileges conferred by statutes. As more citizens take part in government welfare and insurance programs and as the government regulates business firms in greater detail, more conflicts arise that cannot be settled without litigation. Perhaps another part of the trend is caused by the impersonality of urban life. Disputes, which once could be settled by face-to-face negotiations between people who knew each other well, now take place between strangers and their representatives. Whatever the cause, the trend creates difficult problems for the courts. Expanding court facilities is politically difficult: the court system is a weak competitor for the increased public funds that would be needed. Moreover, increasing court facilities may make judicial resolution of conflicts relatively more attractive and bring still more litigation into court. An alternative is to streamline court procedures so that less courtroom time is required to settle a dispute. However, experience with several such schemes thus far indicates that they save relatively little time; even more problematic, many such schemes sacrifice the due process safeguards that make judicial procedures distinctive and especially valued by potential litigants. It seems fair to conclude that, for the present, no satisfactory solution exists for the overload problem. It is likely to become worse before it becomes better.

At the same time that litigation volume is rising, its technical complexity is also increasing. First, the law itself is becoming increasingly technical, in part because it seeks to regulate in considerable detail so many more aspects of everyday life. The leading example of this tendency is the complexity of tax law, but many aspects of commercial law have similarly become more complicated. Second, the courts must contend with the increased complexity of cases that often involve factual situations requiring a considerable understanding of one or several disciplines — chemistry, physics, biology, accounting, economics, political science, sociology, and so forth. Restraint of trade, a central concept in antitrust law, rests on complex and disputed economic theory. To determine when a person may be considered dead (even though the heart may still be beating with the aid of mechanical devices) requires considerable knowledge of biology. Product liability disputes generally require technical knowledge; even personal injury suits arising from automobile accidents require considerable understanding of medical testimony.

Frequently, judges do not possess the technical training required for judging such disputes. Because few courts hear enough cases of a single type to provide on-the-job training, judges are unlikely to acquire it on the bench. The judge's technical naiveté provides a degree of external neutrality, because he does not share the assumptions and preconceptions often produced by technical training and work, but it also produces unnecessary suspicion about scientific evidence and sometimes leads to wrong conclusions. This problem may in time solve itself; disputants may become less willing to bring their conflicts to court if courts cannot effectively deal with the technical requirements. In such cases, disputants will create their own dispute-settling procedures that will bypass public courts. The price the public pays for such a development is that the public interest, presently represented by the judge, may be neglected.

Threats to the political independence of American courts have recurred throughout the country's history. The major threats in the future probably will not involve questions of the selection of judges. This process is firmly ensconced in politics and should remain so if courts are to be at all responsive to the mainstream of political developments. Rather, the main threats are likely to come from the growth of administrative tribunals and from the unwillingness of executive officials to carry out court orders. The latter is an old theme of American history; however, since executive power has grown enormously in the twentieth century, the temptation to extend its domination over the judiciary also grows. The notion of "executive privilege," so brazenly and vigorously advocated by the Nixon administration, presents serious dangers to the power of the judiciary to contribute to the resolution of public disputes. At the same time, an increasing number of disputes will be diverted from the general courts to administrative tribunals. Their decisions are less likely to be disinterested, if only because they are frequently linked to the agencies that they must judge.

It is by no means clear that developments in the near future will improve the administration of justice in the United States. Many of the problems facing the courts are intractable; they are rooted in the economic and social framework of American life and do not respond to superficial structural changes in governmental institutions like the courts. Nevertheless, the courts in the United States provide relief to millions of persons seeking redress of grievances that they cannot obtain elsewhere. While far from perfect, courts in the United States provide more equal treatment to American citizens than do most social and governmental institutions. The quest for more perfect justice must continue, but it must not blind us to the considerable achievements that American courts have already attained.

Index of Authors and Cases

Abington School District v.
  Schempp, 36n, 158n
Abraham, Henry J., 113n
Adamany, David W., 133n, 248n
Alfini, James J., 196n
Alker, Hayward R., 139n
Alschuler, Albert W., 190n, 191n,
  192n
Andenaes, Johannes, 186n
Anderson, William, 124n, 163n,
  171n
Argersinger v. Hamlin, 36n, 204n
Armstrong, Scott, 243n
Arnold, Thurman W., 11n
Aronson, Robert L., 139n
Auerbach, Carl, 163n
Aumann, Frances R., 128n

Baar, Carl, 18n
Balbus, Isaac D., 7n
Barrett, James D., 128n
Barton, Allen H., 155n

Bashful, Emmett W., 123n
Bickel, Alexander M., 243n, 247n
Biddle, Francis, 89n
Bing, Stephen R., 185n
Bird, Frederick C., 128n
Black, Donald J., 185n
Blaustein, Albert P., 54n, 55n,
  58n, 59n, 83n
Bloustein, Edward J., 74n, 75n
Blumberg, Abraham S., 74n
Blumrosen, Alfred W., 36n
Bohannon, Wayne E., 143n
Boland, Barbara, 186n
Borkin, Joseph, 110n, 128n
Botein, Bernard, 106n, 108n
Bozeman, Adda B., 9n
Brereton, David, 208n
Broeder, D. W., 141n, 143n,
  144n, 145n, 149n, 155n
Brown, Esther L., 55n, 87n
Brown, Michael K., 184n
Brownell, Emory A., 70n

Brown v. Board of Education,
36n, 249
Buchholz, Bernard, 105n, 107n,
145n
Buckley v. Valeo, 5n
Buckner, George, 2d, 68n, 69n
Bumiller, Kristin, 214n
Burt, Jeffrey A., 89n, 90n
Byrd, Elbert M., Jr., 164n

Campbell, Bruce, 68n
Canon, Bradley C., 122n
Caplovitz, David, 221n, 224n
Cappell, Charles L., 49n
Cardozo, Benjamin N., 111n
Carlin, Jerome, 59n, 61n, 62n,
76, 80n, 81n
Carp, Robert A., 165n, 188n
Carpenter, William S., 128n,
129n, 177n
Carter, Lief, 190n
Casanova, Kenneth, 121n
Casper, Jonathan, 75n, 205n,
208n
Cathcart, Darlene, 60n
Chase, Harold W., 66n, 114n
Choper, Jesse H., 74n, 75n
Christenson, Barlow F., 68n
Cicourel, Aaron V., 203n
Clayton, James E., 157n, 241n
Cook, Beverly Blair, 164n
Crow, John E., 122n
Curran, Barbara, 49n, 58n, 68n,
77n, 85n

Danelski, David J., 158n, 242n
Davies, Thomas Y., 110n, 240n
Davis, Claude J., 125n
Davis, I. R., 111n, 164n
Dix, George E., 177n
Dodge, Emily P., 77n, 79n
Dorf, Michael C., 60n

Downing, Rondal G., 126n
Dubois, Philip L., 122n, 124n,
133n

Egan, Leo, 130
Eisenstein, James, 88n, 142n,
185n, 188n, 189n, 190n,
191n, 192n, 193n, 194n,
195n, 197n, 199n, 202n,
204n, 205n, 206n, 207n
Eisen v. Carlisle and Jacquelin,
16n
Eldridge, William B., 207n
Emerson, Robert M., 19n, 203n
Engel v. Vitale, 36n, 157
Engstrom, Richard L., 96n
Epstein, Lee, 41n, 151n
Erie R.R. v. Tompkins, 163n
Eulau, Heinz, 81n
Evan, William M., 36n, 55n,
143n
Ewers, Thomas A., 123n

Farrand, Max, 177n
Fay v. Noia, 170n
Feeley, Malcolm M., 75n, 175n,
186n, 196n, 197n, 205n, 208n
Ferguson, Edward, III, 238n
Ferguson v. Skrupa, 63n
Fertitta, Robert S., 96n
Flanagan, Timothy J., 31n
Flemming, Roy B., 186n
Flynn, W. J., 148n
Forst, Martin L., 208n
Fox, Cyril A., Jr., 68n
Frank, Jerome, 132, 140n
Frank, John P., 110n, 241n
Frankel, Jack E., 129n
Frankfurter, Felix, 28n, 29n,
162n, 163n, 171n, 177n
Fried, Michael, 140n
Friedman, Lawrence M., 14n,
15n

Friendly, Alfred, 155n

Garrison, Lloyd K., 163n
Gerbner, George, 153n, 156n
Gibbs, Jack P., 200n
Gibson, James C., 202n
Gideon v. Wainwright, 36n,
    204n, 245n
Glick, Henry Robert, 180n, 238n
Goldfarb, Ronald, 154n, 155n
Goldman, Jerry, 163n, 231n,
    234n, 250n
Goldman, Sheldon, 66n, 115n,
    120n, 121n, 122n, 131n
Gottfredson, Michael R., 31n
Goulden, Joseph C., 77n
Gove, Samuel K., 176n
Graber, Doris, 153n
Greenberg, David F., 200n
Greene, Nathan, 28n, 29n
Greenwood, Peter W., 96n, 195n
Grossman, Joel B., 65n, 114n,
    115n, 116n, 117n, 118n, 248n

Hachten, William A., 157n
Hagan, John, 202n
Hall, F. H., 156n
Halliday, Terence C., 49n
Handler, Joel F., 77n, 151n
Harno, Albert J., 53n, 55n
Harris, Joseph P., 114n
Harris, Richard, 15n, 92n
Hawkins, Gordon J., 200n
Heiberg, Robert A., 123n, 124n
Heinz, John P., 49n, 78n, 80n
Henderson, Bancroft C., 123n,
    125n, 131n
Hennessey, Patricia, 221n, 224n
Hepburn v. Griswold, 119
Herndon, James, 124n
Heumann, Milton, 189n
Higgins, Timothy G., 124n

Horowitz, Donald L., 44n
Horwitz, Morton J., 35n
Hosticka, Carl, 139n
Howard, J. Woodford, Jr., 110n,
    231n, 232n, 233n, 234n, 235n
Hunting, Roger B., 68n
Hurst, James Willard, 14n, 50n,
    53n, 56n, 65n, 76n, 163n

In re Gault, 36n

Jacob, Herbert, 15n, 96n, 122n,
    123n, 126n, 142n, 148n,
    149n, 153n, 178n, 184n,
    185n, 186n, 188n, 189n,
    190n, 191n, 192n, 193n,
    194n, 195n, 197n, 199n,
    202n, 204n, 205n, 206n,
    207n, 220n, 223n, 231n, 239n
Jahnige, Thomas P., 131n
James, Rita M., 143n
Janowitz, Robert J., 70n
Jennings, John B., 196n

Kalven, Harry, Jr., 59n, 105n,
    107n, 144n, 145n
Kamisar, Yale, 74n, 75n
Kaplan, Kalman J., 140n
Karlen, Delmar, 232n, 236n,
    237n
Katznelson, Susan, 202n
Kaufman, Herbert, 15n, 98n,
    111n, 112n, 122n, 123n,
    129n, 130n, 180n
Kelling, George L., 186n
Klaw, Spencer, 77n
Klein, Katherine W., 140n
Klein, Malcolm W., 203n
Kort, Fred, 111n, 164n
Krislov, Samuel, 93n, 151n, 152n
Kuh, Richard, 98n

Ladinsky, Jack, 80n
LaFave, Wayne R., 185n
Landis, James M., 162n, 163n, 171n, 177n
Langner, James E., 234n
Larson, R. L., 94n
Laumann, Edward O., 49n, 78n, 80n
Leflar, Robert A., 126n
Lehman, Warren, 74n
Lepawsky, Albert, 175n, 215n
Levine, James P., 191n, 204n, 205n
Lewis, Anthony, 245n
Lineberry, Robert L., 153n
Lippman, David, 188n
Locke, J. W., 205n
Logan, Charles H., 200n
Lortie, Dan C., 80n

McElwain, Edwin, 242n
McIntyre, Donald M., 188n
McKean, Dayton, 51n, 52, 52n, 58n
McMurray, Carl D., 128n
Mann, Richard D., 143n
Manwaring, David R., 39n, 158n, 246n
Marbury v. Madison, 4
Marks, F. Raymond, 60n
Marks, Merton E., 63n
Mars, David, 111n, 164n
Martin, Edward M., 65n, 125n
Martin v. Hunter's Lessee, 162n
Massachusetts v. Laird, 43n
Mather, Lynn, 195n
Mayer, Martin, 77n
Mayers, Lewis, 215n
Mayhew, Leon H., 71n, 219n, 220n
Meglio, John J., 96n
Mermin, Samuel, 163n

Miller, Arthur Selwyn, 36n
Miller, Ben R., 125n
Mills, Carol J., 143n
Mills, Edwin S., 139n
Milner, Neal, 75n, 250n
Miranda v. Arizona, 36n
Mitchell, Michael, 139n
Molinari, John B., 236n
Montague, R. L., 94n
Moos, Malcolm C., 124n
Morris, Norval, 202n
Mullen, Joan, 31n
Muraskin, Matthew, 110n
Murphy, Walter F., 119n, 158n, 168n, 178n, 242n, 243n, 247n

Nagel, Ilene H., 202n
Nagel, Stuart S., 133n, 134n, 162n, 204n
Neal, David, 208n
Nebraska Press Association v. Stuart, 4n, 155n
Nedrud, Duane P., 95n
Neuwirth, Gloria S., 68n
Newland, Chester A., 151n, 157n
Nimmer, Raymond T., 60n, 61n, 176n
Nixon v. U.S., 5n

Oaks, Dallin H., 74n
O'Connor, Karen, 41n, 151n
O'Gorman, Hubert J., 228n
Orren, Karen, 150n
Osthus, Marlin O., 236n

Padawer-Singer, Alice M., 155n
Partridge, Anthony, 207n
Peltason, Jack W., 119n
Pieczenik, Roberta R., 191n, 194n, 204n
Platt, Anthony, 14n
Pope, Carl E., 202n

Porter, Charles O., 54n, 55n, 58n, 59n, 83n
Pritchett, C. Herman, 119n, 158n, 168n, 242n, 246n

Rathbun v. United States, 241
Reed, Alfred Z., 54n
Rich, Michael, 186n
Richardson, Richard J., 14n, 121n, 231n, 234n
Robinson, W. S., 139n
Roemer, Ruth, 232n
Roe v. Wade, 7, 36n
Rogge, O. John, 204n
Roper, Robert T., 140n
Rosen, Daniel, 110n
Rosenberg, Maurice, 105n, 107n, 217n
Rosenblum, Victor G., 54n, 57n
Rosenfeld, S. Stephen, 185n
Rosenheim, Margaret K., 14n, 178n
Ross, H. Laurence, 216n
Rowland, C. K., 165n
Rubenstein, Jonathan, 184n
Rubenstein, Michael J., 206n
Rutherford, M. Louise, 50n, 54n, 57n, 63n, 64n, 65n
Ryan, Frances M., 128n
Ryan, John P., 102n, 103n, 105n, 196n
Ryerson, Ellen, 14n, 178n

Sackett, Howard A., II, 112n
Sales, Bruce D., 102n, 103n, 105n
Salomon, Leon I., 89n, 90n
Sarat, Austin, 221n
Sayre, Wallace S., 15n, 98n, 111n, 112n, 122n, 123n, 129n, 130n, 180n
Schaalman, Michael H., 49n

Scheff, Thomas J., 175n
Schick, Marvin, 110n
Schlesinger, Joseph A., 81n, 93n
Schloss, Irving, 89n, 90n
Schmidhauser, John P., 114n, 120n, 132n, 247n
Schubert, Glendon, 110n, 119n, 121n, 241n, 246n, 247n
Schulman, Sidney, 64n, 111n, 125n, 180n
Scigliano, Robert, 137n
Shane-Dubow, Sandra, 102n, 103n, 105n
Shapiro, Martin, 36n, 43n
Sheppard v. Maxwell, 154n
Shinnar, Raoul, 200n
Shinnar, Shlomo, 200n
Silverstein, Lee, 74n
Simon, Rita James, 125n, 140n, 143n, 155n, 202n, 203n
Sinclair, T. C., 123n, 125n, 131n
Slotnick, Elliot E., 65n, 116n
Smigel, Erwin O., 77n, 81n
Smith, Bradford, 31n
Solomon, Freda F., 202n
Sprague, John D., 81n, 247n
State v. J. C. Penney Co., 37n
Steele, Eric H., 60n, 61n
Steffen, Roscoe T., 59n
Steiner, Gilbert Y., 176n
Stern, Robert L., 89n
Steude, William L., 94n
Stewart, James B., 77n, 226n
Strodtbeck, Fred L., 55n, 143n, 145n
Stumpf, Harry P., 70n, 72n
Summers, Marvin R., 139n, 214n
Sunderland, Edson R., 50n
Swank, Duane, 153n

Talarico, Susette, 68n
Talbott, Forrest, 124n, 163n, 171n

Tanenhaus, Joseph, 110n
Taylor, Jean G., 204n
Thompson, E. P., 7n
Tinnelly, Joseph T., 54n
Tittle, Charles R., 200n
Todd, A. L., 117n
Tonry, Michael, 202n
Truman, David, 149n, 150n
Twiss, Benjamin, 152n

Ulmer, S. Sidney, 133n, 237n, 248n

van Alstyne, David J., 31n
Vanderbilt, Arthur T., 108n, 109n, 110n, 140n, 147n, 167n, 170n, 171n, 172n, 173n, 232n, 237n
van Maanem, John, 184n
Vines, Kenneth N., 14n, 15n, 121n, 123n, 169n, 178n, 214n, 231n, 234n, 235n, 239n
Virtue, Maxine, 175n
Vose, Clement E., 39n, 151n

Wald, Patricia M., 204n
Wanner, Craig, 212n, 223n, 224n
Wardwall, Walter J., 81n

Warren, Charles, 50n
Wasby, Stephen L., 239n, 240n, 242n, 248n
Watson, Richard W., 94n, 126n
Watson, Robert H., 144n
Weaver, Suzanne, 89n
Wheeler, Michael, 228n
White, Teresa J., 206n
Wilcox, Bertram F., 232n
Wilkinson, J. Harvey, III, 243n
Willcox, Bertram F., 74n, 75n
Williams, Kristen M., 199n
Wilson, James Q., 184n, 186n
Witte, Edwin E., 28n, 29n
Wood, A. L., 78n
Wood, Arthur J., 81n
Woodward, Bob, 243n
Wright, Skelly, 107–108

Yankelovich, Skelly, and White, Inc., 148n
Yngvesson, Barbara, 221n, 224n

Zeisel, Hans, 105n, 107n, 144n, 145n
Zemans, Frances K., 54n, 57n
Zimring, Franklin E., 200n

Subject Index

ABA, 50, 51, 54, 57, 59, 65, 66–
  67, 83
  and judicial appointments,
    115–118
Abortion, 5, 6, 16
Abscam, 30
Adversary process, 11, 12
Alien and Sedition Acts, 8
Ambulance chasing, 220
American Bar Association. *See*
  ABA
Amicus curiae, 41–42, 151, 244
Appeals, costs of, 232–233
Appeals courts. *See* Courts of
  appeals
Arizona, 63
Arrest, 183, 185
Assigned counsel, 72–74
Attorneys. *See* Lawyers
Attorneys general, in states, 93–
  95

Bail reform, 204, 205

Baker v. Carr, 36, 40
Baltimore, 142, 195, 197, 199,
  212
Bar, admission to, 56–59
Bar associations, 50–52
  integrated, 51–52
  and politics, 63–67
Bar examinations, 57–59
Bench trials, 195
Black Panthers, 140
Blacks, 7, 8, 45, 214, 235, 247
  discrimination against, by
    criminal courts, 201–202
Brandeis, Louis, 117n
Budgets, for courts, 104
Burger, Warren, 119, 157, 179,
  239, 240
Burger Court, 41

Calendars, court, 105
California, 27, 52, 55n, 58, 69n,
  129, 164n, 202
Carswell, G. Harrold, 118

Carter, Jimmy, 120, 121
Case load, 27, 28, 258–259
  of Supreme Court, 239
Cases, management of, 104–106
Certiorari, writ of, 240
Chase, Salmon P., 56
Chicago, 30, 74n, 99, 142, 144,
  169, 194, 197, 199, 202, 206,
  224
Civil courts, 8
  proceedings in, 213–218
Civil law, 26
Clark, Ramsey, 20
Cleveland, 212
Code of Professional
  Responsibility, 59–61
Colorado, 156
Compliance with Supreme Court
  decisions, 249–250
Conferences of Supreme Court,
  241–242
Connecticut, 112, 164n
Constitution, U.S., 4, 38
Continuances, 105
Courts
  administrative organization of,
    170–173
  appellate, 166–168
  civil, 8, 213–218
  criminal, 8, 186–196
  jurisdiction of, 162
  reorganization of, 63–64
  structure of, 13–14, 164–168
Courts of appeals
  federal, 231–236
  state, 236–239
Crime problem, scope of, 183–
  186
Crime rate, 31
Criminal courts, 8
  proceedings in, 186–196
Criminal law, 26

Decision making, in Supreme
  Court, 246–248
Defense counsel, 191–192
Delay in courts, 205–206
Desegregation of schools, 19, 36,
  41, 235
Detroit, 142, 195, 197, 199, 202,
  224
Discretion
  by police, 32, 33, 184, 185
  by judges, 32–34, 109–110
Dismissal of charges, 197, 198
District attorney, 95–100, 190–
  191
Diversity cases, 162, 213–215

Eisenhower, Dwight D., 19, 65,
  116, 119, 121
Enforcement of norms, 25–34
Exclusionary rule, 15
Executive privilege, 4–5

Florida, 55n, 69n, 123, 125
Ford, Gerald, 122
Ford administration, 71
Fortas, Abe, 18

Grand jury, 137, 188
Guilty pleas, 182, 188

Haynsworth, Clement F., Jr., 118
Hispanics, 7
Holmes, Oliver Wendell, 119
House counsel, 78

Illinois, 206
Independence of judiciary, 20
Indictment, 188
Innocence, presumption of, 11
Interest groups, 39–42, 149–152
Iowa, 55n, 123

Jehovah's Witnesses, 40, 45
Jenner, Albert, 60
Johnson, Lyndon B., 18, 119,
    120, 121
Judges
    administrative functions of,
        104–106
    in appeals, 109–111
    appointment of federal, 114–
        122
    and bar primaries, 124–125
    in criminal proceedings, 189–
        200
    election of, 113, 122–125
    impeachment of, 128
    merit selection of, 64, 113,
        125–126
    nonjudicial functions of, 111–
        112
    partisan affiliation of, 121–122
    and patronage, 111–112
    recruitment of, 18, 113–127
    removal of, 127–130
    selection of, 64–66
    selection of state, 122–127
    terms of, 127
    at trials, 108–109
Judicial review, 4–5, 38
Juries, 136–149
    in civil cases, 218
    grand. See Grand jury
    instructions to, 108, 141
    and media, 153–155
Jurisdiction of courts, 162
Justice Department, U.S., 87–92
Juveniles, 203

Kennedy, Edward M., 30
Kennedy, John F., 115, 117, 119,
    121, 153
Kentucky, 128

Labor relations, 28–30
Law clerks of Supreme Court,
    243–244
Law firms, 77–78
Lawmaking, by courts, 32–34
Lawyers, 12–13, 49–100
    assigned, 72–74
    continuing education of, 55–56
    disciplinary proceedings
        against, 60–61
    ethics of, 59–62, 80
    in federal government, 85–92
    fees of, 68
    in politics, 81
    specialization of, 69
    training of, 52–56
    work of, 76–82
Legal aid, 70–72
Legal culture, 9–13
Legal education. See Lawyers,
    training of
Legal ethics, 59–62, 80
Legal profession. See Lawyers
Legal services, availability of,
    67–75
Legal Services Corporation, 71
Litigiousness, 218–223
Los Angeles, 74, 96, 123n
Louisiana, 123n, 238

Marshall, Thurgood, 118
Maryland, 164n
Massachusetts, 208
Media, and courts, 152–158
Merit selection of judges, 64,
    113, 125–126
Michigan, 52, 123, 133n, 237
Milwaukee, 98, 212, 221, 222
Minnesota, 55n, 123, 124, 170
Miranda v. Arizona, 204, 204n
Missouri, 149, 168

Missouri Plan. *See* Merit
  selection of judges
Mitchell, John P., 20
Motions, 106

NAACP (National Association for
  the Advancement of Colored
  People), 40, 41
New Haven, 196, 197
New Jersey, 4, 111, 172, 178, 238
New Mexico, 69n
New Orleans, 99
New York City, 98, 99, 112, 125,
  196, 224
New York State, 37, 123, 127,
  129, 130, 148, 170n, 172,
  180, 196, 207–208
Nixon, Richard, 4, 18, 41, 61,
  118, 119, 120, 121, 131, 258,
  260
Nixon administration, 8, 43, 71,
  92
No-fault laws
  for auto insurance, 227
  for divorce, 227–228
Norm enforcement, 25–34
North Carolina, 58
North Dakota, 51

O'Connor, Sandra Day, 18, 120
Oklahoma, 51
Opinions
  of appellate courts, 237–238
  dissenting, 238, 243
  majority, 238
  Supreme Court, 242–243
Oral argument, 234, 237, 240–
  241

Pennsylvania, 111, 125n, 180,
  180n
Per curiam decisions, 240, 246

Plea bargaining, 194, 206, 207
Poverty, and litigation, 223, 224,
  229
Prayer, in school, 36
Preliminary hearing, 188
Presidency, and courts, 4
Presumption of innocence, 11
Pretrial conferences, 107–108,
  228–229
Preventive detention, 15
Prisons, 31
Prison sentences, 199
Probable cause, 188
Prosecuting attorney. *See* District
  attorney
Public defender, 72, 74–75, 191,
  205

Racism, 7–9
Reagan, Ronald, 18, 66, 120, 121,
  258
Reagan administration, 71
Reapportionment of legislatures,
  36, 40–41
Rehnquist, William, 18
Release on recognizance, 204
Remedies, civil, 219
Rights of defendants, 36
Ritual, 10–11
Roe v. Wade, 249
Roosevelt, Franklin D., 121
Roosevelt, Theodore, 119
Rules, in judicial proceedings,
  10, 15

Sentences, 109
  determinate, 207
  disparities in, 207–208
  to prison, 199
Settlements, in civil cases, 216–
  218
  judges' role in, 106–108

Solicitor General, U.S., 90, 91
Staff attorneys, in appellate
    courts, 110, 233
Statutes, interpretation of, 37–38
Stevenson, Adlai, III, 5
Supreme Court, U.S., 110, 120,
    121, 167–168, 239–248
Symbolic issues, 6–7

Taft, William Howard, 178
Test case, 39, 40, 42, 151
Texas, 55n, 69n, 123n, 125n
Thompson, James, 5, 30

Unauthorized practice of law,
    62–63

Warren, Earl, 19, 30, 41, 119,
    134, 231, 242
Washington, Harold, 30
Washington, D.C., 199
Watergate, 4
White-collar crimes, 8
Wilson, Woodrow, 119
Wisconsin, 37, 55n, 96, 124, 131,
    148, 149, 163, 173
Women and crime, 202–203